LAW, LEGISLATION AND LIBERTY

Volume 3

THE POLITICAL ORDER OF A FREE PEOPLE

Law, Legislation and Liberty

Volume 1   Rules and Order
Volume 2   The Mirage of Social Justice
Volume 3   The Political Order of a Free People

By the same author

(ed.) Capitalism and the Historians
The Constitution of Liberty
New Studies in Philosophy, Politics, Economics
    and the History of Ideas
The Pure Theory of Capital
The Road to Serfdom
The Sensory Order: An Inquiry into the
    Foundations of Theoretical Psychology
Studies in Philosophy, Politics and Economics

LAW, LEGISLATION AND LIBERTY

*A new statement of the liberal principles
of justice and political economy*

VOLUME 3

THE POLITICAL ORDER
OF A FREE PEOPLE

Friedrich A. Hayek

The University of Chicago Press

The University of Chicago Press, Chicago 60637
Routledge & Kegan Paul Ltd., London and Henley

16 15 14 13 12 11 10 09 08 07   10 9 8 7

Library of Congress Cataloging-in-Publication Data

Hayek, Frederich August von, 1899–1992
  The political order of a free people.

  (Law, legislation, and liberty; v. 3)
  Includes bibliographical references and indexes.
  1. Liberty.   2. Democracy.   3. Rule of law.   4. Economic policy.
I. Title.

JC585.H294 1979   321.8   78-25905

ISBN-13: 978-0-226-32090-8 (paper)
ISBN-10: 0-226-32090-1 (paper)

⊗ The paper used in this publication meets the minimum requirements of the
American National Standard for Information Sciences—Permanence of Paper
for Printed Library Materials, ANSI Z39.48-1992.

A constitution that achieves the greatest possible freedom by framing the laws in such a way that the freedom of each can coexist with the freedom of all.

Immanuel Kant (*Critique of Pure Reason,* II, i.1)

CONTENTS

18 THE CONTAINMENT OF POWER AND THE
    DETHRONEMENT OF POLITICS

EPILOGUE: THE THREE SOURCES OF HUMAN
VALUES

CONTENTS

PREFACE

Again unforeseen circumstances have delayed somewhat longer than I had expected the publication of this last volume of a work on which I had started more than seventeen years ago. Except for what are now the last two chapters, most of it was in fairly finished form as long ago as the end of 1969 when indifferent health forced me to suspend the efforts to complete it. It was then, indeed, doubt whether I would ever succeed in doing so which made me decide to publish separately as volume 1 the first third of what had been intended to form a single volume, because it was in completely finished form. When I was able to return to systematic work I discovered, as I have explained in the preface to volume 2, that at least one chapter of the original draft of that part required complete re-writing.

Of the last third of the original draft only what was intended to be the last chapter (chapter 18) had not been completed at the time when I had discontinued work. But while I believe I have now more or less carried out the original intention, over the long period which has elapsed my ideas have developed further and I was reluctant to send out what inevitably must be my last systematic work without at least indicating in what direction my ideas have been moving. This has had the effect that not only what was meant to be the concluding chapter contains a good deal of, I hope, improved re-statements of arguments I have developed earlier, but that I found it necessary to add an Epilogue which expresses more directly the general view of moral and political evolution which has guided me in the whole enterprise. I have also inserted as chapter 16 a brief recapitulation of the earlier argument.

There were also other causes which have contributed to delay completion. As I had hesitated whether I ought to publish volume 2 without taking full account of the important work of John Rawls, *A Theory of Justice* (Oxford, 1972), two new important books in the field have since appeared which, if I were younger, I should feel I must fully digest before completing my own survey of the same kind of problems: Robert Nozik, *Anarchy, State and Utopia* (New York, 1974) and Michael Oakeshott, *On Human Conduct* (Oxford, 1975). Rightly or wrongly I finally decided that if I made an effort fully to absorb their argument before concluding my own exposition, I would probably never do this. But I regard it as my duty to tell the younger readers that they cannot fully comprehend the present state of thought on these issues unless they make that effort which I must postpone until I have completed the statement of the conclusions at which I had arrived before I became acquainted with these works.

The long period over which the present work has been growing also had the effect that I came to regard it as expedient to change my terminology on some points on which I should warn the reader. It was largely the growth of cybernetics and the related subjects of information and system theory which persuaded me that expression other than those which I habitually used may be more readily comprehensible to the contemporary reader. Though I still like and occasionally use the term 'spontaneous order', I agree that 'self-generating order' or 'self-organizing structures' are sometimes more precise and unambiguous and therefore frequently use them instead of the former term. Similarly, instead of 'order', in conformity with today's predominant usage, I occasionally now use 'system'. Also 'information' is clearly often preferable to where I usually spoke of 'knowledge', since the former clearly refers to the knowledge of particular facts rather than theoretical knowledge to which plain 'knowledge' might be thought to refer. Finally, since 'constructivist' appears to some people still to carry the commendatory connotation derived from the adjective 'constructive', 'I felt it advisable, in order clearly to bring out the deprecatory sense in which I use that term (significantly of Russian origin) to employ instead the, I am afraid, still more ugly term 'constructivistic'. I should perhaps add that I feel some regret that I have not had the courage consistently to employ certain other neologisms I had suggested, such as 'cosmos', 'taxis', 'nomos', 'thesis', 'catallaxy' and 'demarchy'. But what the exposition has thereby lost in precision it will probably have gained in ready intelligibility.

Perhaps I should also again remind the reader that the present work was never intended to give an exhaustive or comprehensive exposition of the basic principles on which a society of free man could be maintained, but was rather meant to fill the gaps which I discovered after I had made an attempt to restate, in *The Constitution of Liberty,* for the contemporary reader the traditional doctrines of classical liberalism in a form suited to contemporary problems and thinking. It is for this reason a much less complete, much more difficult and personal but, I hope, also more original work than the former. But it is definitely supplementary to and not a substitute for it. To the non-specialist reader I would therefore recommend reading *The Constitution of Liberty* before he proceeds to the more detailed discussion or particular examination of problems to which I have attempted solutions in these volumes. But they are intended to explain why I still regard what have now long been treated as antiquated beliefs as greatly superior to any alternative doctrines which have recently found more favour with the public.

The reader will probably gather that the whole work has been inspired by a growing apprehension about the direction in which the political order of what used to be regarded as the most advanced countries is tending. The growing conviction, for which the book gives the reasons, that this threatening development towards a totalitarian state is made inevitable by certain deeply entrenched defects of construction of the generally accepted type of 'democratic' government has forced me to think through alternative arrangements. I would like to repeat here that, though I profoundly believe in the basic principles of democracy as the only effective method which we have yet discovered of making peaceful change possible, and am therefore much alarmed by the evident growing disillusionment about it as a desirable *method* of government – much assisted by the increasing abuse of the word to indicate supposed *aims* of government – I am becoming more and more convinced that we are moving towards an impasse from which political leaders will offer to extricate us by desperate means.

When the present volume leads up to a proposal of basic alteration of the structure of democratic government, which at this time most people will regard as wholly impractical, this is meant to provide a sort of intellectual stand-by equipment for the time, which may not be far away, when the breakdown of the existing institutions becomes unmistakable and when I hope it may show a way out. It should enable us to preserve what is truly valuable in democracy and at the same time free us of its objectionable features which most people still accept only because they regard them as inevitable. Together with the similar stand-by scheme I have proposed for depriving government of the monopolistic powers of control of the supply of money, equally necessary if we are to escape the nightmare of increasingly totalitarian powers, which I have recently outlined in another publication (*Denationalisation of Money*, 2nd edn, Institute of Economic Affairs, London, 1978), it proposes what is a possible escape from the fate which threatens us. I shall be content if I have persuaded some people that if the first experiment of freedom we have tried in modern times should prove a failure, it is not because freedom is an impracticable ideal, but because we have tried it the wrong way.

I trust the reader will forgive a certain lack of system and some unnecessary repetitions in an exposition which has been written and re-written over a period of fifteen years, broken by a long period of indifferent health. I am very much aware of this, but if I tried in my eightieth year to recast it all, I should probably never complete the task.

In the preface to the first volume I expressed my thanks to Professor Edwin McClellan of the University of Chicago who had been most helpful in stylistically revising the unfinished text as it stood seven years ago. So much has been changed since that I must now absolve him from any responsibility for the wording of the version which I now submit to the public. But I have incurred a new obligation to Professor Arthur Shenfield of London who has kindly gone through the final text of the present volume and corrected a variety of substantive as well as stylistic points, and to Mrs Charlotte Cubitt who in preparing the typescript has further polished the text. I am also much indebted to Mrs Vernelia Crawford of Irvington-on-Hudson, New York, who has again applied her proven skill and understanding in preparing the subject index for all the three volumes which will be found at the end of this one.

CORRIGENDA TO VOLUME 2

p.61, line 14: for 'fiction's' read 'fictitious'
p.27, line 25: for 'their' read 'there'
p.73, line 12 from foot: for 'or' read 'nor'
p.145, line 16: for 'long before' read 'at about the same time as'
p.160, line 26: for 'or' read 'o'
p.161, line 9 from foot: replace quotation by: H. Lévy-Ullmann, *La Définition du droit* (Paris, 1917), p.165: 'Nous definirons donc le droit: la délimitation de ce que le hommes et leurs groupements ont la liberté de faire et de ne pas faire, sans encourir une condemnation, une saisie, une mise en jeu particulière de la force.'
p.163, line 21: for 'd'empecher' read 'd'empêcher'
p.176, line 13 from foot: for 'constitutione' read 'costituzione'
p.187, line 6 from foot: 'for *'Republica'* read *'Re Publica'*

TWELVE

MAJORITY OPINION AND CONTEMPORARY DEMOCRACY

> But the great number [of the Athenian Assembly] cried out that it was monstrous if the people were to be prevented from doing whatever they wished. . . . Then the Prytanes, stricken with fear, agreed to put the question—all of them except Socrates, the son of Sophroniscus; and he said that in no case would he act except in accordance with the law.
>
> Xenophon*

The progressive disillusionment about democracy

When the activities of modern government produce aggregate results that few people have either wanted or foreseen this is commonly regarded as an inevitable feature of democracy. It can hardly be claimed, however, that such developments usually correspond to the desires of any identifiable group of men. It appears that the particular process which we have chosen to ascertain what we call the will of the people brings about results which have little to do with anything deserving the name of the 'common will' of any substantial part of the population.

We have in fact become so used to regard as democratic only the particular set of institutions which today prevails in all Western democracies, and in which a majority of a representative body lays down the law *and* directs government, that we regard this as the only possible form of democracy. As a consequence we do not care to dwell on the fact that this system not only has produced many results which nobody likes, even in those countries in which on the whole it has worked well, but also has proved unworkable in most countries where these democratic institutions were not restrained by strong traditions about the appropriate tasks of the representative assemblies. Because we rightly believe in the basic ideal of democracy we feel usually bound to defend the particular institutions

1

which have long been accepted as its embodiment, and hesitate to criticize them because this might weaken the respect for an ideal we wish to preserve.

It is no longer possible, however, to overlook the fact that in recent times in spite of continued lip-service and even demands for its further extension, there has arisen among thoughtful persons an increasing disquiet and serious alarm about the results it often produces.[1] This does not everywhere take the form of that cynical realism which is characteristic of some contemporary political scientists who regard democracy merely as just another form of an inevitable struggle in which it is decided 'who gets what, when, and how'.[2] Yet that there prevails deep disillusionment and doubt about the future of democracy, caused by a belief that those developments of it which hardly anybody approves are inevitable, can scarcely be denied. It found its expression many years ago in Joseph Schumpeter's well known contention that, although a system based on the free market would be better for most, it is doomed beyond hope, while socialism, though it cannot fulfil its promises, is bound to come.[3]

It seems to be the regular course of the development of democracy that after a glorious first period in which it is understood as and actually operates as a safeguard of personal freedom because it accepts the limitations of a higher nomos, sooner or later it comes to claim the right to settle any particular question in whatever manner a majority agrees upon. This is what happened to the Athenian democracy at the end of the fifth century, as shown by the famous occurrence to which the quotation at the head of this chapter refers; and in the next century Demosthenes (and others) were to complain that 'our laws are no better than so many decrees; nay, you will find that the laws which have to be observed in drafting the decrees are later than the decrees themselves.'[4]

In modern times a similar development started when the British Parliament claimed sovereign, that is unlimited, powers and in 1766 explicitly rejected the idea that in its particular decisions it was bound to observe any general rules not of its own making. Though for a time a strong tradition of the rule of law prevented serious abuse of the power that Parliament had arrogated to itself, it proved in the long run the great calamity of modern development that soon after representative government was achieved all those restraints upon the supreme power that had been painfully built up during the evolution of constitutional monarchy were successively dismantled

2

as no longer necessary. That this in effect meant the abandonment of constitutionalism which consists in a limitation of all power by permanent principles of government was already seen by Aristotle when he maintained that 'where the laws are not sovereign . . . since the many are sovereign not as individuals but collectively . . . such a democracy is not a constitution at all';[5] and it was recently pointed out again by a modern author who speaks of 'constitutions which are so democratic that they are properly speaking no longer constitutions'.[6] Indeed, we are now told that the 'modern conception of democracy is a form of government in which no restriction is placed on the governing body'[7] and, as we have seen, some have already drawn the conclusion that constitutions are an antiquated survival which have no place in the modern conception of government.[8]

Unlimited power the fatal defect of the prevailing form of democracy

The tragic illusion was that the adoption of democratic procedures made it possible to dispense with all other limitations on governmental power. It also promoted the belief that the 'control of government' by the democratically elected legislation would adequately replace the traditional limitations,[9] while in fact the necessity of forming organized majorities for supporting a programme of particular actions in favour of special groups introduced a new source of arbitrariness and partiality and produced results inconsistent with the moral principles of the majority. As we shall see, the paradoxical result of the possession of unlimited power makes it impossible for a representative body to make the general principles prevail on which it agrees, because under such a system the majority of the representative assembly, in order to remain a majority, *must* do what it can to buy the support of the several interests by granting them special benefits.

So it came about that with the precious institutions of representative government Britain gave to the world also the pernicious principle of parliamentary sovereignty[10] according to which the representative assembly is not only the highest but also an unlimited authority. The latter is sometimes thought to be a necessary consequence of the former, but this is not so. Its power may be limited, not by another superior 'will' but by the consent of the people on which all power and the coherence of the state rest. If that consent approves only of the laying down and enforcement of general rules of just conduct, and nobody is given power to coerce except for the enforcement of these rules (or temporarily during a violent disruption of order by some cataclysm), even the highest constituted power may be limited. Indeed, the claim of Parliament to sovereignty at first meant only that it recognized no other will above it; it only gradually came to mean that it could do whatever it liked—which does not necessarily follow from the first, because the consent on which the unity of the state and therefore the power of any of its organs are founded may only restrain power but not confer positive power to act. It is allegiance which creates power and the power thus created extends only so far as it has been extended by the consent of the people. It was because this was forgotten that the sovereignty of law became the same thing as the sovereignty of Parliament. And while the conception of the rule (reign, sovereignty or supremacy) of law presupposes a concept of law defined by the attributes of the rules, not by their source, *today legislatures are no longer so called because they make the laws, but laws are so called because they emanate from legislatures,* whatever the form or content of their resolutions.[11]

If it could be justly contended that the existing institutions produce results which have been willed or approved by a majority, the believer in the basic principle of democracy would of course have to accept them. But there are strong reasons to think that what those institutions in fact produce is in a great measure an unintended outcome of the particular kind of machinery we have set up to ascertain what we believe to be the will of the majority, rather than a deliberate decision of the majority or anybody else. It would seem that wherever democratic institutions ceased to be restrained by the tradition of the Rule of Law, they led not only to 'totalitarian democracy' but in due time even to a 'plebiscitary dictatorship'.[12] This should certainly make us understand that what is a precious possession is not a particular set of institutions that are easily enough copied, but some less tangible traditions; and that the degeneration of these institutions may even be a necessary result wherever the inherent logic of the machinery is not checked by the predominance of the prevailing general conceptions of justice. May it not be true, as has been well said, that 'the belief in democracy presupposes belief in things higher than democracy'?[13] And is there really no other way for people to maintain a democratic government than by handing over unlimited power to a group of elected representatives whose decisions must be guided by the exigencies of a bargaining process in which they bribe a sufficient number of voters to support an organized group of themselves numerous enough to outvote the rest?

The true content of the democratic ideal

Though a great deal of nonsense has been and still is being talked about democracy and the benefits its further extension will secure, I am profoundly disturbed by the rapid decline of faith in it. This sharp decrease of the esteem in which democracy is held by critical minds ought to alarm even those who never shared the unmeasured and uncritical enthusiasm it used to inspire until recently, and which made the term describe almost anything that was good in politics. As seems to be the fate of most terms expressing a political ideal, 'democracy' has been used to describe various kinds of things which have little to do with the original meaning of the term, and now is even often used where what is really meant is 'equality'. Strictly speaking it refers to a method or procedure for determining governmental decisions and neither refers to some substantial good or aim of government (such as a sort of material equality), nor is it a method that can be meaningfully applied to non-governmental organizations (such as educational, medical, military or commercial establishments). Both of these abuses deprive the word 'democracy' of any clear meaning.[14]

But even a wholly sober and unsentimental consideration which regards democracy as a mere convention making possible a peaceful change of the holders of power[15] should make us understand that it is an ideal worth fighting for to the utmost, because it is our only protection (even if in its present form not a certain one) against tyranny. Though democracy itself is not freedom (except for that indefinite collective, the majority of 'the people') it is one of the most important safeguards of freedom. As the only method of peaceful change of government yet discovered, it is one of those paramount though negative values, comparable to sanitary precautions against the plague, of which we are hardly aware while they are effective, but the absence of which may be deadly.

The principle that coercion should be allowed only for the purpose of ensuring obedience to rules of just conduct approved by most, or at least by a majority, seems to be the essential condition for the absence of arbitrary power and therefore of freedom. It is this principle which has made possible the peaceful co-existence of men in a Great Society and the peaceful change of the directors of organized power. But that whenever common action is necessary it should be guided by the opinion of the majority, and that no power of coercion is legitimate unless the principle guiding it is approved by at least a majority, does not imply that the power of the majority must be unlimited—or even that there must be a possible way of ascertaining what it called the will of the majority on every conceivable subject. It appears that we have unwittingly created a machinery which makes it possible to claim the sanction of an alleged majority for measures which are in fact not desired by a majority, and which may even be disapproved by a majority of the people; and that this machinery produces an aggregate of measures that not only is not wanted by anybody, but that could not as a whole be approved by any rational mind because it is inherently contradictory.

If all coercive power is to rest on the opinion of the majority, then it should also not extend further than the majority can genuinely agree. This does not mean that there must exist specific approval by the majority of any particular action of the government. Such a demand would clearly be impossible to fulfil in a complex modern society so far as the current direction of the detail of the government machinery is concerned, that is for all the day-to-day decisions about how the resources placed at the disposal of government are to be used. But it does mean that the individual should be bound to obey only such commands as necessarily follow from the general principles approved by the majority, and that the power of the representatives of the majority should be unrestricted only in the administration of the particular means placed at their disposal.

The ultimate justification of the conferment of a power to coerce is that such a power is required if a viable order is to be maintained, and that all have therefore an interest in the existence of such a power. But this justification does not extend further than the need. There is clearly no need that anybody, not even the majority, should have power over all the particular actions or things occurring in society. The step from the belief that only what is approved by the majority should be binding for all, to the belief that all that the majority approves shall have that force, may seem small. Yet it is the transition from one conception of government to an altogether different one: from the conception by which government has definite limited tasks required to bring about the formation of a spontaneous order, to the conception that its powers are unlimited; or a transition from a system in which through recognized procedures we decide how certain common affairs are to be arranged, to a system in which one group of people may declare anything they like as a matter of common concern and on this ground subject it to those procedures. While the first conception refers to necessary common decisions requisite for the maintenance of peace and order, the second allows some organized sections of the people to control everything, and easily becomes the pretext of oppression.

There is, however, no more reason to believe in the case of the majority that because they want a particular thing this desire is an expression of their sense of justice, than there is ground for such a belief in the case of individuals. In the latter we know only too well that their sense of justice will often be swayed by their desire for particular objects. But as individuals we have generally been taught to curb illegitimate desires, though we sometimes have to be restrained by authority. Civilization largely rests on the fact that the individuals have learnt to restrain their desires for particular objects and to submit to generally recognized rules of just conduct. Majorities, however, have not yet been civilized in this manner because they do not have to obey rules. What would we not all do if we were genuinely convinced that our desire for a particular action proves that it is just? The result is not different if people are persuaded that the agreement of the majority on the advantage of a particular measure proves that it is just. When people are taught to believe that what they agree is necessarily just, they will indeed soon cease to ask whether it is so. Yet the belief that all on which a majority can agree is by definition just has for several generations been impressed upon popular opinion. Need we be surprised that in the conviction that what they resolve is necessarily just, the existing representative assemblies have ceased even to consider in the concrete instances whether this is really so?[16]

While the agreement among many people on the justice of a particular *rule* may indeed be a good though not an infallible test of its justice, it makes nonsense of the conception of justice if we define as just whatever particular measure the majority approves— justifiable only by the positivist doctrine that there are no objective tests of justice (or rather injustice—see chapter 8 above). There exists a great difference between what a majority may decide on any particular question and the general principle relevant to the issue which it might be willing to approve if it were

7

put to it, as there will exist among individuals. There is, therefore, also great need that a majority be required to prove its conviction that what it decides is just by *committing* itself to the universal application of the rules on which it acts in the particular case; and its power to coerce should be confined to the enforcement of rules to which it is prepared to commit itself.

The belief that the will of the majority on particular matters determines what is just leads to the view, now widely regarded as self-evident, that the majority cannot be arbitrary. This appears to be a necessary conclusion only if, according to the prevalent interpretation of democracy (and the positivistic jurisprudence as its foundation), the source from which a decision emanates rather than its conformity with a rule on which the people agree, is regarded as the criterion of justice, and 'arbitrary' is arbitrarily defined as not determined by democratic procedure. 'Arbitrary' means, however, action determined by a particular will unrestrained by a general rule—irrespective of whether this will is the will of one or a majority. It is, therefore, not the agreement of a majority on a particular action, nor even its conformity with a constitution, but only the willingness of a representative body to commit itself to the universal application of a rule which requires the particular action, that can be regarded as evidence that its members regard as just what they decide. Today, however, the majority is not even asked whether it regards a particular decision as just; nor could its individual members assure themselves that the principle that is applied in the particular decision will also be applied in all similar instances. Since no resolution of a representative body binds it in its future decisions, it is in its several measures not bound by any general rules.

The weakness of an elective assembly with unlimited powers

The crucial point is that votes on rules applicable to all, and votes on measures which directly affect only some, have a wholly different character. Votes on matters that concern all, such as general rules of just conduct, are based on a lasting strong opinion and thus something quite different from votes on particular measures for the benefit (and often also at the expense) of unknown people— generally in the knowledge that such benefits will be distributed from the common purse in any case, and that all the individual can do is to guide this expenditure in the direction he prefers. Such a system is bound to produce the most paradoxical results in a Great Society, however expedient it may be for arranging local affairs where all are fairly familiar with the problems, because the number and complexity of the tasks of the administration of a Great Society far exceed the range where the ignorance of the individual could be remedied by better information at the disposal of the voters or representatives.[17]

The classical theory of representative government assumed that the deputies

> when they make no laws but what they themselves and their posterity must be subject to; when they can give no money, but what they must pay their share of; when they can do no mischief, but what must fall upon their own heads in common with their countrymen; their principals may expect then good laws, little mischief, and much frugality.[18]

But the electors of a 'legislature' whose members are mainly concerned to secure and retain the votes of particular groups by procuring special benefits for them will care little about what others will get and be concerned only with what they gain in the haggling. They will normally merely agree to something being given to others about whom they know little, and usually at the expense of third groups, as the price for having their own wishes met, without any thought whether these various demands are just. Each group will be prepared to consent even to iniquitous benefits for other groups out of the common purse if this is the condition for the consent of the others to what this group has learnt to regard as its right. The result of this process will correspond to nobody's opinion of what is right, and to no principles; it will not be based on a judgment of merit but on political expediency. Its main object is bound to become the sharing out of funds extorted from a minority. That this is the inevitable outcome of the actions of an unrestrained 'interventionist' legislature was clearly foreseen by the early theorists of representative democracy.[19] Who indeed would pretend that in modern times the democratic legislatures have granted all the special subsidies, privileges and other benefits which so many special interests enjoy because they regard these demands as just? That A be protected against the competition of cheap imports and B against being undercut by a less highly trained operator, C against a reduction in his wages, and D against the loss of his job is not in the general interest, however much the advocates of such a measure pretend that this is so. And it is not chiefly because the voters are convinced that it is in the general interest but because they want the support of those who make these demands that they are in turn prepared to support *their* demands. The creation of the myth of 'social justice' which we have examined in the last volume is indeed largely the product of this particular democratic machinery, which makes it necessary for the representatives to invent a moral justification for the benefits they grant to particular interests.

Indeed people often come genuinely to believe that it must in some sense be just if the majority regularly concedes special benefits to particular groups—as if it had anything to do with justice (or any moral consideration) if every party that wants majority support must promise special benefits to some particular groups (such as the farmers or peasants, or legal privileges to the trade unions) whose votes may shift the balance of power. Under the existing system thus every small interest group can enforce its demands, not by persuading a majority that the demands are just or equitable, but by threatening to withhold that support which the nucleus of agreed individuals will need to become a majority. The pretence that the democratic legislatures have granted all the special subsidies, privileges and other benefits which so many particular interests today enjoy because they thought these to be just would of course be simply ridiculous. Though skilful propaganda may occasionally have moved a few soft-hearted individuals on behalf of special groups, and though it is of course useful to the legislators to claim that they have been moved by considerations of justice, the artefacts of the voting machinery which we call the will of the majority do certainly not correspond to any opinion of the majority about what is right or wrong.

An assembly with power to vote on benefits to particular groups must become one in which bargains or deals among the majority rather than substantive agreement on the merits of the different claims will decide.[20] The fictitious 'will of the majority' emerging from this bargaining process is no more than an agreement to assist its supporters at the expense of the rest. It is to the awareness of this fact that policy is largely determined by a series of deals with special interests that 'politics' owes its bad reputation among ordinary men.

Indeed, to the high-minded who feel that the politician should concern himself exclusively with the common good the reality of constant assuaging of particular groups by throwing them titbits or more substantial gifts must appear as outright corruption. And the

10

fact that majority government does not produce what the majority wants but what each of the groups making up the majority must concede to the others to get their support for what it wants itself amounts to that. That this is so is today accepted as one of the commonplaces of everyday life and that the experienced politician will merely pity the idealist who is naive enough to condemn this and to believe it could be avoided if only people were more honest, is therefore perfectly true so far as the existing institutions are concerned, and wrong only in taking it as an inevitable attribute of all representative or democratic government, an inherent corruption which the most virtuous and decent man cannot escape. It is however not a necessary attribute of all representative or democratic government, but a necessary product only of all unlimited or omnipotent government dependent on the support of numerous groups. Only limited government can be decent government, because there does not exist (and cannot exist) general moral rules for the assignments of particular benefits (as Kant put it, because 'welfare has no principle but depends on the material content of the will and therefore is incapable of a general principle'.[21] It is not democracy or representative government as such, but the particular institution, chosen by us, of a single omnipotent 'legislature' that make it necessarily corrupt.

Corrupt at the same time weak: unable to resist pressure from the component groups the governing majority *must do what it can do* to gratify the wishes of the groups from which it needs support, however harmful to the rest such measures may be—at least so long as this is not too easily seen or the groups who have to suffer are not too popular. While immensely and oppressively powerful and able to overwhelm all resistance from a minority, it is wholly incapable of pursuing a consistent course of action, lurching like a steam roller driven by one who is drunk. If no superior judiciary authority can prevent the legislature from granting privileges to particular groups there is no limit to the blackmail to which government will be subject. If government has the power to grant their demands it becomes their slave—as in Britain where they make impossible any policy that might pull the country out of its economic decline. If government is going to be strong enough to maintain order and justice we must deprive the politicians of that cornucopia the possession of which makes them believe that they can and ought 'to remove all sources of discontent.'[22] Unfortunately, every necessary adaptation to changed circumstances is bound to cause widespread

11

discontent, and what will be mainly demanded from politicians is to make these unwelcome changes unnecessary for the individuals.

One curious effect of this condition in which the granting of special benefits is guided not by a general belief of what is just but by 'political necessity' is that it is apt to create erroneous beliefs of the following kind: if a certain group is regularly favoured because it may swing the balance of the votes the myth will arise that it is generally agreed that it deserves this. But it would of course be absurd to conclude if the farmers, the small business men, or the municipal workers got their demands regularly satisfied that they must have a just claim, if in reality this merely happens because without the support of a substantial part of these groups no government would have a majority. Yet there seems to be a paradoxical reversal of what democratic theory assumes to happen: that the majority is not guided by what is generally believed to be right, but what it thinks it is necessary to do in order to maintain its coherence is being regarded as just. It is still believed that consent of the majority is proof of the justice of a measure, although most members of the majority will often consent only as payment of the price for the fulfilment of their own sectional demands. Things come to be regarded as 'socially just' merely because they are regularly done, not because anyone except the beneficiaries regards them as just on their own merits. But the necessity of constantly wooing splinter groups produces in the end purely fortuitous moral standards and often leads people to believe that the favoured social groups are really specially deserving because they are regularly singled out for special benefits. Sometimes we do encounter the argument that 'all modern democracies have found it necessary to do this or that', used as if it were proof of the desirability of a measure rather than merely the blind result of a particular mechanism.

Thus the existing machinery of unlimited democratic government produces a new set of 'democratic' pseudo-morals, an artifact of the machinery which makes people regard as socially just what is regularly done by democracies, or can by clever use of this machinery be extorted from democratic governments. The spreading awareness that more and more incomes are determined by government action will lead to ever new demands by groups whose position is still left to be determined by market forces for similar assurance of what they believe they deserve. Every time the income of some group is increased by government action a legitimate claim for similar treatment is provided for other groups. It is merely the expectations of many which legislatures have created by the boons they have already conferred on certain groups that they will be treated in the same manner that underlies most of the demands for 'social justice'.

Coalitions of organized interests and the apparatus of para-government

So far we have considered the tendency of the prevailing democratic institutions only in so far as it is determined by the necessity to bribe the individual voter with promises of special benefits for his group, without taking into account a factor which greatly accentuates the influence of some particular interests, their ability to organize and to operate as organized pressure groups.[23] This leads to the particular political parties being united not by any principles but merely as coalitions or organized interests in which the concerns of those pressure groups that are capable of effective organization greatly preponderate over those that for one reason or another cannot form effective organizations.[24] This greatly enhanced influence of the organizable groups further distorts the distribution of benefits and makes it increasingly unrelated to the requirements of efficiency or any conceivable principle of equity. The result is a distribution of incomes chiefly determined by political power. The 'incomes policy' nowadays advocated as a supposed means to combat inflation is in fact largely inspired by the monstrous idea that all material benefits should be determined by the holders of such power.[25]

It is part of this tendency that in the course of this century an enormous and exceedingly wasteful apparatus of para-government has grown up, consisting of trade associations, trades unions and professional organizations, designed primarily to divert as much as possible of the stream of governmental favour to their members. It has come to be regarded as obviously necessary and unavoidable, yet has arisen only in response to (or partly as defence against being disadvantaged in) the increasing necessity of an all-mighty majority government maintaining its majority by buying the support of particular small groups.

Political parties in these conditions become in fact little more than coalitions of organized interests whose actions are determined by the inherent logic of their mechanics rather than by any general principles or ideals on which they are agreed. Except for some ideological parties in the West who disapprove of the system now

13

prevailing in their countries and aim at wholly replacing these by some imaginary utopia, it would indeed be difficult to discern in the programmes, and even more in the actions, of any major party a consistent conception of the sort of social order on which its followers agree. They are all driven, even if that is not their agreed aim, to use their power to impose some particular structure upon society i.e. some form of socialism, rather than create the conditions in which society can gradually evolve improved formations.[26]

The inevitability of such developments in a system where the legislature is omnipotent is cleary seen if we ask how a majority united on common action and capable of directing current policy can be formed. The original democratic ideal was based on the conception of a common opinion on what is right being held by most of the people. But community of opinion on basic values is not sufficient to determine a programme for current governmental action. The specific programme that is required to unite a body of supporters of a government, or to hold together such a party, must be based on some aggregation of different interests which can only be achieved by a process of bargaining. It will not be an expression of common desire for the particular results to be achieved; and, as it will be concerned with the use of the concrete resources at the disposal of government for particular purposes, it will generally rest on the consent of the several groups to particular services rendered to some of them in return for other services offered to each of the consenting groups.

It would be mere pretence to describe a programme of action thus decided upon in a bargaining democracy as in any sense an expression of the common opinion of the majority. Indeed, there may exist nobody who desires or even approves of all the things contained in such a programme; for it will often contain elements of such contradictory character that no thinking person could ever desire them all for their own sake. Considering the process by which such programmes for common action are agreed upon, it would indeed be a miracle if the outcome were anything but a conglomerate of the separate and incoherent wishes of many different individuals and groups. On many of the items included in the programme most members of the electorate (or many of the representative assembly) will have no opinion at all because they know nothing of the circumstances involved. Towards many more they will be indifferent or even adversely disposed, but prepared to consent as payment for the realization of their own wishes. For most individuals the choice between party programmes will therefore be mainly a choice between evils, namely between different benefits to be provided for others at their expense.

The purely additive character of such a programme for governmental action stands out most clearly if we consider the problem that will face the leader of the party. He may or he may not have some chief objective for which he deeply cares. But whatever his ultimate objective, what he needs to achieve it is power. For this he needs the support of a majority which he can get only by enlisting people who are little interested in the objectives which guide him. To build up support for his programme he will therefore have to offer effective enticements to a sufficient number of special interests to bring together a majority for the support of his programme as a whole.

The agreement on which such a programme for governmental action is based is something very different from that common opinion of a majority which it was hoped would be the determining force in a democracy. Nor can this kind of bargaining be regarded as the kind of compromise that is inevitable whenever people differ and must be brought to agree on some middle line which does not wholly satisfy anybody. A series of deals by which the wishes of one group are satisfied in return for the satisfaction of the wishes of another (and frequently at the expense of a third who is not consulted) may determine aims for common action of a coalition, but does not signify popular approval of the overall results. The outcome may indeed be wholly contrary to any principles which the several members of the majority would approve if they ever had an opportunity to vote on them.

This domination of government by coalitions of organized interests (when they were first observed they were generally described as 'sinister interests') is usually regarded by the outsider as an abuse, or even a kind of corruption. It is, however, the inescapable result of a system in which government has unlimited powers to take whatever measures are required to satisfy the wishes of those on whose support it relies. A government with such powers cannot refuse to exercise them and still retain the support of a majority. We have no right to blame the politicians for doing what they must do in the position in which we have placed them. We have created conditions in which it is known that the majority has power to give any particular section of the population whatever it demands. But a government that possesses such unlimited powers can stay in office

15

only by satisfying a sufficiently large number of pressure groups to assure itself of the support of a majority.

Government, in the narrow sense of the administration of the special resources set aside for the satisfaction of common needs, will to some extent always have that character. Its task is to hand out particular benefits to different groups, which is altogether distinct from that of legislation proper. But while this weakness is comparatively innocuous as long as government is confined to determining the use of an amount of resources placed at its disposal according to rules it cannot alter (and particularly when, as in local government, people can escape exploitation by voting with their feet), it assumes alarming proportions when government and rulemaking come to be confused and the persons who administer the resources of government also determine how much of the total resources it ought to control. To place those who ought to define what is right in a position in which they can maintain themselves only by giving their supporters what they want, is to place at their disposal all the resources of society for whatever purpose they think necessary to keep them in power.

If the elected administrators of a certain share of the resources of a society were under a law which they could not alter, though they would have to use them so as to satisfy their supporters, they could not be driven beyond what can be done without interfering with the freedom of the individual. But if they are at the same time also the makers of those rules of conduct, they will be driven to use their power to organize not only the resources belonging to government, but all the resources of society, including the individual's, to serve the particular wishes of their constituents.

We can prevent government from serving special interests only by depriving it of the power to use coercion in doing so, which means that we can limit the powers of organized interests only by limiting the powers of government. A system in which the politicians believe that it is their duty, and in their power, to remove all dissatisfaction,[27] must lead to a complete manipulation of the people's affairs by the politicians. If that power is unlimited, it will and must be used in the service of particular interests, and it will induce all the organizable interests to combine in order to bring pressure upon government. The only defence that a politician has against such pressure is to point to an established principle which prevents him from complying and which he cannot alter. No system in which those who direct the use of the resources of government are not

16

bound by unalterable rules can escape becoming an instrument of the organized interests.

Agreement on general rules and on particular measures

We have repeatedly stressed that in a Great Society nobody can possess knowledge of, or have any views about, all the particular facts which might become the object of decisions by government. Any member of such a society can know no more than some small part of the comprehensive structure of relationships which makes up the society; but his wishes concerning the shaping of the sector of the overall pattern to which he belongs will inevitably conflict with the wishes of the others.

Thus, while nobody knows all, the separate desires will often clash in their effects and must be reconciled if agreement is to be reached. Democratic *government* (as distinguished from democratic legislation) requires that the consent of the individuals extend much beyond the particular facts of which they can be aware; and they will submit to a disregard of their own wishes only if they have come to accept some general rules which guide all particular measures and by which even the majority will abide. That in such situations conflict can be avoided only by agreement on general rules while, if agreement on the several particulars were required, conflicts would be irreconcilable, seems to be largely forgotten today.

True general agreement, or even true agreement among a majority, will in a Great Society rarely extend beyond some general principles, and can be maintained only on such particular measures as can be known to most of its members.[28] Even more important, such a society will achieve a coherent and self-consistent overall order only if it submits to general rules in its particular decisions, and does not permit even the majority to break these rules unless this majority is prepared to commit itself to a new rule which it undertakes henceforth to apply without exception.

We have seen earlier that commitment to rules is in some degree necessary even to a single individual who endeavours to bring order into a complex of actions he cannot know in detail in advance. It is even more necessary where the successive decisions will be made by different groups of people with reference to different parts of the whole. Successive votes on particular issues would in such conditions not be likely to produce an aggregate result of which anyone would approve, unless they were all guided by the same general rules.

It has in a great measure been an awareness of the unsatisfactory results of the established procedures of democratic decision-making that has led to the demand for an overall plan whereby all government action will be decided upon for a long period ahead. Yet such a plan would not really provide a solution for the crucial difficulty. At least, as it is usually conceived, it would still be the result of a series of particular decision on concrete issues and its determination would therefore raise the same problems. The effect of the adoption of such a plan is usually that it becomes a substitute for real criteria of whether the measures for which it provides are desirable.

The decisive facts are that not only will a true majority view in a Great Society exist only on general principles, but also that a majority can exercise some control over the outcome of the market process only if it confines itself to the laying down of general principles and refrains from interfering with the particulars even if the concrete results are in conflict with its wishes. It is inevitable that, when for the achievement of some of our purposes we avail ourselves of a mechanism that responds in part to circumstances unknown to us, its effects on some particular results should be contrary to our wishes, and that there will therefore often arise a conflict between the general rules we wish to see obeyed and the particular results that we desire.

In collective action this conflict will manifest itself most conspicuously because, while as individuals we have in general learned to abide by rules and are able to do so consistently, as members of a body that decides by majority votes we have no assurance that future majorities will abide by those rules which might forbid us to vote for particulars which we like but which are obtainable only by infringing an established rule. Though as individuals we have learnt to accept that in pursuing our aims we are limited by established rules of just conduct, when we vote as members of a body that has power to alter these rules, we often do not feel similarly restrained. In the latter situation most people will indeed regard it as reasonable to claim for themselves benefits of a kind which they know are being granted to others, but which they also know cannot be granted universally and which they would therefore perhaps prefer not to see granted to anybody at all. In the course of the particular decisions on specific issues the voters or their representatives will therefore often be led to support measures in conflict with principles which they would prefer to see generally observed. So long as there exist no rules that are binding on those who decide on the particular measures, it is thus inevitable that majorities will approve measures of a kind which, if they were asked to vote on the principle, they would probably prohibit once and for all.

The contention that in any society there will usually exist more agreement on general principles than on particular issues will at first perhaps appear contrary to ordinary experience. Daily practice seems to show that it is usually easier to obtain agreement on a particular issue than on a general principle. This, however, is a consequence merely of the fact that we usually do not explicitly know, and have never put into words, those common principles on which we know well how to act and which normally lead different persons to agree in their judgments. The articulation or verbal formulation of these principles will often be very difficult. This lack of conscious awareness of the principles on which we act does not disprove, however, that in fact we usually agree on particular moral issues only because we agree on the rules applicable to them. But we will often learn to express these common rules only by the examination of the various particular instances in which we have agreed, and by a systematic analysis of the points on which we agree.

If people who learn for the first time about the circumstances of a dispute will generally arrive at similar judgements on its merits, this means precisely that, whether they know it or not, they are in fact guided by the same principles, while, when they are unable to agree, this would seem to show that they lack such common principles. This is confirmed when we examine the nature of the arguments likely to produce agreement among parties who first disagreed on the merits of a particular case. Such arguments will always consist of appeals to general principles, or at least to facts which are relevant only in the light of some general principle. It will never be the concrete instance as such, but always its character as one of a class of instances, or as one that falls under a particular rule, that will be regarded as relevant. The discovery of such a rule on which we can agree will be the basis for arriving at an agreement on the particular issue.

THIRTEEN

THE DIVISION OF DEMOCRATIC POWERS

The most urgent problem of our age for those who give most urgency to the preservation of democratic institutions is that of restraining the vote-buying process.

W. H. Hutt*

The loss of the original conception of the functions of a legislature

It cannot be our task here to trace the process by which the original conception of the nature of democratic constitutions gradually was lost and replaced by that of the unlimited power of the democratically elected assembly. That has been done recently in an important book by M. J. C. Vile in which it is shown how during the English Civil War the abuse of its powers by Parliament 'had shown to men who had previously seen only the royal power as a danger, that parliament could be as tyrannical as a king' and how this led to 'the realisation that legislatures must also be subjected to restriction if individual freedom was not to be invaded'.[1] This remained the doctrine of the old Whigs until far into the eighteenth century. It found its most famous expression in John Locke who argued in effect that 'the legislative authority is the authority *to act in a particular way*'. Furthermore, Locke argued, those who wield this authority should make only general rules. 'They are to govern by promulgated established Laws, not to be varied in particular cases.'[2] One of the most influential statements is met with in *Cato's Letters* by John Trenchard and Thomas Gordon in which, in a passage already quoted in part, the former could maintain in 1721 that

> when the deputies thus act for their own interest, by acting for the interest of their principals; when they can make no laws but what they themselves, and their posterity must be subject to; when

20

they can give no money, but what they must pay their share of; when they can do no mischief but what fall upon their own heads in common with their countrymen; their principals may then expect good laws, little mischief, and much frugality.[3]

Even towards the end of the century, moral philosophers could still regard this as the basic principle of the British constitution and argue, as William Paley did in 1785, that when the legislative and the judicial character

are united in the same person or assembly, particular laws are made for particlar cases, springing oftentimes from partial motives, and directed to private ends: whilst they are kept separate, general laws are made by one body of men, without foreseeing whom they may affect; and when made must be applied by the other, let them affect whom they will . . . .

When the parties and the interests to be affected by the law were known, the inclinations of the law-makers would inevitably attach on one side or the other . . . .

Which dangers, by the division of the legislative and judicial functions, are effectually provided against. Parliament knows not the individuals upon whom its acts will operate; it has no cases or parties before it, no private designs to serve; consequently its resolutions will be suggested by the consideration of universal effects and tendencies, which always produces impartial and commonly advantageous regulations.[4]

No doubt this theory was an idealization even then and in fact the arrogation of arbitrary powers by Parliament was regarded by the spokesmen of the American colonies as the ultimate cause of the break with the mother country. This was most clearly expressed by one of the profoundest of their political philosophers, James Wilson, who

rejected Blackstone's doctrine of parliamentary sovereignty as outmoded. The British do not understand the idea of a constitution which limits and superintends the operations of the legislature. This was an improvement in the science of government reserved to the Americans.[5]

We shall not further consider here the American attempts to limit in their Constitution the powers of the legislature, and its limited success. It in fact did no more to prevent Congress from becoming primarily a governmental rather than a truly legislative institution and from developing in consequence all the characteristics which this chief preoccupation is apt to impress on an assembly and which must be the chief topic of this chapter.

Existing representative institutions have been shaped by the needs of government, not of legislation

The present structure of democratic governments has been decisively determined by the fact that we have charged the representative assemblies with two altogether different tasks. We call them 'legislatures' but by far the greater part of their work consists not in the articulation and approval of general rules of conduct but in the direction of the measures of government concerning particular matters.[6] We want, and I believe rightly, that both the laying down of general rules of conduct binding upon all and the administration of the resources and machinery placed at the disposal of government be guided by the wishes of the majority of the citizens. This need not mean, however, that these two tasks should be placed into the hands of the same body, nor that every resolution of such a democratically elected body must have the validity and dignity that we attach to the appropriately sanctioned general rules of conduct. Yet by calling 'law' every decision of that assembly, whether it lays down a rule or authorizes particular measures, the very awareness that these are different things has been lost.[7] Because most of the time and energy of the representative assemblies is taken up by the task of organizing and directing government, we have not only forgotten that government is different from legislation but have come to think that an instruction to government to take particular actions is the normal content of an act of law-giving. Probably the most far-reaching effect of this is that the very structure and organization of the representative assemblies has been determined by the needs of their governmental tasks but is unfavourable to wise rule-making.

It is important to remember in this connection that the founders of modern representative government were almost all apprehensive of political parties (or 'factions', as they usually called them), and to understand the reasons for their apprehension. The political theorists were still concerned chiefly with what they conceived to be the main task of a legislature, that is, the laying down of rules of just conduct for the private citizen, and did not attach much importance to its other task, the directing or controlling of government or

22

administration. For the former task clearly a body widely representative of the various shades of opinion but not committed to a particular programme of action would seem desirable.

But, as government rather than legislation became the chief task of the representative assemblies, their effectiveness for this task demanded the existence within them of a majority of members agreed on a programme of action. The character of modern parliamentary institutions has in fact been wholly shaped by these needs of democratic *government* rather than by those of democratic *legislation* in the strict sense of the latter term. The effective direction of the whole apparatus of government, or the control of the use of all the personal and material resources placed under its supervision, demands the continuous support of the executive authority by an organized majority committed to a coherent plan of action. Government proper will have to decide constantly what particular demands of interests it can satisfy; and even when it is limited to the use of those particular resources which are entrusted to its administration, it must continually choose between the requirements of different groups.

All experience has shown that if democratic government is to discharge these tasks effectively it must be organized on party lines. If the electorate is to be able to judge its performance, there must exist an organized group among the representatives that is regarded as responsible for the conduct of government, and an organized opposition that watches and criticizes and offers an alternative government if the people become dissatisfied with the one in power.

It is, however, by no means true that a body organized chiefly for the purpose of directing government is also suited for the task of legislation in the strict sense, i.e. to determine the permanent framework of rules of law under which it has to move its daily tasks.

Let us recall once more how different the task of government proper is from that of laying down the universally applicable rules of just conduct. Government is to act on concrete matters, the allocation of particular means to particular purposes. Even so far as its aim is merely to enforce a set of rules of just conduct given to it, this requires the maintenance of an apparatus of courts, police, penal institutions, etc., and the application of particular means to particular purposes. But in the wider sphere of government, that of rendering to the citizens other services of various kinds, the employment of the resources at its command will require constant choosing of the particular ends to be served, and such decisions must be largely a matter of expediency. Whether to build a road along one route or another one, whether to give a building one design or a different one, how to organize the police or the removal of rubbish, and so on, are all not questions of justice which can be decided by the application of a general rule, but questions of effective organization for satisfying the needs of various groups of people, which can be decided only in the light of the relative importance attached to the competing purposes. If such questions are to be decided democratically, the decisions will be about whose interests are to prevail over those of others.

Administration of common means for public purposes thus requires more than agreement on rules of just conduct. It requires agreement on the relative importance of particular ends. So far as the administration of those resources of society that are set aside for the use of government is concerned, somebody must have power to decide for which ends they are to be used. Yet the difference between a society of free men and a totalitarian one lies in the fact that in the former this applies only to that limited amount of resources that is specifically destined for governmental purposes, while in the latter it applies to all the resources of society including the citizens themselves. The limitation of the powers of government that a free society presupposes requires thus that even the majority should have unrestricted power only over the use of those resources which have been dedicated to common use, and that the private citizen and his property are not subject to specific commands (even of the legislature), but only to such rules of conduct as apply equally to all.

Since the representative assemblies which we call legislatures are predominantly concerned with governmental tasks, these tasks have shaped not only their organization but also the entire manner of thinking of their members. It is today often said that the principle of the separation of powers is threatened by the increasing assumption of legislative function by the administration. It was in fact largely destroyed much earlier, namely when the bodies called legislatures assumed the direction of government (or, perhaps more correctly, legislation was entrusted to existing bodies mainly concerned with government). The separation of powers has been supposed to mean that every coercive act of government required authorization by a universal rule of just conduct approved by a body not concerned with the particularly momentary ends of government. If we now call 'law' also the authorization of particular acts of government by a resolution of the representative assembly, such 'legislation' is not legislation in the sense in which the concept is used in the theory of the separation of powers; it means that the democratic assembly exercises executive powers without being bound by laws in the sense of general rules of conduct it cannot alter.

Bodies with powers of specific direction are unsuited for law-making

Though, if we want democratic government, there is evidently need for a representative body in which the people can express their wishes on all the issues which concern the actions of government, a body concerned chiefly with these problems is little suited for the task of legislation proper. To expect it to do both means asking it to deprive itself of some of the means by which it can most conveniently and expeditiously achieve the immediate goals of government. In its performance of governmental functions it will in fact not be bound by any general rules, for it can at any moment make the rules which enable it to do what the momentary task seems to require. Indeed, any particular decision it would make on a specific issue will automatically abrogate any previously existing rule it infringes. Such a combination of governmental and rule-making power in the hands of one representative body is evidently irreconcilable, not only with the principle of the separation of powers, but also with the ideals of government under the law and the rule of law.

If those who decide on particular issues can make for any purpose whatever law they like, they are clearly not under the rule of law; and it certainly does not correspond to the ideal of the rule of law if, whatever particular group of people, even if they be a majority, decide on such an issue is called a law. We can have a rule of law or a rule of majority, we can even have a rule of laws made by a majority which also governs[8] but only so long as the majority itself, when it decided particular matters, is bound by rules that it cannot change *ad hoc*, will the rule of law be preserved. Government subject to the control of a parliamentary assembly will assure a government under the law only if that assembly merely restrains the powers of the government by general rules but does not itself direct the actions of government, and by doing so make legal anything it orders government to do. The existing situation is such that even the awareness has been lost of the distinction between law in the sense of rules of just conduct and law in the sense of the expression of the majority's will on some particular matter. The conception that law is whatever the so-called legislature decides in the manner prescribed by the constitution is a result of the peculiar institutions of European democracy, because these are based on the erroneous belief that the recognized representatives of the majority of the people must have of necessity unlimited powers. American attempts to meet this difficulty have provided only a limited protection.

An assembly whose chief task is to decide what particular things should be done, and which in a parliamentary democracy supervises its executive committee (called government) in the carrying out of a programme of action approved by it, has no inducement or interest to tie itself by general rules. It can adapt the particular rules it lays down to the needs of the moment, and these rules will in general tend to serve the needs of the organization of government rather than the needs of the self-generating order of the market. Where it concerns itself with rules of just conduct, this will mostly be by-products of government and subservient to the needs of government. Such legislation will tend progressively to increase the discretionary powers of the government machinery and, instead of imposing limitations on government, become a tool to assist in the achievement of its particular ends.

The ideal of a democratic control of government and that of the limitation of government by law are thus different ideals that certainly cannot be both achieved by placing into the hands of the same representative body both rule-making and governmental powers. Though it would be possible to assure the realization of both these ideals, no nation has yet succeeded in doing this effectively by constitutional provisions; peoples have approached this state only temporarily thanks to the prevailing of certain strong political traditions. In recent times the effect of the existing institutional set up has been progressively to destroy what had remained of the tradition of the rule of law.

During the early periods of the representative government members of parliament could still be regarded as representatives of the general and not of the particular interests.[9] Though governments needed the confidence of the majority of parliament, this did not yet mean that an organized majority had to be maintained for the carrying out of a programme of policy. In peace-time at least most of the current activities of government were chiefly of a routine character for which little parliamentary authorization was needed beyond the approval of the annual budget; and this became the chief instrument through which the British House of Commons directly guided the activities of government.

The character of existing 'legislatures' determined by their governmental tasks

Although anyone even remotely familiar with modern politics has long come to take the present character of parliamentary proceedings for granted, when we come to think of it it is really astounding how far the reality of the concerns and practices of modern legislature differs from the image that most reasonable persons would form of an assembly which has to decide on the grave and difficult questions of the improvement of the legal order, or of the framework of rules within which the struggle of divergent interests ought to be conducted. An observer who was not used to the existent arrangements would probably soon come to the conclusion that politics as we know it is a necessary result of the fact that it is in the same arena that those limits are laid down and the struggle is conducted which they ought to restrain, and that the same persons who compete, for votes by offering the special favours are also supposed to lay down the limits of governmental power. There exists clearly an antagonism between these two tasks and it is illusory to expect the delegates to deprive themselves of those powers of bribing their mandatories by which they preserve their position.

It is hardly an exaggeration to say that the character of existing representative bodies has in the course of time been shaped almost entirely by their governmental tasks. From the methods of election of the members, the periods for which they are elected, the division of the assembly into organized parties, its order of business and rules of procedure, and above all the mental attitudes of the members, everything is determined by the concern with governmental measures, not with legislation. At least in the lower houses the budget, which is of course as far from legislation proper as anything can be, is the main event of the year.

All this tends to make the members agents of the interests of their constituents rather than representatives of public opinion. The election of an individual becomes a reward for having delivered the goods rather than an expression of confidence that the good sense, honesty and impartiality which he has shown in his private dealings will still guide him in his service to the public. People who hope to be re-elected on the basis of what their party during the preceding three or four years has conferred in conspicuous special benefits on their voters are not in the sort of position which will make them pass the kind of general laws which would really be most in the public interest.

It is a well-known fact that as a result of his double task the typical representative has neither time nor interest nor the desire or competence to preserve, and still less to improve, those limits to the coercive powers of government which is one of the chief purposes of law (the other being the protection against violence or coercion of people by their fellows)—and therefore, one may hope, of legislation. The governmental task of the popular assemblies, however, not only interferes with but often is in outright conflict with the aims of the law-maker.

We have earlier quoted the comments of one of the closest observers of British Parliament (a former Parliamentary Counsel of the Treasury) that 'For lawyer's law, parliament has neither time nor taste'.[10] It is worth while now to quote Sir Courtenay Ilbert's fuller account of the position in the British Parliament at the beginning of the century:

> The bulk of the members are not really interested in technical questions of law, and would always prefer to let the lawyers develop their rules and procedures in their own way. The substantial business of Parliament as a legislature [!] is to keep the machinery of State in working order. And the laws which are required for this purpose belong to the domain, not of private or of criminal law, but what is called on the Continent administrative law. . . . The bulk of the Statute book of each year will usually consist of administrative regulations, relating to matters which lie outside the ordinary reading and practice of the barrister.[11]

While this was already true of the British Parliament at the beginning of the century, I know of no contemporary democratic legislature of which it is not now equally true. The fact is that the legislators are in general largely ignorant of law proper, the lawyer's law which constitutes the rules of just conduct, and they concern themselves mostly with certain aspects of administrative law which progressively created for them a separate law even in England, where it was once understood that the private law limited the powers of governmental agents as much as those of the ordinary citizens. The result is that the British (who at one time flattered themselves that such a thing as administrative law was unknown in their country) are now subject to hundreds of administrative agencies capable of issuing binding orders.

The almost exclusive concern of the representatives with government rather than legislation is a consequence of the fact that they know that their re-election depends chiefly on the record of their party in government and not on legislation. It is the voters' satisfaction with the immediate effects of governmental measures, not their judgement of the effect of alterations in the law, noticeable only in the long run, which they will express at the polls. Since the individual representative knows that his re-election will depend chiefly on the popularity of his party and the support he will receive from his party, it will be the short run effects of the measures taken by it that will be his chief concern. Considerations about the principles involved may affect his initial choice of party, but since, once he has been elected for one party, a change of party may end his political career, he will in general leave such worries to the leaders of his party and immerse himself in the daily work arising out of the grievances of his constituents, dealing in its course with much routine administration.

His whole bias will thus be towards saying 'yes' to particular demands while the chief task of a true legislator ought to be to say 'no' to all claims for special privileges and to insist that certain kinds of things simply are not done. Whatever may have been the ideal described by Edmund Burke, a party today in general is not agreed on values but united for particular purposes. I do not wish to deny that even present day parties often form around a nucleus united by common principles or ideals. But since they must attract a following by promising other things, they can rarely if ever remain true to their principles and achieve a majority. It certainly is helpful to a party if it has principles by which it can justify the granting of special advantages to a sufficient number of groups to obtain a majority support.

The socialists have in this respect an advantage and, until they have accomplished their first aim and, having achieved control of the means of production, they have to face the task of assigning particular shares of the product to the different groups, are tied together by their belief in a common principle—or at least a form of words like 'social justice', the emptiness of which they have not yet discovered. They can concentrate on creating a new machinery rather than its use, and direct all their hopes to what the new machinery will achieve when completed. But they also are of course from the outset, as we have seen, agreed on the destruction of law in the sense of general rules of just conduct and its replacement by administrative orders. A socialist legislature would therefore be a purely governmental body—probably confined to rubber stamping the work of the planning bureaucracy.

For the task of laying down the limits of what government may do clearly a type of person is wanted wholly different from those whose main interest is to secure their re-election by getting special benefits for their supporters. One would have to entrust this not to men who have made party politics their life's concern and whose thinking is shaped by their preoccupation with their prospects of re-election, but to persons who have gained respect and authority in the ordinary business of life and who are elected because they are trusted to be more experienced, wise and fair, and who are then enabled to devote all their time to the long run problems of improving the legal framework of all actions, including those of government. They would have ample time to learn their jobs as legislators and not be helpless before (and the object of contempt of) that bureaucracy which makes in fact today the laws because the representative assemblies have not the time to do so.

Nothing indeed is more conspicuous in those assemblies than that what is supposed to be the chief business of a legislature is constantly crowded out, and that more and more of the tasks which the man in the street imagines to be the main occupation of the legislators are in fact performed by civil servants. It is largely because the legislatures are preoccupied by what in effect is discretionary administration that the true work of legislation is increasingly left in the hands of the bureaucracy, which of course has little power of restraining the governmental decision of the 'legislatures' which are too busy to legislate.

No less significant is it that when parliaments have to deal with true legislation concerning problems on which strong moral convictions exist and which many representatives regard as matters of conscience, such as the death penalty, abortion, divorce, euthanasia, the use of drugs (including alcohol and tobacco), pornography and the like, parties find it necessary to relax control over the voting of their members—in effect in all cases where we really want to find out what is dominant *opinion* on major issues rather

30

than the views on particular measures. It shows that there exist in fact no simple lines dividing the citizens into distinct groups of people who agree among themselves on a variety of principles as the party organization suggests. Agreement to obey certain principles is a different thing from agreeing to the manner of distributing various benefits.

An arrangement by which the interest of the highest authority is directed chiefly to government and not to law can only lead to a steady growth of the preponderance of government over law—and the progressive growth of the activities of government is largely a result of this arrangement. It is an illusion to expect from those who owe their positions to their power to hand out gifts that they will tie their own hands by inflexible rules prohibiting all special privileges. To leave the law in the hands of elective governors is like leaving the cat in charge of the cream jug—there soon won't be any, at least no law in the sense in which it limits the discretionary powers of government. Because of this defect in the construction of our supposedly constitutional democracies we have in fact again got that unlimited power which the eighteenth-century Whigs represented as 'so wild and monstrous a thing that however natural it be to desire it, it is as natural to oppose it'.[12]

Party legislation leads to the decay of democratic society

A system which may place any small group in the position to hold a society to ransom if it happens to be the balance between opposing groups, and can extort special privileges for its support of a party, has little to do with democracy or 'social justice'. But it is the unavoidable product of the unlimited power of a single elective assembly not precluded from discrimination by a restriction of its powers either to true legislation or to government under a law which it cannot alter.

Not only will such a system produce a government driven by blackmail and corruption, but it will also produce laws which are disapproved by the majority and in their long-run effects may lead to the decline of the society. Who would seriously maintain that the most fateful law in Britain's modern history, the Trade Disputes Act of 1906, was an expression of the will of the majority?[13] With the Conservative opposition wholly opposed, it is more than questionable whether even the majority of the members of the governing Liberal party approved of a bill 'drawn up by the first generation of Labour MPs'.[14] Yet the majority of the Liberal party depended on Labour support, and although the bill shocked the leading representatives of the British constitutional tradition probably more than any other act of modern legislative history,[15] the spectacular legal privileges granted in it to the trades unions has since become the chief cause of the progressive decline of the British economy.

Nor is there, with the present character of the existing Parliament, much hope that they will prove more capable of dealing intelligently with such crucial future tasks of legislation as the limits to the powers of all corporate bodies or the prohibition of restraints on competition. It is to be feared that they will be decided mainly by the popularity or unpopularity of the particular groups that are directly affected rather than by an understanding of the requirements of a functioning market order.

A further peculiar sort of bias of government created by the necessity to gain votes by benefiting particular groups or activities operates indirectly through the need to gain the support of those second-hand dealers of ideas, mainly in what are now called the 'media', who largely determine public opinion. This expresses itself among other manifestations in a support of modern art which the majority of the people certainly does not care for in the least, and certainly also in some of the governmental support to technological advance (the flight to the moon!) for which such support is certainly very questionable but by which a party can secure the sympathy and the support of those intellectuals who run the 'media'.

Democracy, so far as the term is not used simply as a synonym for egalitarianism, is increasingly becoming the name for the very process of vote-buying, for placating and remunerating those special interests which in more naive times were described as the 'sinister interests'. What we are concerned with now is, however, to show that what is responsible for this is not democracy as such but the particular form of democracy which we are practising today. I believe in fact that we should get a more representative sample of the true opinion of the people at large if we picked out by drawing lots some five hundred mature adults and let them for twenty years devote themselves to the task of improving the law, guided only by their conscience and the desire to be respected, than by the present system of auction by which every few years we entrust the power of legislation to those who promise their supporters the greatest special benefits. But, as we shall show later, there are better alternative systems of democracy than that of a single omnipotent assembly with unlimited powers which has produced the blackmail and corruption system of politics.

The constructivistic superstition of sovereignty

The conception that the majority of the people (or their elected representatives) ought to be free to decree whatever they can agree upon, and that in this sense they must be regarded as omnipotent, is closely connected with the conception of popular sovereignty. Its error lies not in the belief that whatever power there is should be in the hands of the people, and that their wishes will have to be expressed by majority decisions, but in the belief that this ultimate source of power must be unlimited, that is, the idea of sovereignty itself. The pretended logical necessity of such an unlimited source of power simply does not exist. As we have already seen, the belief in such a necessity is a product of the false constructivistic interpretation of the formation of human institution which attempts to trace them all to an original designer or some other deliberate act of will. The basic source of social order, however, is not a deliberate decision to adopt certain common rules, but the existence among the people of certain opinions of what is right and wrong. What made the Great Society possible was not a deliberate imposition of rules of conduct, but the growth of such rules among men who had little idea of what would be the consequence of their general observance.

Since all power rests on pre-existing opinions, and will last only so long as those opinions prevail, there is no real personal source of this power and no deliberate will which has created it. The conception of sovereignty rests on a misleading logical construction which starts from the initial assumption that the existing rules and institutions derive from a uniform will aiming at their creation. Yet, far from arising from such a pre-existing will capable of imposing upon the people whatever rules it likes, a society of free men presupposes that all power is limited by the common beliefs which made them join, and that where no agreement is present no power exists.[16]

Except where the political unit is created by conquest, people submit to authority not to enable it to do what it likes, but because they trust somebody to act in conformity with certain common conceptions of what is just. There is not first a society which then gives itself rules, but it is common rules which weld dispersed bands

33

into a society. The terms of submission to the recognized authority become a permanent limit of its powers because they are the condition of the coherence and even existence of the state—and these terms of submission were understood in the liberal age to be that coercion could be used only for the enforcement of recognized general rules of just conduct. The conception that there must be an unlimited will which is the source of all power is the result of a constructivistic hypostasation, a fiction made necessary by the false factual assumptions of legal positivism but unrelated to the actual sources of allegiance.

The first question we should always ask in contemplating the structure of governmental powers is not who possesses such and such a power, but whether the exercise of such a power by any agency is justified by the implicit terms of submission to that agency. The ultimate limit of power is therefore not somebody's will on particular matters, but something quite different: the concurrence of opinions among members of a particular territorial group on rules of just conduct. The famous statement by Francis Bacon which is the ultimate source of legal positivism, that 'a supreme and absolute power cannot conclude itself, neither can that which is in its true nature revocable be fixed'[17] thus wrongly presupposes a derivation of all power from some act of purposive will. But the resolve that 'we will let us by governed by a good man, but if he is unjust we will throw him out' does not mean that we confer on him unlimited powers or powers which we already have! Power does not derive from some single seat but rests on the support by common opinion of certain principles and does not extend further than this support. Though the highest source of deliberate decisions cannot effectively limit its own powers, it is itself limited by the source from which its power derives which is not another act of will but a prevailing state of opinion. There is no reason why allegiance, and therefore the authority of the state, should survive the arrogation of arbitrary powers which has neither the support of the public nor can be effectively enforced by the usurping government.

In the Western world unlimited sovereignty was scarcely ever claimed by anyone since antiquity until the arrival of absolutism in the sixteenth century. It was certainly not conceded to medieval princes and hardly ever claimed by them. And although it was successfully claimed by the absolute monarchs of the European Continent, it was not really accepted as legitimate until after the advent of modern democracy which in this respect has inherited the

34

tradition of absolutism. Till then the conception was still kept alive that legitimacy rested in the last resort on the approval by the people at large of certain fundamental principles underlying and limiting all government, and not on their consent to particular measures. But when this explicit consent that was devised as a check upon power came to be regarded as the sole source of power, the conception of unlimited power was for the first time invested with the aura of legitimacy.

The idea of the omnipotence of some authority as a result of the source of its power is thus essentially a degeneration that, under the influence of the constructivistic approach of legal positivism, appeared wherever democracy had existed for any length of time. It is, however, by no means a necessary consequence of democracy, but a consequence only of the deceptive belief that, once democratic procedures have been adopted, all the results of the machinery of ascertaining the will of the majority in fact correspond to the *opinion* of a majority, and that there is no limit to the range of question on which agreement of the majority can be ascertained by this procedure. It was helped by the naive belief that in this way the people were 'acting together'; and a sort of fairy tale spread that 'the people' are doing things and that this is morally preferable to the separate actions by individuals. In the end this fantasy led to the curious theory that the democratic decision-making process always is directed towards the common good—the common good being defined as the conclusions which the democratic procedures produces. The absurdity of this is shown by the fact that different but equally justifiable procedures for arriving at a democratic decision may produce very different results.

The requisite division of the powers of representative assemblies

The classical theory of representative government assumed that its aim could be achieved by allowing the division between the legislature and the administration to coincide with the division between an elected representative assembly and an executive body appointed by it. It failed to do so because there was of course as strong a case for democratic government as for democratic legislation and the sole democratically elected assembly inevitably claimed the right to direct government as well as the power to legislate. It thus came to combine the powers of legislation with those of government. The result was the revival of the monstrous establishment of an absolute power not restricted by any rules. I trust there will come a time when people will look with the same horror at the idea of a body of men, even one authorized by the majority of the citizens, who possesses power to order whatever it likes, as we feel today about most other forms of authoritarian government. It creates a barbarism, not because we have given barbarians power, but because we have released power from the restraint of rules, producing effects that are inevitable, whoever the people to whom such power is entrusted. It may well be that common people often have a stronger sense of justice than any intellectual élite guided by the lust for new deliberate construction; yet when unrestricted by any rules they are likely to act more arbitrarily than any élite or even a single monarch who is so bound. This is so, not because the faith in the common man is misplaced, but because he is thereby given a task which exceeds human capacities.

Though government proper in the performance of its characteristic tasks cannot be strictly tied to rules, its powers for this very reason ought always to be limited in extent and scope, namely confined to the administration of a sharply circumscribed range of means entrusted to its care. All power, however, that is not thus confined to a particular mass of material things but is unlimited in extent should be confined to the enforcement of general rules; while those who have the rule-making power should be confined to providing for the enforcement of such general rules and have no power of deciding on particular measures. All ultimate power should, in other words, be subject to the test of justice, and be free to do what it desires only in so far as it is prepared to commit itself to a principle that is to be applied in all similar instances.

The aim of constitutions has been to prevent all arbitrary action. But no constitution has yet succeeded in achieving this aim. The belief that they have succeeded in this has however led people to regard the terms 'arbitrary' and 'unconstitutional' as equivalent. Yet the prevention of arbitrariness, though one of the aims, is by no means a necessary effect of obeying a constitution. The confusion on this point is a result of the mistaken conception of legal positivism. The test of whether a constitution achieves what constitutions are meant to do is indeed the effective prevention of arbitrariness; but this does not mean that every constitution provides an adequate test of what is arbitrary, or that something that is permitted by a constitution may not still be arbitrary.

If the supreme power must always prove the justice of its intentions by committing itself to general rules, this requires institutional arrangements which will secure that general rules will always prevail over the particular wishes of the holders of authority— including even the case where a very large majority favours a particular action but another, much smaller majority would be prepared to commit itself to a rule which would preclude that action. (This is not incompatible with the former, since it would be entirely rational to prefer that actions of the kind in question be prohibited altogether, yet so long as they are permitted to favour a particular one.) Or, to put this differently, even the largest majority should in its coercive acts be able to break a previously established rule *only* if it is prepared explicitly to abrogate it and to commit itself to a new one. Legislation in the true sense ought always to be a commitment to act on stated principles rather than a decision how to act in a particular instance. It must, therefore, essentially aim at effects in the long run, and be directed towards a future the particular circumstances of which are not yet known; and the resulting laws must aim at helping unknown people for their equally unknown purposes. This task demands for its successful accomplishment persons not concerned with particular situations or committed to the support of particular interests, but men free to look at their tasks from the point of view of the long run desirability of the rules laid down for the community as a whole.

Though true legislation is thus essentially a task requiring the long view, even more so than that of the designing of a constitution, it differs from the latter in that it must be a continuous task, a persistent effort to improve the law gradually and to adapt it to new conditions—essentially helping where jurisdiction cannot keep pace with a rapid development of facts and opinions. Though it may require formal decisions only at long intervals, it demands constant application and study of the kind for which politicians busy wooing their supporters and fully occupied with pressing matters demanding rapid solution will not really have time.

The task of legislation proper differs from the task of constitution-making also in that it will be concerned with rules of greater generality than those contained in a constitution. A constitution is chiefly concerned with the organization of government and the allocation of the different powers to the various parts of this organization. Though it will often be desirable to include in the formal

37

documents 'constituting' the organization of the state some principles of substantive justice in order to confer upon these special protection, it is still true that a constitution is essentially a superstructure erected to serve the enforcement of existing conceptions of justice but not to articulate them: it presupposes the existence of a system of rules of just conduct and merely provides a machinery for their regular enforcement.

We need not pursue this point further at this stage since all that we want to point out here is that the task of true legislation is as different from that of constitution-making as it is from that of governing, and that it ought to be as little confused with the former as with the latter. It follows from this that, if such confusion is to be avoided, a three-tiered system of representative bodies is needed, of which one would be concerned with the semi-permanent framework of the constitution and need act only at long intervals when changes in that framework are considered necessary, another with the continuous task of gradual improvement of the general rules of just conduct, and a third with the current conduct of government, that is, the administration of the resources entrusted to it.

Democracy or demarchy?

We cannot consider here further the changes which the meaning of the concept of democracy has undergone by its increasingly common transfer from the political sphere in which it is appropriate to other spheres in which it is very doubtful whether it can be meaningfully applied:[18] and whether its persistent and deliberate abuse by the communists as in such terms as 'people's democracies', which of course lack even the most basic characteristics of a democracy, does not make it unsuitable to describe the ideal it was originally meant to express. These tendencies are mentioned here merely because they are contributing further to deprive the term 'democracy' of clear meaning and turn it into a word-fetish used to clothe with an aura of legitimacy any demands of a group that wishes to shape some feature of society to its special wishes.

The legitimacy of the demands for more democracy becomes particularly questionable when they are directed to the manner in which organizations of various kinds are conducted. The problems which arise here show themselves at once when it is asked who are to be regarded as the 'members' of such organizations for whom a share in their direction is claimed. It is by no means obvious that a person who finds it in his interest to sell his services should thereby also acquire a voice in its conduct or in determining the purposes towards which this organization is to be directed. We all know that the conduct of the campaign of an army could not be directed democratically. It is the same with such simple operations as the building of a house or the conduct of an enterprise of the bureaucratic machinery of government.

And who are the 'members' of a hospital, or an hotel, or a club, a teaching institution or a department store? Those who serve these institutions, those whom these institutions serve, or those who provide the material means required to render the services? I ask these questions here simply to make clear that the term democracy, though we all still use it and feel we ought to defend the ideal it describes, has ceased to express a definite conception to which one can commit oneself without much explanation, and which in some of the senses in which it is now frequently used has become a serious threat to the ideals it was once meant to depict. Though I firmly believe that government ought to be conducted according to principles approved by a majority of the people, and must be so run if we are to preserve peace and freedom, I must frankly admit that *if* democracy is taken to mean government by the unrestricted will of the majority I am not a democrat, and even regard such government as pernicious and in the long run unworkable.

A question which has arisen here is whether those who believe in the original ideal of democracy can still usefully avail themselves of that old name to express their ideal. I have come seriously to doubt whether this is still expedient and feel more and more convinced that, if we are to preserve the original ideal, we may have to invent a new name for it. What we need is a word which expresses the fact that the *will* of the greater number is authoritative and binding upon the rest only if the former prove their intention of acting justly by committing themselves to a general rule. This demands a name indicating a system in which what gives a majority legitimate power is not bare might but the proven conviction that it regards as right what it decrees.

It so happens that the Greek word 'democracy' was formed by combining the word for the people (*demos*) with that of the two available terms for power, namely *kratos* (or the verb *kratein*) which had not already been used in such a combination for other purposes. *Kratein*, however, unlike the alternative verb *archein* (used in such compounds as monarchy, oligarchy, anarchy, etc.) seems to stress brute force rather than government by rule. The reason why in ancient Greece the latter root could not be used to form the term *demarchy* to express a rule by the people was that the term *demarch* had (at least in Athens) been preempted by an earlier use for the office of the head of a local group or district (the *deme*), and thus was no longer available as a description of government by the people at large. This need not prevent us today from adopting the term *demarchy* for the ideal for which *democracy* was originally adopted when it gradually supplanted the older expression *isonomy*, describing the ideal of an equal law for all.[19] This would give us the new name we need if we are to preserve the basic ideal in a time when, because of the growing abuse of the term democracy for systems that lead to the creation of new privileges by coalitions or organized interests, more and more people will turn against that prevailing system. If such a justified reaction against abuse of the term is not to discredit the ideal itself, and lead people in their disillusionment to accept much less desirable forms of government, it would seem necessary that we have a new name like demarchy to describe the old ideal by a name that is not tainted by long abuse.

FOURTEEN

THE PUBLIC SECTOR AND THE PRIVATE SECTOR

> The distinction between legislation and taxation is essential to liberty.
>
> William Pitt, Earl of Chatham*

The double task of government

Since in this book we are mainly concerned with the limits that a free society must place upon the coercive powers of government, the reader may get the mistaken impression that we regard the enforcement of the law and the defence against external enemies as the only legitimate functions of government. Some theorists in the past have indeed advocated such a 'minimal state'.[1] It may be true that in certain conditions, where an undeveloped government apparatus is scarcely yet adequate to perform this prime function, it would be wise to confine it to it, since an additional burden would exceed its weak powers and the effect of attempting more would be that it did not even provide the indispensable conditions for the functioning of a free society. Such considerations are not relevant, however, to advanced Western societies, and have nothing to do with the aim of securing individual liberty to all, or with making the fullest use of the spontaneous ordering forces of a Great Society.

Far from advocating such a 'minimal state',[2] we find it unquestionable that in an advanced society government ought to use its power of raising funds by taxation to provide a number of services which for various reasons cannot be provided, or cannot be provided adequately, by the market. Indeed, it could be maintained that, even if there were no other need for coercion, because everybody voluntarily obeyed the traditional rules of just conduct, there would still exist an overwhelming case for giving the territorial authorities power to make the inhabitants contribute to a common fund from which such services could be financed. The contention

41

that where the market can be made to supply the services required it is the most effective method of doing so does not imply that we may not resort to other methods where the former is not applicable. Nor can it be seriously questioned that where certain services can be provided only if all beneficiaries are made to contribute to their costs, because they cannot be confined to those to pay for them, only the government should be entitled to use such coercive powers.

Any adequate discussion of the manner in which the service activities of the government should be regulated, or the raising and the administration of the material means placed at the disposal of government for these services controlled, would require another volume of about the same size as the present one. All we can attempt here in a single chapter is to indicate the wide range of such wholly legitimate activities which, as the administrator of common resources, government may legitimately undertake. The purpose of such a sketch can be no more than to prevent the impression that by limiting the *coercive* activities and the monopoly of government to the enforcement of rules of just conduct, defence, and the levying of taxes to finance its activities, we want to restrict government wholly to those functions.

While it is the possession of coercive powers which enables government to obtain the means for rendering services which cannot be rendered commercially, this should not mean that as the supplier or organizer of such services it ought to be able to use the coercive powers. We shall see that the necessity of relying on the coercive powers to raise the finance does not even necessarily mean that those services ought also to be organized by government. That organization by government is sometimes the most expedient way of providing them certainly does not mean that as the provider of the services government need or ought to claim any of those attributes of authority and reverence which it traditionally and rightly enjoys in its authoritative functions (and which particularly in the German tradition have found their most marked expression in the mystique of *Hoheit* and *Herrschaft*). It is indeed most important that we keep clearly apart these altogether different tasks of government and do not confer upon it in its service functions the authority which we concede to it in the enforcement of the law and defence against enemies. There is no reason whatsoever why such authority or exclusive right should be transferred to the purely utilitarian service agencies entrusted to government simply because it alone can finance them. There is nothing reprehensible in treating these agencies as a purely utilitarian device, quite as useful as the butcher and the baker but no more so—and somewhat more suspect, because of the powers of compulsion which they can employ to cover their costs. If modern democracy often fails to show that respect for the law which is due to it, it also tends unduly to extol the role of the state in its service functions and to claim for it in this role privileges which it ought to possess only as the upholder of law and order.

Collective goods

The effectiveness of the market order and of the institution of several property rests on the fact that in most instances the producers of particular goods and services will be able to determine who will benefit from them and who pay for their costs. The conditions that the benefits due to a person's activities can be confined to those willing to pay for them, and withheld from those not willing (and, correspondingly, that all harm done has to be paid for), is largely satisfied so far as material commodities in private possessions are concerned: ownership of a particular movable subject generally confers on the owner control over most of the beneficial or harmful effects of its use. But as soon as we turn from commodities in the narrow sense to land, this is true only to a limited degree. It is often impossible to confine the effects of what one does to one's own land to this particular piece; and hence arise those 'neighbourhood effects' which will not be taken into account so long as the owner has to consider only the effects on his property. Hence also the problems which arise with respect to the pollution of air or water and the like. In these respects calculation by the individuals which takes into account only the effects upon their protected domain will not secure that balancing of costs and benefits which will in general be achieved where we have to do with the use of particular movable things with regard to which the owner alone will experience the effects of their use.

In some instances the conditions which the market requires in order to perform its ordering function will be satisfied only with respect to some of the results of activities of the individuals. These will on the whole still be effectively guided by the price mechanism, even though some of the effects of these activities will spill over on others who either do not pay for the benefits they receive or are not compensated for damage done to them. In these instances the economists speak of (positive or negative) *external* effects. In other instances, however, it is either technically impossible, or would be prohibitively costly, to confine certain services to particular persons, so that these services can be provided only for all (or at least will be provided more cheaply and effectively if they are provided for all). To this category belong not only such obvious instances as the protection against violence, epidemics, or such natural forces as floods or avalanches, but also many of the amenities which make life in modern cities tolerable, most roads (except some long-distance highways where tolls can be charged), the provision of standards of measure, and of many kinds of information ranging from land registers, maps, and statistics to the certification of the quality of some goods or services offered in the market. In many instances the rendering of such services could bring no gain to those who do so, and they will therefore not be provided by the market. These are the collective or public goods proper, for the provision of which it will be necessary to devise some method other than that of sale to the individual users.

It might at first be thought that for such purposes coercion would be unnecessary, because the recognition of a common interest that can be satisfied only by common action would lead a group of reasonable people voluntarily to join in the organizing of such services and pay for them. But, though this is likely to happen in comparatively small groups, it is certainly not true of large groups. Where large numbers are involved, most individuals, however much they may wish that the services in question should be made available, will reasonably believe that it will make no difference to the results whether they themselves agree to contribute to the costs or not. Nor will any individual who consents to contribute have the assurance that the others will also do so and that therefore the object will be attained. Indeed, wholly rational considerations will lead each individual, while wishing that all the others would contribute, to refuse himself to do so.[3] If, on the other hand, he knows that compulsion can be applied only if it is applied to all including himself, it will be rational for him to agree to be compelled, provided this compulsion is also applied to others. This will in many instances be the only way in which collective goods can be provided which are desired by all or at least by a large majority.

The morality of this kind of coercion to positive action is, perhaps, not as obvious as the morality of the rules which merely prevent the individual from infringing the protected domain of others. Particularly where the collective good in question is not wanted by all or at least by a considerable majority, this does raise serious problems. Yet it will clearly be in the interest of the different individuals to agree that the compulsory levying of means to be used also for purposes for which they do not care so long as others are similarly made to contribute to ends which they desire but the others do not. Though this looks as if the individuals were made to serve purposes for which they do not care, a truer way of looking at it is to regard it as a sort of exchange: each agreeing to contribute to a common pool according to the same uniform principles on the understanding that his wishes with regard to the services to be financed from that pool will be satisfied in proportion to his contributions. So long as each may expect to get from this common pool services which are worth more to him than what he is made to contribute, it will be in his interest to submit to the coercion. Since in the case of many collective goods it will not be possible to ascertain with any precision who will benefit from them or to what extent, all we can aim at will be that each should feel that in the aggregate all the collective goods which are supplied to him are worth at least as much as the contribution he is required to make.

With many collective goods which satisfy the needs only of the inhabitants of a particular region or locality, this aim can be more closely approached if not only the administration of the services but also the taxation is placed in the hands of a local rather than a central authority. If in the greater part of this book, for the sake of brevity, we shall as a rule have to speak of government in the singular and must stress that only government ought to possess the power of raising funds by compulsion, this must not be misunderstood to mean that such power should be concentrated in a single central authority. A satisfactory arrangement for the provision of collective goods seems to require that the task be to a great extent delegated to local and regional authorities. Within the scope of this book we shall have little opportunity to consider the whole issue of centralization versus decentralization of government, or of unitary government versus federalism. We can merely emphasize here that our stress on coercion being a monopoly of government by no means necessarily implies that this power of coercion should be concentrated in a single central government. On the contrary, the delegation of all powers that can be exercised locally to agencies whose powers are confined to the locality is probably the best way of securing that the burdens of and the benefits from government action will be approximately proportional.

Two points must chiefly be remembered throughout the following discussion of the public sector. The first is that, contrary to an assumption often tacitly made, the fact that some services must be financed by compulsory levies by no means implies that such services should also be administered by government. Once the problem of finance is solved, it will often be the more effective method to leave the organization and management of such services to competitive enterprise and rely on appropriate methods of apportioning the funds raised by compulsion among the producers in accordance with some expressed preference of the users. Professor Milton Friedman has developed an ingenious scheme of this kind for the financing of education through vouchers to be given to the parents of the children and to be used by them as total or partial payment for the services rendered by schools of their choice, a principle capable of application in many other fields. [4]

The second important point to be remembered throughout is that in the case of collective goods proper, as well as in some instances of these 'external effects' which make part of the effects of individual activities a kind of collective good (or collective nuisance), we are resorting to an *inferior* method of providing these services because the conditions necessary for their being provided by the more efficient method of the market are absent. Where the services in question will be most effectively provided if their production is guided by the spontaneous mechanism of the market, it will still be desirable to rely on it, and to use the coercive method of central determination only for the raising of the funds but leave the organization of the production of these services and the distribution of the available means among the different producers still as far as possible to the forces of the market. And one of the guiding considerations in resorting to the technique of deliberate organization where this is indispensable for the achievement of particular goals, must always be that we do not do so in a manner which impairs the functioning of the spontaneous market order on which we remain dependent for many other and often more important needs.

The delimitation of the public sector

If government has the exclusive right of coercion this will often mean that it is alone able to provide certain services which must be financed by coercive levies. This ought not to mean, however, that the right of providing such services should be reserved to government if other means can be found for providing them. The current distinction between the public sector and the private is sometimes erroneously taken to mean that some services beyond the enforcement of rules of just conduct should be reserved to government by law. There is no justification for this. Even if in given circumstances only government is in fact able to supply particular services, this is no reason for prohibiting private agencies from trying to find methods of providing these services without the use of coercive powers. It is even important that the manner in which government provides such services should not be such that it makes it impossible for others to provide them. New methods may be found for making a service saleable which before could not be restricted to those willing to pay for it, and thus make the market method applicable to areas where before it could not be applied. Wireless broadcasting is an instance: so long as the transmission of any station can be received by anybody, a sale to the particular users of a programme is impossible. But technical advance might well open the possibility of confining reception to those using particular equipment, making the operation of the market possible.

What is generally described as the public sector ought thus not to be interpreted as a set of functions or services reserved to the government; it should rather be regarded as a circumscribed amount of material means placed at the disposal of government for the rendering of services it has been asked to perform. In this connection government needs no other special power than that of compulsory raising means in accordance with some uniform principle, but in administering these means it ought not to enjoy any special privileges and should be subject to the same general rules of conduct and potential competition as any other organization.

The existence of such a public sector[5] comprising all the personal and material resources placed under the control of government, and all the institutions and facilities provided and maintained by it for general use, creates problems of regulation which are determined today by legislation. The 'laws' which are made for this purpose are, however, of a very different character from those universal rules of conduct which we have so far considered as *the law*. They regulate the rendering, and the use by private persons, of such public facilities as roads and the various other public services that are provided by government for general use. The rules required will clearly be in the nature of rules of organization aiming at particular results, rather than rules of just conduct delimiting private spheres; and their content will be determined chiefly by considerations of efficiency or expediency rather than of justice. They are affairs of government, not of legislation proper; and though in establishing such rules for the use of the services it provides, government ought to be bound by certain general requirements of justice, such as the avoidance of arbitrary discrimination, the substantive content of the rules will be determined mainly by considerations of expediency or the efficiency of the services to be rendered.

A good example of such rules for the use of public institutions that is often but misleadingly cited as an instance of rules of just conduct is the Rule of the Road, or the whole system of traffic regulations. Though these rules also have the form of rules of conduct, they differ from the universal rules of just conduct in not delimiting private domains and not applying universally but only to the use of certain facilities provided by government. (The Rule of the Road, for example, does not apply to the traffic in a private park closed to the general public.)

Though such special regulations for the use of facilities provided by government for the public are undoubtedly necessary, we must guard against the prevailing tendency to extend this conception of regulation to other so-called public places which are provided commercially by private enterprise. A privately owned theatre, factory, department store, sports ground or general purpose building does not become a public place in the strict sense because the public at large is invited to use it. There exists unquestionably a strong case for the establishment of uniform rules under which such places may be thrown open to the public: it is evidently desirable that on entering such a place one may presume that certain requirements of safety and health are met. But such rules which must be observed in throwing private institutions open for general use fall into a somewhat different category from those made for the use and conduct of institutions provided and maintained by government. Their content will not be determined by the purpose of the institution, and their aim will merely be to protect the persons using its facilities by informing them what they may count upon in any place they are invited to enter for their own purposes, and what they will be allowed to do there. The particular owner will of course be free to add to these legal requirements for any place open to the general public his own special terms on which he is prepared to admit customers. And most of the special regulations that will be laid down for the use of particular services provided by government are of this kind rather than general laws.

The independent sector

That the 'public sector' should not be conceived of as a range of purposes for the pursuit of which government has a monopoly, but rather as a range of needs that government is asked to meet so long and in so far as they cannot be met better in other ways, is particularly important to remember in connection with another important issue which we can only even more briefly touch upon here. Though government may have to step in where the market fails to supply a needed service, the use of the coercive powers of government for raising the required means is often not the only, or the best, alternative. It may be the most effective means of providing collective goods in those intances where they are wanted by a majority, or at least by a section of the population sufficiently numerous to make its weight felt politically. There will at all times be many services wanted, however, which are needed by many and which have all the characteristics of collective goods, but for which only relatively small numbers care. It is the great merit of the market that it serves minorities as well as majorities. There are some fields, particularly those usually described as 'cultural' concerns, in which it must even appear doubtful whether the views of majorities ought to be allowed to gain a preponderant influence, or those of small groups overlooked—as is likely to happen when the political organization becomes the only channel through which some tastes can express themselves. All new tastes and desires are necessarily at first tastes and desires of a few, and if their satisfaction were dependent on approval by a majority, much of what the majority might learn to like after they have been exposed to it might never become available.

It should be remembered that long before government entered those fields, many of the now generally recognized collective needs were met by the efforts of the public-spirited individuals or groups providing means for public purposes which they regarded as important. Public education and public hospitals, libraries and museums, theatres and parks, were not first created by governments. And although in these fields in which private benefactors have led the way, governments have now largely taken over,[6] there is still need for initiative in many areas whose importance is not yet generally recognized and where it is not possible or desirable that government take over.

In the past it has been initially the churches, but more recently, and especially in the English-speaking world, it has been to a great extent foundations and endowments, private associations and the innumerable private charities and welfare agencies, that have led the way. To some extent these have had their origin in the dedication of large private fortunes for various philanthropic purposes. But many are due to idealists with small means who have devoted their organizational and propagandist talents to a particular cause. There can be no doubt that we owe to such voluntary efforts the recognition of many needs and the discovery of many methods of meeting them which we could never have expected from the government; and that in some fields voluntary effort is more effective and provides outlets for valuable energies and sentiments of individuals that otherwise would remain dormant. No governmental agency has ever thought out or brought into being so effective an organization as Alcoholics Anonymous. It seems to me that local efforts at rehabilitation offer more hope for the solution of the urgent problems of our cities than governmental 'urban renewal'.[7] And there would be many more such developments if the habit of appealing to government, and a short-sighted desire to apply at once and everywhere the now visible remedies, did not so often lead to the whole field being preempted by government whose often clumsy first attempts then block the way for something better.

In this respect the accepted two-fold division of the whole field into a private and a public sector is somewhat misleading. As R. C. Cornuelle has forcefully argued,[8] it is most important for a healthy society that we preserve between the commercial and the governmental a third, *independent sector* which often can and ought to provide more effectively much that we now believe must be provided by government. Indeed, such an independent sector could to a great extent, in direct competition with government for public service, mitigate the gravest danger of governmental action, namely the creation of a monopoly with all the powers and inefficiency of a monopoly. It just is not true that, as J. K. Galbraith tells us, 'there is no alternative to public management'.[9] There often is, and at least in the USA people owe to it much more than they are aware of. To develop this independent sector and its capacities is in many fields the only way to ward off the danger of complete domination of social life by government. R. C. Cornuelle has shown the way; and his optimism regarding what the independent sector could achieve if deliberately cultivated and developed, though it may at first seem illusionary, does not appear excessive. His small book on the subject seems to me to be one of the most promising developments of political ideas in recent years.

Though the actual and potential achievements of this independent sector would constitute a very good illustration of one of the basic contentions of the present book, we can, since our aim is chiefly to devise effective limits to governmental powers, give only passing attention to them. I wish I could write about the subject at length, even if it were only to drive home the point that public spirit need not always mean demand for or support of government action. I must, however, not stray too far from the proper subject of this chapter, which is the service functions which government might usefully perform, not those which it need not take upon itself.

Taxation and the size of the public sector

The degrees of interest of different individuals in the various services provided by government differ a great deal; true agreement between them is likely to be achieved only on the volume of such services to be rendered, provided that each may expect that he will get approximately as much in services as he pays in taxes. This, as we have seen, ought to be interpreted not as each agreeing to pay the costs of all government services, but rather as each consenting to pay according to the same uniform principle for the services which he receives at the expense of the common pool. It ought therefore to be the decision on the level of taxation that should determine the total size of the public sector.

But if it is only through agreement on the total volume of government services, that is, agreement on the total of resources to be entrusted to government, that a rational decision regarding the services which government is to render can be achieved, this presupposes that every citizen voting for a particular expenditure should know that he will have to bear his predetermined share in the cost. Yet the whole practice of public finance has been developed in an endeavour to outwit the taxpayer and to induce him to pay more

51

than he is aware of, and to make him agree to expenditure in the belief that somebody else will be made to pay for it. Even in the theory of public finance all possible considerations have been advanced for determining the principles of taxation, except the one that seems to be the most important in a democracy: that the decision procedure should lead to a rational limitation of the volume of public expenditure. This would seem to require that the principles on which the burden is to be shared by the individuals be determined in advance, and that whoever votes in favour of a particular expenditure knows that he will have to contribute to it at a predetermined rate and thus be able to balance advantages against costs.

The main concern of public finance, however, has from the beginning been to raise the largest sums with the least resistance; and what should have been the main consideration, namely that the method of raising the means should operate as a check on total expenditure, has been little considered. But a method of taxation that encourages the belief that 'the other fellow will pay for it', together with the admission of the principle that any majority has the right to tax minorities in accordance with rules which do not apply to the former (as in any overall progression of the tax burden), must produce a continuous growth of public expenditure beyond what the individual really desires. A rational and responsible decision on the volume of public expenditure by democratic vote presupposes that in each decision the individual voters are aware that they will have to pay for the expenditure determined. Where those who consent to an item of expenditure do not know that they will have to pay for it, and the question that is considered is rather to whom the burden can be shifted, and where the majority in consequence feel that their decisions refer to expenditure to be paid for from other people's pockets, the result is that it is not expenditure which is adjusted to available means, but that means will be found to meet an expenditure which is determined without regard to costs. This process leads in the end to a general attitude which regards political pressure, and the compulsion of others, as the cheap way of paying for most services one desires.

A rational decision on the volume of public expenditure is to be expected only if the principles by which the contribution of each is assessed assures that in voting on any expenditure he will take the costs into account, and therefore only if each voter knows that he will have to contribute to all expenditure he approves in accordance with a predetermined rule, but cannot command anything to be done at somebody else's expense. The prevailing system provides instead a built-in inducement to irresponsible and wasteful expenditure.

The tendency of the public sector to grow progressively and indefinitely led, almost a hundred years ago, to the formulation of a 'law of growing government expenditure'.[10] In some countries such as Great Britain the growth has now reached the point where the share of national income controlled by government amounts to more than 50 per cent. This is but a consequence of that built-in bias of the existing institutions towards the expansion of the machinery of government; and we can hardly expect it to be otherwise in a system in which the 'needs' are fixed first and the means then provided by the decision of people who are mostly under the illusion that they will not have to provide them.

While there is some reason to believe that with the increase in general wealth and of the density of population, the share of all needs that can be satisfied only by collective action will continue to grow, there is little reason to believe that the share which governments, and especially central governments, already control is conducive to an economic use of resources. What is generally overlooked by those who favour this development is that every step made in this direction means a transformation of more and more of the spontaneous order to society that serves the varying needs of the individuals, into an organization which can serve only a particular set of ends determined by the majority—or increasingly, since this organization is becoming far too complex to be understood by the voters, by the bureaucracy in whose hands the administration of those means is placed.

In recent times it has been seriously maintained that the existing political institutions lead to an insufficient provision for the public sector.[11] It is probably true that some of those services which the government ought to render are provided inadequately. But this does not mean that the aggregate of government expenditure is too small. It may well be true that having assumed too many tasks, government is neglecting some of the most important ones. Yet the present character of the procedure by which it is determined what share of the resources ought to be entrusted to government seems to make it more likely that the total is already much larger than most individuals approve or are even aware of. This seems to be more than confirmed by the results of the various opinion polls, the most recent one for Great Britain indicating that about 80 per cent of all the various classes and age groups desire a decrease and no more than 5 per cent of any age group favour an increase in the rate of the income tax—the only burden concerning the magnitude of which they seemed to have at least an approximately correct idea.[12]

Security

There is no need here to enlarge further on the second unquestioned task of government that it would have to perform even in a 'minimal state', that of defence against external enemies. Together with the whole field of external relations it has to be mentioned merely as a reminder of how big is the sphere of those government activities which cannot be strictly bound by general rules (or even effectively guided by a representative assembly), and where the executive must be given far-reaching discretionary powers. It may be useful to recall at this point that it has always been the desire to make central governments strong in their dealings with other countries that has led to their being entrusted also with other tasks which could probably be more efficiently performed by regional or local authorities. The main cause of the progressive centralization of government powers has always been the danger of war.

But the danger from foreign enemies (or possibly internal insurrection) is not the only danger to all members of society which can be effectively dealt with only by an organization with compulsory powers. Few people will question that only such an organization can deal with the effects of such natural disasters as storms, floods, earthquakes, epidemics and the like, and carry out measures to forestall or remedy them. This again is mentioned only to remind us of another reason why it is important that government be in control of material means which it is largely free to use at discretion.

There is, however, yet another class of common risks with regard to which the need for government action has until recently not been generally admitted and where as a result of the dissolution of the ties of the local community, and of the development of a highly mobile open society, an increasing number of people are no longer closely associated with particular groups whose help and support they can count upon in the case of misfortune. The problem here is chiefly the fate of those who for various reasons cannot make their living in the market, such as the sick, the old, the physically or mentally defective, the widows and orphans—that is all people suffering from adverse conditions which may affect anyone and against which most individuals cannot alone make adequate provision but in which a society that has reached a certain level of wealth can afford to provide for all.

The assurance of a certain minimum income for everyone, or a sort of floor below which nobody need fall even when he is unable to provide for himself, appears not only to be a wholly legitimate protection against a risk common to all, but a necessary part of the Great Society in which the individual no longer has specific claims on the members of the particular small group into which he was born. A system which aims at tempting large numbers to leave the relative security which the membership in the small group has given would probably soon produce great discontent and violent reaction when those who have first enjoyed its benefits find themselves without help when, through no fault of their own, their capacity to earn a living ceases.[13]

It is unfortunate that the endeavour to secure a uniform minimum for all who cannot provide for themselves has become connected with the wholly different aims of securing a 'just' distribution of incomes, which, as we have seen, leads to the endeavour to ensure to the individuals the particular standard they have reached. Such assurance would clearly be a privilege that could not be granted to all and could be granted to some only at the expense of worsening the prospects of others. When the means needed for this purpose are raised by general taxation, it even produces the unintended effect of increasing inequality beyond the degree that is the necessary condition of a functioning market order; because, in contrast to the case in which such pensions to the old, disabled or dependents are provided either by the employer as part of the contract of service (i.e. as a sort of deferred payment) or by voluntary or compulsory insurance, there will be no corresponding reduction of the remuneration that is received while the more highly priced services are rendered, with the result that the continued payment of this higher income out of public funds after the services have ceased will constitute a net addition to the higher income that has been earned in the market.

Even the recognition of a claim by every citizen or inhabitant of a country to a certain minimum standard, dependent upon the average level of wealth of that country, involves, however, the recognition of a kind of collective ownership of the resources of the country which is not compatible with the idea of an open society and which raises serious problems. It is obvious that for a long time to come it will be wholly impossible to secure an adequate and uniform minimum standard for all human beings everywhere, or at least that the wealthier countries would not be content to secure for their citizens no higher standards than can be secured for all men. But to confine to the citizens of particular countries provisions for a minimum standard higher than that universally applied makes it a privilege and necessitates certain limitations on the free movement of men across frontiers. There exist, of course, other reasons why such restrictions appear unavoidable so long as certain differences in national or ethnic traditions (especially differences in the rate of propagation) exist—which in turn are not likely to disappear so long as restrictions on migration continue. We must face the fact that we here encounter a limit to the universal application of those liberal principles of policy which the existing facts of the present world make unavoidable. These limits do not constitute fatal flaws in the argument since they imply merely that, like tolerance in particular, liberal principles can be consistently applied only to those who themselves obey liberal principles, and cannot always be extended to those who do not. The same is true of some moral principles. Such necessary exceptions to the general rule do therefore provide no justification for similar exceptions within the sphere in which it is possible for government consistently to follow liberal principles.

We cannot attempt here to consider any of the technical details of the appropriate arrangement of an apparatus of 'social security' which will not destroy the market order or infringe on the basic principles of individual liberty. We have attempted to do so on another occasion.[14]

Government monopoly of services

There are two very important fields of services in which governments have for so long claimed a monopoly (or prerogative) that this has come to be regarded as a necessary and natural attribute of government, although these monopolies neither have been introduced for, nor have ever redounded to, the benefit of the public: the exclusive right of issuing money and of providing postal services. They were not established in order that people should be served better, but solely to enhance the powers of government; and

56

as a result the public is not only much worse served than it would otherwise be, but, at least in the case of money, exposed to hazards and risks in their ordinary efforts of gaining a living which are inseparable from a political control of money and which they would soon have discovered a way of preventing if they had only been allowed to.

So far as the postal monopoly (in the USA only with respect to the delivery of letters) is concerned, all that need be said is that it owes its existence solely to, and has no other justification than, the government's desire to control communications between citizens.[15] It was not government which first created it but it took over what private enterprise had provided. Far from assuring better communications, or even revenue for the government, it has in recent times all over the world steadily deteriorated and is becoming not only an increasing burden on the taxpayer but a serious handicap to business. For having discovered that government is the most helpless of employers, the labour unions in public employments have achieved an increasing power to blackmail all and sundry by paralysing public life. But even apart from strikes and the like the increasing inefficiency of the governmental postal services is becoming a real obstacle to the efficient use of resources. There apply to it also all the other objections against the policy of running the various other 'public unitilities' in transport, communications and power supplies as government monopolies which we shall have to consider later.

The problem of proper monetary arrangements, on the other hand, is too big and difficult to deal with adequately in the present context.[16] To understand what is involved here requires freeing oneself of deeply ingrained habits, and a rethinking of much monetary theory. If the abolition of the government monopoly led to the general use of several competing currencies, that would in itself be an improvement on a governmental monetary monopoly which has without exception been abused in order to defraud and deceive the citizens; but its main purpose would be to impose a very necessary discipline upon the governmental issue of currency through the threat of its being displaced by a more reliable one. In that case the ordinary citizen would still be able in his daily transactions to use the kind of money with which he is now familiar but one which he could at last trust. Government would then be deprived not only of one of the main means of damaging the economy and subjecting individuals to restrictions of their freedom but also of one of the chief causes of its constant expansion. It is of course nonsense that government is ever needed to 'protect' the money used in a country against any threat (except counterfeiting which, like all fraud, the ordinary rules of law forbid) other than that which comes from government itself: it is against the state that money must primarily be protected. The exporters of money, or providers of another kind of money, and the like, against whom the responsible politicians skilfully direct the indignation of the public, are in fact the best watchdogs who, if they are allowed freely to practice their trade, will force government to provide honest money. Exchange control and the like merely serve government to continue with their nefarious practices of competing on the market with the citizen for resources by spending money manufactured for the purpose.

There is no justification for the assiduously fostered myth that there must be within a given territory a uniform sort of money or legal tender. Government may at one time have performed a useful function when it certified weight and fineness of coins, although even that was done at least as reliably and honestly by some respected merchants. But when the princes claimed the minting prerogative, it was for the gain from seignorage and in order to carry their image to the remotest corners of their territory and show the inhabitants to whom they were subject. They and their successors have shamelessly abused this prerogative as an instrument of power and fraud. Further, the blind transfer of rights relating coinage to modern forms of money was claimed solely as an instrument of power and finance and not because of any belief that it would benefit the people. The British government gave the Bank of England in 1694 a (slightly limited) monopoly of the issue of bank notes because it was paid for it, not because it was for the common good. And though the illusion that government monopoly would secure for the countries a better money than the market has governed all the development of monetary institutions ever since, the fact is of course that wherever the exercise of this power was not limited by some such automatic mechanism as the gold standard, it was abused to defraud the people. A study of the history of money shows that no government that had direct control of the quantity of money can be trusted for any length of time not to abuse it. We shall not get a decent money until others are free to offer us a better one than the government in charge does. So long as the defalcating practices are not prevented by the prompt desertion of the official currency by the people, governments will again and again be driven to such practices by the false belief that they can, and therefore must, ensure full employment by monetary manipulation—which has even been adduced as the reason why we are irrevocably committed to a 'planned', 'directed', 'guided', or 'steered' economy. Of course experience has once more confirmed that it is the very inflationary policies to which governments resort which cause the malady they seek to cure; for though they may reduce unemployment for the moment, they do so only at the price of much greater unemployment later on.

Similar considerations apply to the monopolies of rendering other services which government, mostly local government, can usefully render but which any monopolist is likely to abuse, indeed will probably be forced to abuse. The most harmful abuse here is not that which the public most fears, namely demanding extortionate prices, but on the contrary the political coercion to make uneconomic use of resources. The monopolies in transport, communications, and energy supply which not only prevent competition but make politically determined tariffs necessary, which are determined by supposed considerations of equity, are chiefly responsible for such phenomena as the sprawling of the cities. This is of course the inevitable result if anybody, at however a remote and inaccessible place he chooses to live, is supposed to have a just claim to be served, in disregard of costs, at the same prices as those who live in the centre of a densely occupied city.

On the other hand, it is merely common sense that government, as the biggest spender and investor whose activities cannot be guided wholly by profitability, and which for finance is in a great measure independent of the state of the capital market, should so far as practicable distribute its expenditure over time in such a manner that it will step in when private investment flags, and thereby employ resources for public investment at the least cost and with the greatest benefit to society. The reason why this old prescription has in fact been so little acted upon, hardly any more effectively since it has become fashionable than when it was supported by only a few economists, are of a political and administrative kind. To bring about the required changes in the rate of governmental investment promptly enough to act as a stabilizer, and not, as is usually the case, with such delays that they do more harm than good, would require that the whole investment programme of government be so designed that the speed of its execution could be accelerated or delayed at short notice. To achieve this it would be necessary that all capital expenditure of government be

59

fixed at a certain average rate for as long a period ahead as five or seven years, with the provision that this was to be only the average speed. If we call this 'speed 3' it would then on central direction have to be temporarily increased by all departments by 20 or 40 per cent to 'speed 4' or 'speed 5' or reduced by 20 or 40 per cent to 'speeds 2' or '1'. Each department or section would know that it would later have to make up for this increase or reduction and to endeavour to let the brunt of these changes fall on those activities where the costs of such variations was least, and particularly where it would gain most from adapting to the temporary abundance or scarcity of labour and other resources. It need hardly be pointed out how difficult an effective execution of such a programme would be, or how far we still are from possessing the kind of governmental machinery required for such a task.

Information and education

This, also, is a field which we can only briefly touch on here. The reader will find a fuller treatment of it in my earlier discussion of the subject.[17]

Information and education of course shade into each other. The argument for the provision at public expense is similar in the two cases, but not quite the same as that in the case of public goods. Though information and education can be sold to particular people, those who do not possess either often will not know that it would be to their advantage to acquire them; yet it may be to the advantage of others that they should possess them. This is evident so far as the knowledge is concerned which the individuals must possess if they are to obey the law and take part in the democratic procedures of government. But the market process, though one of the most efficient instruments for conveying information, will also function more effectively if the access to certain kinds of information is free. Also useful knowledge that could assist the individuals in their efforts accrues incidentally in the process of government, or can be obtained only by government, such as that contained in statistics, land registers, etc. Again, much knowledge once acquired is in its nature no longer a scarce commodity and could be made generally available at a fraction of the costs of first acquiring it. This is not necessarily a valid argument for entrusting its distribution to government: we certainly would not wish government to acquire a dominating position in the distribution of news; and the conferment in some countries of a monopoly of wireless broadcasting to governments is probably one of the most hazardous political decisions made in modern times.

But even though it is often very doubtful whether government is the most effective agency for distributing any particular kind of information, and though there is the danger that by preempting this task it may prevent others from performing it better, it would be difficult to maintain that government should not enter this field at all. The real problem is in what form and to what extent government should provide such services.

With regard to education the primary argument in support of its being assisted by government is that children are not yet responsible citizens and cannot be assumed to know what they need, and do not control resources which they can devote to the acquisition of knowledge; and that parents are not always able or prepared to invest in the children's education as much as would make the returns on this intangible capital correspond to those on material capital. This argument applies to children and minors only. But it is supplemented by a further consideration which applies also to adults, namely that education may awaken in those who receive it capacities they did not know they possessed. Here, too, it may often be the case that only if the individual is assisted during the first stages will he be able to develop his potentialities further by his own initiative.

The strong case for a government finance of at least general education does not however imply that this education should also be managed by government, and still less that government should acquire a monopoly of it. At least so far as general education rather than advanced training for the professions is concerned, Professor Milton Friedmann's proposal mentioned before[18] for giving the parents vouchers with which they can pay for their children's education at schools of their own choosing seems to have great advantages over the prevailing system. Though the choice of the parents would have to be limited to a range of schools meeting certain minimum standards, and the vouchers would cover fully the fees of only some of these schools, the system would have the great advantage over schools managed by authority that it would allow parents to pay for the additional costs of a special preferred form of education. In the special training for the professions, etc., where the problems arise after the students have reached the age of discretion, a system of students' loans repayable out of the higher earnings to

61

which such training leads, such as developed by Mr Richard Cornuelle's United Student Aid Fund, Inc., offer alternative and probably preferable possibilities.[19]

Other critical issues

Several other important issues which would need consideration even in a cursory survey of the field of legitimate government policy can however be barely mentioned here. One is that of the problem of *certification* by government or others of the quality of some goods and services which may include a kind of *licensing* of particular activities by government. It can hardly be denied that the choice of the consumer will be greatly facilitated, and the working of the market improved, if the possession of certain qualities of things or capacities by those who offer services is made recognizable for the inexpert though it is by no means obvious that only the government will command the confidence required. Building regulations, pure food laws, the certification of certain professions, the restrictions on the sale of certain dangerous goods (such as arms, explosives, poisons and drugs), as well as some safety and health regulations for the processes of production and the provision of such public institutions as theatres, sports grounds, etc., certainly assists intelligent choice and sometimes may be indispensable for it. That the goods offered for human consumption satisfy certain minimum standards of hygiene, as for example that pork is not trichinuous or milk not tuberculous, or that somebody who describes himself by a term generally understood to imply a certain competence, such as a physician, really possesses that competence, will be most effectively assured by some general rules applying to all who supply such goods or services. It is probably merely a question of expediency whether it will be sufficient to have a generally understood manner in which such goods and services can be described, or whether to permit the sale of such goods only if they are thus certified. All that is required for the preservation of the rule of law and of a functioning market order is that everybody who satisfies the prescribed standards has a legal claim to the required certification, which means that the control of admissions authorities must *not* be used to regulate supply.

A problem which raises particular difficulties is that of the regulation of *expropriation* or *compulsory purchase*, a right which seems to be needed by government for some of its desirable functions. At

62

least for the purpose of providing an adequate system of communications such a right seems to be indispensable and under the name of 'eminent domain' it appears indeed to have been granted to government at all times.[20] So long as the grant of such powers is strictly limited to instances that can be defined by general rules of law, payment of compensation at full value is required, and the decisions of the administrative authorities subject to the control of independent courts, such powers need not seriously interfere with the working of the market process or with the principles of the rule of law. It is not to be denied, however, that in this connection a *prima facie* conflict arises between the basic principles of a libertarian order and what appear to be unquestioned necessities of governmental policy, and that we still lack adequate theoretical principles for a satisfactory solution of some of the problems which arise in this field.

There are also probably several fields in which government has not yet given the private individual the protection he needs if he is to pursue his ends most effectively and to the greatest benefit of the community. One of the most important of these seems to be the *protection of privacy and secrecy* which only the modern increase of the density of population has raised in acute form and with respect to which government has so far clearly failed to provide appropriate rules or to enforce them.[21] The delimitation of some such fields in which the individual is protected against the inquisitiveness of his neighbours or even the representatives of the public at large, such as the press, seems to me an important requirement of full liberty.

Finally we must once more remind the reader that to reduce the discussion of these problems to manageable dimensions it was necessary to discuss them in terms of a unitary, central government. Yet one of the most important conclusions to be derived from our general approach is the desirability of devolving many of these functions of government to regional or local authorities. Indeed, much is to be said in favour of limiting the task of whatever is the supreme authority to the essentially limited one of enforcing law and order on all the individuals, organizations and sectional government bodies, and leaving all rendering of positive services to smaller governmental organizations. Most of the service functions of government would probably be much more effectively performed and controlled if those local authorities had, under a law they could not alter, to compete for residents. It has been the unfortunate necessity of making central governments strong for the task of defence against external enemies that has produced the situation in which the laying down of general rules and the rendering of particular services have been placed into the same hands, with the result that they have become increasingly confused.

FIFTEEN

GOVERNMENT POLICY AND THE MARKET

The pure market economy assumes that government, the social apparatus of compulsion and coercion, is intent upon preserving the operation of the market system, abstains from hindering its functioning, and protects it against encroachment on the part of other people.

Ludwig von Mises*

The advantages of competition do not depend on it being 'perfect' [1]

In certain conditions competition will bring about an allocation of the resources for the production of the different commodities and services which leads to an output of that particular combination of products as large as that which could be brought about by a single mind who knew all those facts actually known only to all the people taken together, and who was fully capable of utilizing this knowledge in the most efficient manner. The special case in which these results follow from the competitive market process has been found intellectually so satisfying by economic theorists that they have tended to treat it as paradigmatic. The case for the competition has in consequence regularly been stated as if competition were desirable because as a rule it achieves these results, or even as if it were desirable only when in fact it does so. From basing the argument for the market on this special case of 'perfect' competition it is, however, not far to the realization that it is an exceptional case approached in only a few instances, and that, in consequence, if the case for competition rested on what it achieves under those special conditions, the case for it as a general principle would be very weak indeed. The setting of a wholly unrealistic, over-high standard of what competition should achieve thus often leads to an erroneously low estimate of what in fact it does achieve.

This model of perfect competition rests on assumptions of facts which do not exist except in a few sectors of economic life and which in many sectors it is not in our power to create and would sometimes not even be desirable to create if we could. The crucial assumption on which that model is based is that any commodity of service that differs significantly from others can be supplied to most consumers at the same cost by a large number of producers, with the result that none of the latter can deliberately determine the price because, if he tried to change more than his marginal costs, it would be in the interests of others to undersell him. This ideal case, in which for each competitor the price is given, and where his interests will induce him to increase his production until the marginal costs are equal to price, came to be regarded as the model and was used as a standard by which the achievement of competition in the real world was judged.

It is true that, if we could bring about such a state, it would be desirable that the production of each article should be extended to the point where prices equalled marginal costs because, so long as this was not so, a further increase of production of the commodity in question would mean that the factors of production required would be used more productively than elsewhere. This, however, does not mean that where we have to use the process of competition to find out what the different people want and are able to do, we are also in a position to bring about the ideal state, or that the results even of 'imperfect' competition will not be preferable to any condition we can bring about by any other known method such as direction by government.

It is evidently neither desirable nor possible that every commodity or service that is significantly different from others should be produced by a large number of producers, or that there should always be a large number of producers capable of producing any particular thing at the same cost. As a rule there will exist at any one time not only an optimum size of the productive unit, below and above which costs will rise, but also special advantages of skill, location, traditions, etc. which only some but not all enterprises will possess. Frequently a few enterprises or perhaps only a single one will be able to supply as much of a particular commodity as can be sold at prices covering its costs which may be cheaper than those of any other firm. In this case a few firms (or the single firm) will not be under the necessity of bringing their prices down to the marginal costs, or of producing such a quantity of their product that they can be sold only at prices just covering its marginal costs. All that their interests will induce the firm to do will be to keep prices below the figure at which new producers would be tempted to enter the market. Within this range such firms (or such a firm) would indeed be free to act as monopolists or obligopolists and to fix their prices (or the quantities of goods produced) at the level which would bring them the highest profits, limited only by the consideration that they must be low enough to keep out others.

In all such instances an omniscient dictator could indeed improve the use of the available resources by requiring the firms to expand production until prices only just covered marginal costs. On this standard, habitually applied by some theorists, most of the markets in the existing world are undoubtedly very imperfect. For all practical problems, however, this standard is wholly irrelevant, because it rests on a comparison, not with some other state that could be achieved by some known procedure, but with one that might have been achieved if certain facts which we cannot alter were other that they in fact are. To use as a standard by which we measure the actual achievement of competition the hypothetical arrangements made by an omniscient dictator comes naturally to the economist whose analysis must proceed on the fictitious assumption that *he* knows all the facts which determine the order of the market. But it does not provide us with a valid test which can meaningfully be applied to the achievements of practical policy. The test should not be the degree of approach towards an unachievable result, but should be whether the results of a given policy exceed or fall short of the results of other available procedures. The real problem is how far we can raise efficiency above the pre-existing level, *not* how close we can come to what would be desirable if the fact were different.

That standard for judging the performance of competition, in other words, must not be the arrangements which would be made by somebody who had complete knowledge of all the facts, but the probability which only competition can secure that the different things will be done by those who thereby produce more of what the others want than they would do otherwise.

Competition as a discovery procedure

Quite generally outside as well as inside the economic sphere, competition is a sensible procedure to employ only if we do not know beforehand who will do best. In examinations or in sport meetings as well as on the market, it will tell us, however, only who did best on the particular occasion, and not necessarily that each did as well as he could have done—though it also provides one of the most effective spurs to achievement. It will produce an inducement to do better than the next best, but if this next best is far behind, the range within which the better one will be free to decide how much to exert himself may be very wide. Only if the next best is pressing on his heels and he himself does not know how much better he really is, will he find it necessary to exert himself to the full. And only if there is a more or less continuous graduation of capacities, and each anxious to achieve as good a place as he can, will each be kept on tiptoe and be looking over his shoulder to see whether the next best is catching up with him.

Competition is thus, like experimentation in science, first and foremost a discovery procedure. No theory can do justice to it which starts from the assumption that the facts to be discovered are already known.[2] There is no pre-determined range of known or 'given' facts which will ever all be taken into account. All we can hope to secure is a procedure that is on the whole likely to bring about a situation where more of the potentially useful objective facts will be taken into account than would be done in any other procedure which we know. It is the circumstances which makes so irrelevant for the choice of a desirable policy all evaluation of the results of competition that starts from the assumption that all the relevant facts are known to some single mind. The real issue is how we can best assist the optimum utilization of the knowledge, skills and opportunities to acquire knowledge, that are dispersed among hundreds of thousands of people, but given to nobody in their entirety. Competition must be seen as a process in which people acquire and communicate knowledge; to treat it as if all this knowledge were available to any one person at the outset is to make nonsense of it. And it is as nonsensical to judge the concrete results of competition by some preconception of the products it 'ought' to bring forth as it would be to judge the results of scientific experimentation by their correspondence with what had been expected. As is true of the results of scientific experimentation, we can judge the value of the results only by the conditions under which it was conducted, not by the results. It therefore cannot be said of competition any more than of any other sort of experimentation that it leads to a maximization of any measurable results. It merely leads, under favourable conditions, to the use of more skill and knowledge than any other known procedure. Though every successful use of skill and knowledge can be regarded as a gain, and therefore each additional act of exchange in which both parties prefer what they get for what they give can be regarded as an advantage, we can never say by what aggregate amount the net benefits available to the people have increased. We have not to deal with measurable or additive magnitudes, but must accept as the possible optimum the results of those general conditions which are most likely to lead to the discovery of the largest number of opportunities.

How any individual will act under the pressure of competition, what particular circumstance he will encounter in such conditions, is not known before even to him and must be still more unknown to anyone else. It is therefore literally meaningless to require him to act 'as if ' competition existed, or as if it were more complete than it is. We shall see in particular that one of the chief sources of error in this field is the conception derived from the fictitious assumption that the individual's 'cost curves' are an objectively given fact ascertainable by inspection, and not something which can be determined only on the basis of his knowledge and judgment—a knowledge which will be wholly different when he acts in a highly competitive market from what it would be if he were the sole producer or one of a very few.

Though to explain the results of competition is one of the chief aims of economic theory (or catallactics), the facts we have considered greatly restrict the extent to which this theory can predict the particular results of competition in the kind of situation in which we are practically interested. Indeed, competition is of value precisely because it constitutes a discovery procedure which we would not need if we could predict its results. Economic theory can elucidate the operation of this discovery procedure by constructing models in which it is assumed that the theoretician possesses all the knowledge which guides all the several individuals whose interaction his model represents. We are interested in such a model only because it tells how a system of this sort will work. But we have to apply it to actual situations in which we do not possess that knowledge of the particulars. What the economist alone can do is to derive from mental models in which he assumes that, as it were, he can look into the cards of all the individual players, certain conclusions about the general character of the result, conclusions which he may perhaps be able to test on artificially constructed models, but which are interesting only in the instances where he cannot test

69

them because he does not possess that knowledge which he would need.

If the factual requirements of 'perfect' competition are absent, it is not possible to make firms act 'as if' it existed

Competition as a discovery procedure must rely on the self-interest of the producers, that is it must allow them to use their knowledge for their purposes, because nobody else possesses the information on which they must base their decision. Where the conditions of 'perfect' competition are absent, some will find it profitable to sell their products at prices above their marginal costs, though they could still make an adequate profit by selling at lower prices. It is this that those object to who regard the condition of perfect competition as the standard. They contend that producers in such conditions ought to be made to act as if perfect competition existed, although their self-interest will not lead them to do so. But we rely on self-interest because only through it can we induce producers to use knowledge which we do not possess, and to take actions the effects of which only they can determine. We cannot at the same time rely on their self-interest to find the most economical method of production and not allow them to produce the kinds and quantities of goods by the methods which best serve their interest. The inducement to improve the manner of production will often consist in the fact that whoever does so first will thereby gain a temporary profit. Many of the improvements of production are due to each striving for such profits even though he knows that they will only be temporary and last only so long as he leads.

If the future costs of production of any producer (and particularly his marginal costs of any additional quantity produced) were an objectively ascertainable magnitude which could unambiguously be determined by a supervising authority, it might be meaningful to demand that producers should be made to sell at marginal costs. But, though we are in the habit of arguing in theory as if costs were a 'datum', that is, given knowledge, the lowest costs at which a thing can be produced are exactly what we want competition to discover. They are not necessarily known to anyone but to him who has succeeded in discovering them—and even he will often not be aware what it is that enables him to produce more cheaply than others can.

It is, therefore, generally also not possible for an outsider to establish objectively whether a large excess of price over costs, manifesting itself in high profits and due to some improvement in technique or organization, is merely an 'adequate' return on investment. 'Adequate' in this connection must mean a return the expectation of which was sufficient to justify the risk incurred. In technologically advanced production the cost of a particular product will quite generally not be an objectively ascertainable fact, but will in a large measure depend on the opinion of the producer about probable future developments. The success of the individual enterprise and its long-run efficiency will depend on the degree of correctness of the expectations which are reflected in the entrepreneur's estimate of costs.

Whether a firm that has made large investments in improving its plant should at once extend production to the point where prices will fall to its new marginal costs will thus depend on judgment about the probability of future developments. It clearly is desirable that some investment in new and more efficient plant should be undertaken that will be profitable only if for some time after they come into operation prices will remain above the cost of operating the already existing plant. The construction of a new plant will only be justified if it is expected that the prices at which the product can be sold will remain sufficiently above marginal costs to provide not only amortization of the capital sunk in it but also to compensate for the risk of creating it. Who can say how great this risk did appear, or ought to have appeared, to those who in the first instance made the decision to build the plant? It would clearly make the running of such risks impossible if, after the venture had proved successful, the firm were required to reduce prices to what would then appear as its long-run marginal costs. Competitive improvement of productive techniques rests largely on the endeavour of each to gain temporary monopolistic profits so long as he leads; and it is in a great measure out of such profits that the successful obtain the capital for further improvements.

Nor is it unreasonable that in such situations some of the benefits which the producers could offer to the consumers will still be served better by the producer with the new equipment than by anybody else, and that is all we can demand so long as we rely on his use of his knowledge. Not to do as well as one could cannot be treated as an offence in a free society in which each is allowed to choose the manner of employing his person and property.

Quite apart from the practical difficulty of ascertaining whether such a *de facto* monopolist does extend his production to the point at which prices will only just cover marginal costs, it is by no means clear that to require him to do so could be reconciled with the general principles of just conduct on which the market order rests. So far as his monopoly is a result of his superior skill or of the possession of some factor of production uniquely suitable for the product in question, this would hardly be equitable. At least so long as we allow persons possessing special skills or unique objects not to use them at all, it would be paradoxical that as soon as they use them for commercial purposes, they should be required to use them to the greatest possible extent. We have no more justification for prescribing how intensively anyone must use his skill or his possessions than we have for prohibiting him from using his skill for solving crossword puzzles or his capital for acquiring a collection of postage stamps. Where the source of a monopoly position is a unique skill, it would be absurd to punish the possessor for doing better than anyone else by insisting that he should do as well as he can. And even where the monopoly position is the result of the possession of some object conferring a unique advantage, such as a particular site, it would seem hardly any less absurd to allow somebody to use for his private swimming pool a spring of water which would provide unique advantages for a brewery or whisky distillery, and then, once he turns it to such purpose, insist that he must not make a monopoly profit from it.

The power to determine the price or the quality of a product at the figure most profitable to the owner of such a rare resource used in its production is a necessary consequence of the recognition of private property in particular things, and cannot be eliminated without abandoning the institution of private property. There is in this respect no difference between a manufacturer or merchant who has built up a unique organization, or acquired a uniquely suitable site, and a painter who limits his output to what will bring him the largest income. There exists no more an argument in justice, or a moral case, against such a monopolist making a monopoly profit than there is against anyone who decides that he will work no more than he finds worth his while.

We shall see that the situation is wholly different where 'market power' consists in a power of preventing others from serving the customers better. In certain circumstances it is true that even the power over prices, etc. may confer upon a monopolist the power of influencing the market behaviour of others in a manner which protects him against unwelcome competition. We shall see that in such cases there is indeed a strong argument for preventing him from doing so.

Sometimes, however, the appearance of a monopoly (or of an obligopoly) may even be a desirable result of competition, that is, competition will have done its best when, for the time being, it has led to a monopoly. Although, except in a special case which we shall consider later, production is not likely to be more efficient *because* it is conducted by a monopoly, it will often be conducted most effectively by one particular enterprise that for some special reason is more efficient than other existing ones.[3] While this does not provide a justification for protecting monopolistic positions or assisting their preservation, it makes it desirable not only to tolerate monopolies but even to allow them to exploit their monopolistic positions—so long as they maintain them solely by serving their customers better than anyone else, and not by preventing those who think they could do still better from trying to do so. So long as any producer is in a monopoly position because he can produce at costs lower than anybody else can, and sells at prices which are lower than those which anybody else can sell, that is all we can hope to achieve—even though we can in theory conceive of a better use of resources which, however, we have no way of realizing.

If such a position appears objectionable to many people this is chiefly due to the false suggestion of the word monopoly that it constitutes a privilege. But the bare fact that one producer (or a few producers) can meet the demand at prices which nobody else can match, does not constitute a privilege so long as the inability of others to do the same is not due to their being prevented from trying. The term privilege is used legitimately only to describe a right conferred by special decree (*privi-legium*) which others do not have, and not for an objective possibility which circumstances offer to some but not others.

So far as monopoly does not rest on privilege in the strict sense, it is indeed always objectionable when it depends on people being prevented from trying to do better than others. But those monopolies or obligopolies of which we have spoken in this section do not rest upon any such discrimination. They rest on the fact that men and things are not perfectly alike and that often a few or even only one of them will possess certain advantages over all others. We know how to induce such individuals or organizations to serve their fellows better than anyone else can do. But we have no means of always making them serve the public as well as they could.

The achievements of the free market

What, then, is it that we want competition to bring about and which it normally does bring about if it is not prevented from doing so? It is a result so simple and obvious that most of us are inclined to take it for granted; and we are wholly unaware that it is a remarkable thing which is brought about and which never could be achieved by any authority telling the individual producer what to do. Competition, if not prevented, tends to bring about a state of affairs in which: *first*, everything will be produced which somebody knows how to produce and which he can sell profitably at a price at which buyers will prefer it to the available alternatives; *second*, everything that is being produced is produced by persons who can do so at least as cheaply as anybody else who in fact is not producing it;[4] and *third*, that everything will be sold at prices lower than, or at least as low as, those at which it could be sold by anybody who in fact does not do so.

There are three points which have to be considered if one wants to see the significance of such a state in its proper light: first, that this is a state of affairs which no central direction could ever bring about; second, that this state is approached remarkably closely in all fields where competition is not prevented by government or where governments do not tolerate such prevention by private persons or organizations; third, that in very large sectors of economic activity this state has never been closely approached because governments have restricted competition or allowed and often assisted private persons or organizations to restrict competition.

Modest as these accomplishments of competition may at first appear, the fact is that we do not know of any other method that would bring about better results; and wherever competition is prevented or impeded the conditions for their achievement are usually very far from being satisfied. Considering that competition has always been prevented in many fields by the deliberate policies of government from achieving this, while the result is very closely approximated wherever competition is allowed to operate, we should certainly be more concerned to make it generally possible than to make it operate in accordance with an unachievable standard of 'perfection'.

To what a great extent in a normally functioning society the result described is in fact achieved in all sectors where competition is not prevented is demonstrated by the difficulty of discovering opportunities for making a living by serving the customers better than is already being done. We know only too well how difficult this in fact is and how much ingenuity is needed in a functioning catallaxy to discover such opportunities.[5] It is also instructive to compare in this respect the situation in a country which possesses a large commercially alert class, where most of the existing opportunities will have been taken advantage of, and in a country where people are less versatile or enterprising and which in consequence will often offer to one with a different outlook great opportunities for rapid gain.[6] The important point here is that a highly developed commercial spirit is itself as much the product as the condition of effective competition, and that we know of no other method of producing it than to throw competition open to all who want to take advantage of the opportunities it offers.

Competition and rationality

Competition is not merely the only method which we know for utilizing the knowledge and skills that other people may possess, but it is also the method by which we all have been led to acquire much of the knowledge and skills we do possess. This is not understood by those who maintain that the argument for competition rests on the assumption of rational behaviour of those who take part in it. But rational behaviour is not a premise of economic theory, though it is often presented as such. The basic contention of theory is rather that competition will make it necessary for people to act rationally in order to maintain themselves. It is based not on the assumption that most or all the participants in the market process are rational, but, on the contrary, on the assumption that it will in general be through competition that a few relatively more rational individuals will make it necessary for the rest to emulate them in order to prevail.[7] In a society in which rational behaviour confers an advantage on the individual, rational methods will progressively be developed and be spread by imitation. It is no use being more rational than the rest if one is not allowed to derive benefits from being so. And it is therefore in general not rationality which is required to make competition work, but competition, or traditions which allow competition, which will produce rational behaviour.[8] The endeavour to do better than can be done in the customary manner is the process in which that capacity for thinking is developed which will later manifest itself in argument and criticism. No society which has not first developed a commercial group within which the improvement of the tools of thought has brought advantage to the individual has ever gained the capacity of systematic rational thinking.

This should be remembered particularly by those who are inclined to argue that competition will not work among people who lack the spirit of enterprise: let merely a few rise and be esteemed and powerful because they have successfully tried new ways, even if they may be in the first instance foreign intruders, and let those tempted to imitate them be free to do so, however few they may be in the first instance, and that spirit of enterprise will emerge by the only method which can produce it. Competition is as much a method for breeding certain types of mind as anything else: the very cast of thinking of the great entrepreneurs would not exist but for the environment in which they developed their gifts. The same innate capacity to think will take a wholly different turn according to the task it is set.

Such a development will be possible only if the traditionalist majority does not have power to make compulsory for everyone those traditional manners and mores which would prevent the experimentation with new ways inherent in competition. This means that the powers of the majority must be limited to the enforcement of such general rules as will prevent the individuals from encroaching on the protected domains of their fellows, and should not extend to positive prescriptions of what the individuals must do. If the majority view, or any *one* view, is made generally to prevail concerning how things must be done, such developments as we have sketched by which the more rational procedures gradually replace the less rational ones become impossible. The intellectual growth of a community rests on the views of a few gradually spreading, even to the disadvantage of those who are reluctant to accept them; and though nobody should have the power to force upon them new views because he thinks they are better, if success proves that they are more effective, those who stick to their old ways must not be protected against a relative or

76

even absolute decline in their position. Competition is, after all, always a process in which a small number makes it necessary for larger numbers to do what they do not like, be it to work harder, to change habits, or to devote a degree of attention, continuous application, or regularity to their work which without competition would not be needed.

If in a society in which the spirit of enterprise has not yet spread, the majority has power to prohibit whatever it dislikes, it is most unlikely that it will allow competition to arise. I doubt whether a functioning market has ever newly arisen under an unlimited democracy, and it seems at least likely that unlimited democracy will destroy it where it has grown up. To those with whom others compete, the fact that they have competitors is always a nuisance that prevents a quiet life; and such direct effects of competition are always much more visible than the indirect benefits which we derive from it. In particular, the direct effects will be felt by the members of the same trade who see how competition is operating, while the consumer will generally have little idea to whose actions the reduction of prices or the improvement of quality is due.

Size, concentration and power

The misleading emphasis on the influence of the individual firm on prices, in combination with the popular prejudice against bigness as such, with various 'social' considerations supposed to make it desirable to preserve the middle class, the independent entrepreneur, the small craftsman or shopkeeper, or quite generally the existing structure of society, has acted against changes caused by economic and technological development. The 'power' which large corporations can exercise is represented as in itself dangerous and as making necessary special governmental measures to restrict it. This concern about size and power of individual corporations more often than perhaps any other consideration produces essentially anti-liberal conclusions drawn from liberal premises.

We shall presently see that there are two important respects in which monopoly may confer on its possessor harmful power. But neither size in itself, nor ability to determine the prices at which all can buy their product is a measure of their harmful power. More important still, there is no possible measure or standard by which we can decide whether a particular enterprise is too large. Certainly the bare fact that one big firm in a particular industry 'dominates' the market because the other firms of the industry will follow its price leadership, is no proof that this position can in fact be improved upon in any way other than by the appearance of an effective competitor—an event which we may hope for, but which we cannot bring about so long as nobody is available who does enjoy the same (or other compensating) special advantages as the firm that is now dominant.

The most effective size of the individual firm is as much one of the unknowns to be discovered by the market process as the prices, quantities or qualities of the goods to be produced and sold. There can be no general rule about what is the desirable size since this will depend on the ever-changing technological and economic conditions; and there will always be many changes which will give advantages to enterprises of what on past standards will appear to be an excessive size. It is not to be denied that the advantages of the size will not always rest on facts which we cannot alter, such as the scarcity of certain kinds of talents or resources (including such accidental and yet unavoidable facts as that somebody has been earlier in the field and therefore has had more time to acquire experience and special knowledge); they will often be determined by institutional arrangements which happen to give an advantage to size which is artificial in the sense that it does not secure smaller social costs of the unit of output. In so far as tax legislation, the law of corporations, or the greater influence on the administrative machinery of government, give to the larger unit differential advantages which are not based on genuine superiority of performance, there is indeed every reason for so altering the framework as to remove such artificial advantages of bigness. But there is as little justification for discrimination by policy against large size as such as there is for assisting it.

The argument that mere size confers harmful power over the market behaviour of competitors possesses a degree of plausibility when we think in terms of one 'industry' within which there may indeed sometimes be room only for one specialised big firm. But the growth of the giant corporation has made largely meaningless the conception of separate industries which one corporation, because of the magnitude of its resources, can dominate. One of the unforeseen results of the increase of size of the individual corporations which the theorists have not yet quite digested is that large size has brought diversification far beyond the bounds of any definable industry. In consequence, the size of the corporations in other industries has become the main check on the power which size might give a single large corporation in one industry. It may well be that, say in the electrical industry of one country, no other corporation has the strength or staying power to 'take on' an established giant intent upon defending its *de facto* monopoly of some of the products. But as the development of the great automobile or chemical concerns in the USA shows, they have no compunction about encroaching on such fields in which the backing of large resources is essential to make the prospects of entry promising. Size has thus become the most effective antidote to the power of size: what will control the power of large aggregations of capital are other large aggregations of capital, and such control will be much more effective than any supervision by government, whose permission of an act carries its authorization, if not outright protection. As I cannot repeat too often, government-supervised monopoly always tends to become government-protected monopoly; and the fight against bigness only too often results in preventing those very developments through which size becomes the antidote of size.

I do not intend to deny that there are real social and political (as distinct from merely economic) considerations which make a large number of small enterprises appear as more desirable or 'healthy' structures than a smaller number of large ones. We have already had occasion to refer to the danger arising from the fact that constantly increasing numbers of the population work in ever larger corporations, and as a result are familiar with the organizational type of order but strangers to the working of the market which co-ordinates the activities of the several corporations. Considerations like this are often advanced in justification of measures designed to curb the growth of individual enterprise or to protect the less efficient smaller firms against their displacement or absorption into a big one.

Yet, even granting that such measures might in some sense be desirable, it is one of those things which, even though in themselves desirable, cannot be achieved without conferring a discretionary and arbitrary power on some authority, and which therefore must give way to the higher consideration that no authority should be given such power. We have already stressed that such a limitation on all power may make impossible the achievement of some particular aims which may be desired by a majority of the people, and that generally, to avoid greater evils, a free society must deny itself certain kinds of power even if the foreseeable consequences of its

79

exercise appear only beneficial and constitute perhaps the only available method of achieving that particular result.

The political aspects of economic power

The argument that the great size of an individual corporation confers great power on its management, and that such power of a few men is politically dangerous and morally objectionable, certainly deserves serious consideration. Its persuasiveness derives, however, in a great measure from a confusion of the different meanings of the word 'power', and from a constant shifting from one of the senses in which the possession of great power is desirable to another in which it is objectionable: power over material things and power over the conduct of other men. These two kinds of power are not necessarily connected and can to a large extent be separated. It is one of the ironies of history that socialism, which gained influence by promising the substitution of the administration of things for the power over men, inevitably leads to an unbounded increase of the power exercised by men over other men.

So long as large aggregations of material resources make it possible to achieve better results in terms of improved or cheaper products or more desirable services than smaller organizations provide, every extension of this kind of power must be regarded as in itself beneficial. The fact that large aggregations of resources under a single direction often increase power of this kind more than in proportion to size is often the reason for the development of very large enterprises. Although size is not an advantage in every respect, and though there will always be a limit to the increase of size which still brings an increase of productivity, there will at all times exist fields in which technological change gives an advantage to units larger than those which have existed before. From the replacement of the cottage weaver by the factory to the growth of the continuous process in steel production and to the supermarket, advances in technological knowledge have again and again made larger units more efficient. But if such increase in size leads to more effective use of resources, it does not necessarily increase the power over the conduct of the people, except the limited power which the head of an enterprise wields over those who join it for their benefit. Even though a mail-order house like Sears Roebuck & Co. has grown to be one

80

of the 100 largest corporations in the world and far exceeds in size any comparable enterprise, and although its activities have profoundly affected the standards and habits of millions, it cannot be said to exercise power in any sense other than that of offering services which people prefer when they become available. Nor would a single corporation gain power over the conduct of other men if it were so efficient in the production of a piece of mechanical equipment as universally employed as, say, ball bearings, that it would drive out all competition: so long as it stood ready to supply everyone awaiting its product on the same terms, even though it thereby made a huge profit, not only would all its customers be better off for its existence, but they could also not be said to be dependent on its power.

In modern society it is not the size of the aggregate of resources controlled by an enterprise which gives it power over the conduct of other people, so much as its capacity to withhold services on which people are dependent. As we shall see in the next section, it is therefore also not only simply power over the price of their products but the power to exact different terms from different customers which confers power over conduct. This power, however, is not directly dependent on size and not even an inevitable product of monopoly—although it will be possessed by the monopolist of any essential product, whether he be big or small, so long as he is free to make a sale dependent on terms not exacted from all customers alike. We shall see that it is not only the power of the monopolist to discriminate, together with the influence he may exercise on government possessing similar powers, which is truly harmful and ought to be curbed. But this power, although often associated with large size, is neither a necessary consequence of size nor confined to large organizations. The same problem arises when some small enterprise, or a labour union, which controls an essential service can hold the community to ransom by refusing to supply it.

Before we consider further the problem of checking these harmful actions of monopolists we must, however, consider some other reasons why size as such is often regarded as harmful.

The fact that the welfare of many more people is affected by the decisions of a big enterprise rather than by those of a small one does not mean that other considerations should enter into those decisions, or that it is desirable or possible in the case of the former to safeguard against mistakes by some sort of public supervision. Much of the resentment against the big corporations is due to the

81

belief that they do not take consequences into account which we think that they could because they are big, although a smaller firm admittedly could not do so: if a large concern closes down an unprofitable local plant, there will be an outcry because it 'could have afforded' to run it at a loss in order to preserve the jobs, while if the same plant had been an independent enterprise everybody would accept its closing down as inevitable. It is, however, no less desirable that an uneconomical plant be closed down if it belongs to a large concern, although it could be kept going out of the profits of the rest of the concern, than if it is an enterprise which cannot draw on such other sources of revenue.

There exists a widespread feeling that a big corporation, because it is big, should take more account of the indirect consequences of its decisions, and that it should be required to assume responsibilities not imposed upon smaller ones. But it is precisely here that there lies the danger of a big enterprise acquiring objectionably large powers. So long as the management has the one overriding duty of administering the resources under its control as trustees for the shareholders and for their benefit, its hands are largely tied; and it will have no arbitrary power to benefit this or that particular interest. But once the management of a big enterprise is regarded as not only entitled but even obliged to consider in its decisions whatever is regarded as the public or social interest, or to support good causes and generally to act for the public benefit, it gains indeed an uncontrollable power—a power which could not long be left in the hands of private managers but would inevitably be made the subject of increasing public control.[9]

In so far as corporations have power to benefit groups of individuals, mere size will also become a source of influencing government, and thus beget power of a very objectionable kind. We shall see presently that such influence, much more serious when it is exerted by the organized interests of groups than when exerted by the largest single enterprise, can be guarded against only by depriving government of the power of benefiting particular groups.

We must finally mention another instance in which it is undeniable that the mere fact of bigness creates a highly undesirable position: namely where, because of the consequences of what happens to a big enterprise, government cannot afford to let such an enterprise fail. At least in so far as the expectation that it will thus be protected makes investment in very big corporations appear less risky than investment in smaller ones, this will produce one of the 'artificial' advantages of bigness which are not based on better performance and which policy ought to eliminate. It seems clear that this can be done only by effectively depriving government of the power of providing such protection, for as long as it has such power it is vulnerable to pressure.

The chief point to remember, which is often obscured by the current talk about monopoly, is that it is not monopoly as such but only the prevention of competition which is harmful. These are so very far from being the same thing that it ought to be repeated that a monopoly that rests entirely on superior performance is wholly praiseworthy—even if such a monopolist keeps prices at a level at which he makes large profits and only just low enough to make it impossible for others to compete with him successfully, because he still uses a smaller amount of resources than others would do if they produced the same quantity of the product. Nor can there be a legitimate claim that such a monopolist is under a moral obligation to sell his product as cheaply as he still could while making a 'normal' profit—as little as we are under a moral obligation to work as hard as possible, or to sell a rare object at a moderate gain. Just as nobody dreams of attacking the 'monopoly' price of the unique skill of an artist or surgeon, so there is no wrong in the 'monopoly' profit of an enterprise capable of producing more cheaply than anybody else.

That it is not monopoly but only the prevention of competition (and all prevention of competition, whether it leads to monopoly or not) which is morally wrong should be specially remembered by those 'neo-liberals' who believe that they must show their impartiality by thundering against all enterprise monopoly as much as against labour monopolies, forgetting that much enterprise monopoly is the result of better performance, while all labour monopoly is due to the coercive suppression of competition. Where enterprise monopoly is based on a similar prevention of competition, it is as reprehensible and in as much need of prevention as those of labour and ought to be severely dealt with. But neither the existence of monopoly nor size as such are on economic or moral grounds undesirable or comparable with any acts aiming at the prevention of competition.

When monopoly becomes harmful

We leave out here deliberately one model case in which it must be admitted that monopolies are likely to arise—the case of scarce and exhaustible resources such as the deposits of certain ores and the like. The reason for the omission is that the problems which arise in this connection are much too complex for any brief discussion to be useful. We need merely note that this one case in which the development of a monopoly may be inevitable is also a case in which it is by no means clear that a monopoly is harmful, since such a monopoly is likely only to spread over a longer period the exploitation of the resource in question, but not to lead to any permanent withholding of goods or services at the expense of the total output.

Quite generally it can probably be said that what is harmful is not the existence of monopolies that are due to greater efficiency or to the control of particular limited resources, but the ability of some monopolies to protect and preserve their monopolistic position after the original cause of their superiority has disappeared. The main reason for this is that such monopolies will be able to use their power, not only over the prices which they charge uniformly to all, but over the prices which it can charge to particular customers. This power over the prices they will charge particular customers, or the power to discriminate, can in many ways be used to influence the market behaviour of these others, and particularly to deter or otherwise influence potential competitors.

It is probably not much of an exaggeration to say that almost all really harmful power of non-privileged monopolies rests on this power of discrimination because it alone, short of violence, gives them power over potential competitors. So long as a monopolist enjoys a monopolistic position because he offers to all better terms than anybody else can, even if these terms are not as favourable as those he could offer, everybody is better off for his existence. But if, because he can supply most people at better terms than anyone else, no other firm is ready to supply the product in question, anyone to whom he refuses to supply at those terms will have no alternative opportunity to satisfy his needs. Though the majority of the people may still be better off for the existence of such a monopolist, anyone may be at his mercy in so far as the nature of the product or service makes aimed discrimination possible and the monopolist chooses to practice it in order to make the buyer behave in some respect in a manner that suits the monopolist. He can, in particular, use this power to keep out a potential competitor by offering specially favourable terms to customers only in that limited region in which a newcomer at first will be able to compete.

84

The task of preventing such use of discrimination is especially difficult because certain kinds of discrimination by a monopolist will often be desirable. We have already mentioned that there is one case in which a monopolist may render better services *because* he is a monopolist. This is the case where his power to discriminate between different users of his product enables him to cover most of his fixed costs from those who can pay a relatively higher price and then to supply others at little more than variable costs. In such fields as transport and public utilities it is at least possible that some services could not be supplied at all at a profit if it were not for the possibility of discrimination such as monopoly confers.

The problem can therefore not be solved by imposing upon all monopolists the obligation to serve all customers alike. Yet since the power of the monopolist to discriminate can be used to coerce particular individuals or firms, and is likely to be used to restrict competition in an undesirable manner, it clearly ought to be curbed by appropriate rules of conduct. Though it would not be desirable to make all discrimination illegal, aimed discrimination intended to enforce a certain market conduct should clearly be prohibited. It is doubtful, however, whether it would be effectively achieved by making it a punishable offence rather than merely the basis of a claim for damages. The knowledge required here in order to prosecute successfully is not the kind of knowledge that any authority is likely to possess.

The problem of anti-monopoly legislation

It would seem more promising to give potential competitors a claim to equal treatment where discrimination cannot be justified on grounds other than the desire to enforce a particular market conduct, and to hold out an inducement for enforcing such claims in the form of multiple damages to all who feel they have been unreasonably discriminated against. Thus to set potential competitors as watchdogs over the monopolist and to give them a remedy against the use of price discrimination would seem a more promising check on such practices than to place enforcement in the hands of a supervising authority. Particularly if the law explicitly authorized that a part of the damages awarded might be collected by the lawyers conducting such cases, in lieu of fees and expenses, highly specialized legal consultants would probably soon grow up who, since they would owe the whole of their business to such suits, would not be inhibited through fear of offending the big corporations.

The same applies largely to the case where not a single monopolist but small groups of firms acting in concert to control the market are concerned. It is generally thought necessary to prohibit such monopolistic combinations or cartels by prohibiting them under penalties. The example set in the USA by Section One of the Sherman Act 1890 has been widely imitated. It seems also that this provision of the Act has been remarkably successful in creating in the business world a climate of opinion which regards as improper such explicit agreements to restrict competition. I have no doubt that such a general prohibition of all cartels, if it were consistently carried through, would be preferable to any discretionary power given to authorities for the purpose of merely preventing 'abuses'. The latter leads to a distinction between good and bad monopolies and usually to governments becoming more concerned with protecting the good monopolies than with combating the bad ones. There is no reason to believe that any monopolistic organization deserves protection against threatening competition, and much reason to believe that some wholly voluntary organizations of firms that do not rely on compulsion are not only not harmful but actually beneficial. It would seem that prohibition under penalties cannot be carried out without a discretionary power of granting exemptions, or of imposing upon courts the difficult task of deciding whether a particular agreement is, or is not, in the public interest. Even in the USA, under the Sherman Act and its various amendments and supplements, a situation has in consequence arisen of which it could be said that 'the law tells some businessmen that they must not cut prices, others that they must not raise prices, and still others that there is something evil in similar prices'.[10] It seems to me; therefore, that a third possibility, less far-reaching than prohibition under penalties, but more general than discretionary surveillance to prevent abuses, would be both more effective and more in conformity with the rule of law than either. This would be to declare invalid and legally unenforceable all agreement in restraint of trade, without any exceptions, and to prevent all attempts to enforce them by aimed discrimination or the like by giving those upon whom such pressures were brought a claim for multiple damages as suggested above.

We need not here again consider the misconception that this would be contrary to the principle of freedom of contract. Freedom of contract, like any other freedom, means merely that what kind of contract is enforceable in the courts depends only on the general rules of law and not on the previous approval by authority of the particular contents of the contract. Many kinds of contracts, such as gambling contracts, or contracts for immoral purposes, or contracts for life-long service, have long been held invalid and unenforceable. There is no reason why the same should not also apply to all contracts in restraint of trade, and no reason why all attempts to make someone, by the threat of withholding usual services, conform to certain rules of conduct should not be treated as unwarranted interference in this private domain which entitles him to damages. The practical solution of our problem may be much facilitated by the necessity which, as we shall see later, will arise of imposing special limitations upon the power of 'legal persons' (corporations and all other formal or informal organizations) which do not apply to private individuals.

The reason why such a modest aim of the law seems to me to promise greater results is that it can be applied universally without exceptions, while all the more ambitious attempts are generally emasculated by so many exceptions that they become not nearly so effective than the general application of a less far-reaching rule would be—not to mention the wholly undesirable discretionary power which, under the first system confers on government the power of determining the character of economic activity.

There is probably no better illustration of the failure of the more ambitious attempt than the German Federal Republic's law against restriction of competition.[11] It begins with a sweeping provision which, wholly in the sense of what has been suggested, declares as invalid all agreements in restraint of competition. But after it has also made such agreements a punishable offence, it ends up by perforating the general rule with so many exceptions, which wholly exempt various kinds of contracts, or confer upon authorities discretionary powers to permit them, and finally confines the application of the law to such a limited sector of the economy, that it deprives the whole of most of its effectiveness. There would have been no need for most of if not for all of these exceptions if the law had confined itself to what it provided in the first paragraph and had not added to the declaration of the invalidity of agreements in restraint of trade a prohibition under penalties.

As there exist undoubtedly all kinds of understandings on standards and the like which are to apply unless other terms are explicitly agreed upon in the particular instances, and which are wholly beneficial so long as adherence to them is purely voluntary and no pressure can be brought on those who find it in their interest to divert from them, any outright prohibition of such agreements would be harmful. Both as regards types of products and terms of the contract the establishment of such norms as it would be in the interest of most to observe in ordinary instances would produce considerable economies. In such instances it will, however, be not so much that the norm is obligatory as that it pays the individual to adhere to an established standard practice which will bring about his conformity. The necessary check on such agreements on standards becoming obstructive will be provided by any individual firms being free explicitly to deviate from the norm in making a contract whenever this is to the interest of both parties to the contract.

Before leaving this particular subject a few words may be added on the curiously contradictory attitude of most governments towards monopoly. While in recent times they have generally endeavoured to control monopolies in the production and distribution of manufactured goods, and have in this field often applied overly rigorous standards, they have at the same time in much larger fields—in transport, public utilities, labour, agriculture, and, in many countries, also finance—deliberately assisted monopoly or used it as an instrument of policy. Also, the anti-cartel or anti-trust legislation has mostly been aimed at the combination of a few big firms and has rarely effectively touched the restrictive practices of the large groups of smaller firms organized in trade associations and the like. If we add to this the extent to which monopolies have been assisted by tariffs, industrial patents, some features of the law of corporations and the principles of taxation, one may well ask whether, if government had merely refrained from favouring monopolies, monopoly would ever have been a serious problem. Though I do believe that it should be one of the aims of the development of law to reduce private power over the market conduct of others, and that some beneficial results would follow from this, it does not appear to me that this compares in importance with what could be achieved by government refraining from assisting monopoly by discriminatory rules or measures of policy.

Not individual but group selfishness is the chief threat

While public indignation and in consequence also legislation has been directed almost entirely against the selfish actions of single monopolists, or of a few conspicuous enterprises acting in concert, what is chiefly threatening to destroy the market order is not the selfish action of individual firms but the selfishness of organized groups. These have gained their power largely through the assistance government has given them to suppress those manifestations of individual selfishness which would have kept their action in check. The extent to which the functioning of the market order has already been impeded, and threatens to become progressively more inoperative, is a result not so much of the rise of large productive units as of the deliberately furthered organization of the units for collective interests. What is increasingly suspending the working of the spontaneous forces of the market is not what the public has in mind when it complains about monopolies, but the ubiquitous associations and unions of the different 'trades'. They operate largely through the pressure they can bring on government to 'regulate' the market in their interest.

It was a misfortune that these problems became acute for the first time in connection with labour unions when widespread sympathy with their aims led to the toleration of methods which certainly could not be generally permitted, and which even in the field of labour will have to be curbed, though most workers have come to regard them as their hard-earned and sacred rights. One need merely ask what the results would be if the same techniques were generally used for political instead of economic purposes (as indeed they sometimes already are) in order to see that they are irreconcilable with the preservation of what we know as a free society.

The very term 'freedom of organization', hallowed by its use as a battle cry not only by labour but also by those political organizations which are indispensable for democratic government, carries overtones which are not in accord but in conflict with the reign of law on which a free society rests. Certainly any control of these activities through a discretionary supervision by government would be incompatible with a free order. But 'freedom of organization' should no more than 'freedom of contract' be interpreted to mean that the activities of organizations must not be subject to rules restricting their methods, or even that the collective action of organizations should not be restricted by rules which do not apply to individuals. The new powers created by the perfection of organizational techniques, and by the right conceded to them by existing laws, will probably require limitations by general rules of law far more narrow than those it has been found necessary to impose by law on the actions of private individuals.

It is easy to see why the weak individual will often derive comfort from the knowledge that he is a member of an organized group comprising individuals with common aims and which, as an organized group, is stronger than the strongest individual. It is an illusion, however, to believe that he would benefit, or that generally the many will benefit at the expense of the few, if all interests were so organized. The effect of such organization on society as a whole would be to make power not less but more oppressive. Though groups may then count for more than individuals, small groups may still be more powerful than large ones, simply because the former are more organizable, or the whole of their produce more indispensable than the whole of the produce of larger groups. And even though to the individual his single most important interest may be enhanced by joining an organization, this single most important interest that is organizable may still be less important to him than the sum of all his other interests which will be encroached upon by other organizations and which he himself cannot defend by joining a corresponding number of other organizations.

The importance attached and the respect paid to the collective bodies is a result of an understandable though erroneous belief that the larger the group becomes the more its interests will correspond to the interest of all. The term 'collective' has become invested with much the same aura of approval which the term 'social' commands. But far from the collective interests of the various groups being nearer to the interests of society as a whole, the exact opposite is true. While as a rough approximation it can legitimately be said that individual selfishness will in most instances lead the individual to act in a manner conducive to the preservation of the spontaneous order of society, the selfishness of a closed group, or the desire of its members to become a closed group, will always be in opposition to the true common interest of the members of a Great Society.[12]

That is what classical economics had already clearly brought out and modern marginal analysis has put into a more satisfying form. The importance of any particular service which any individual renders to the members of society is always only that of the last (or marginal) additions he makes to all the services of that kind; and if, whatever any member of society takes out of the pool of products and services is to leave as much as possible to the others, this requires that not the groups as such but the separate individuals composing them, by their free movement between the groups, strive to make their respective incomes as large as possible. The common interest of the members of any organized group will, however, be to make the value of their services correspond, not to the importance of the last increment, but to the importance which the aggregate of the services rendered by the group has for the users. The producers of food or electrical energy, of transport or medical services, etc., will therefore aim to use their joint power of determining the volume of such services to achieve a price that will be much higher than that which the consumers would be prepared to pay for the last increment. There exists no necessary relationship between the importance of a kind of commodity or service as a whole and the importance of the last addition that is still provided. If to have some food is essential for survival, this does not mean that the last addition to the supply of food is also more important than the production of an additional quantity of some frivolity, or that the production of food should be better remunerated than the production of things whose existence is certainly much less import-ant than the availability of food as such.

The special interest of the producers of food, or electricity, or transport, or medical services will be, however, to be remunerated not merely according to the marginal value of the kind of services they render, but according to the value that the total supply of the services in question has to the users. Public opinion, which still sees the problem in terms of the importance of this kind of service as such, therefore tends to give some support to such demands because it is felt that remuneration should be appropriate to the absolute importance of the commodity in question. It is only through the efforts of the marginal producers who can earn a living by rendering their services much below the value which the consumers would be prepared to pay if the total supply were smaller, that we are assured of plenty and that the chances of all are improved. The collective interests of the organized groups, on the other hand, will always be opposed to this general interest and aim at preventing those marginal individuals from adding to the total supply.

Any control wielded by the members of a trade or profession over the total amount of goods or services to be supplied will therefore always be opposed to the true general interest of society, while the selfish interests of the individual will normally drive them to make those marginal contributions which will cost approximately as much as the price at which they can be sold.

It is a wholly mistaken conception that a bargaining between groups in which the producers and the consumers of each of the different commodities or services respectively are combined would lead to a state of affairs which secures either efficiency in production or a kind of distribution which from any point of view would appear to be just. Even if all the separate interests (or even all 'important' interests) could be organized (which, as we shall see, they cannot), the sort of balance between the strengths of different organized groups which some people expect as the necessary or even desirable outcome of the developments which have been going on for some time, would in fact produce a structure which would be demonstrably irrational and inefficient, and unjust to the extreme in the light of any test of justice which requires a treatment of all according to the same rules.

The decisive reason for this is that in negotiations between existing organized groups the interests of those who bring about the required adjustments to changes, namely those who could improve their position by moving from one group to another, are systematically disregarded. So far as the group to which they wish to move is concerned, it will be its chief aim to keep them out. And the groups they wish to leave will have no incentive to assist their entry into what will often be a great variety of other groups. Thus, in a system in which the organizations of the existing producers of the various commodities and services determine prices and quantities to be produced, those who would bring about the continuous adjustment to change would be deprived of influence on events. It is not true, as the argument in support of the various syndicalist or corporativist systems assumes, that anybody's interest is bound up with the interest of all others who produce the same goods. It may be much more important to some to be able to shift to another group, and these movements are certainly most important for the preservation of the overall order. Yet it is these changes which, possible in a free market, agreements between organized groups will aim to prevent.

The organized producers of particular commodities or services will in general attempt to justify the exclusive policies by pleading that they can still meet the whole demand, and that, if and when they are not able to do so, they will be fully prepared to let others enter the trade. What they do not say is that this means merely that they can meet the demand at prevailing prices which give them what they regard as adequate profits. What is desirable, however, is that the demand be satisfied at the lower prices at which others might be able to supply—leaving those now in the trade perhaps only an income reflecting the fact that their particular skill is no longer scarce, or their equipment no longer up-to-date. In particular, though it should be as profitable for those in possession to introduce improvements in technique as it is for any newcomers, this will involve for the former risks and often the necessity of raising outside capital which will disturb their comfortable established position and seem not worth while unless their position is threatened by those not content with theirs. To allow the established producers to decide when new entrants are to be permitted would normally lead simply to the *status quo* being preserved.

Even in a society in which all the different interests were organized as separate closed groups, this would therefore lead merely to a freezing of the existing structure and as a result, to a gradual decline of the economy as it became progressively less adjusted to the changed conditions. It is therefore not true that such a system is unsatisfactory and unjust only so long as not all groups are equally organized. The belief of such authors as G. Myrdal and J. K. Galbraith[13] that the defects of the existing order are only those of a transitory kind which will be remedied when the process of organization is completed, is therefore erroneous. What makes most Western economies still viable is that the organization of interests is yet only partial and incomplete. If it were complete, we would have a deadlock between these organized interests, producing a wholly rigid economic structure which no agreement between the established interests and only the force of some dictatorial power could break.

The consequences of a political determination of the incomes of the different groups

The interest which is common to all members of a society is not the sum of the interests which are common to the members of the existing groups of producers, but only the interest in the continuous adaptation to changing conditions which some particular groups will always find it in their interests to prevent. The interest of the organized producers is therefore always contrary to the one permanent interest of all the individual members of society, namely the interest in the continuous adaptation to unpredictable changes, an adaptation necessary even if only the existing level of production is to be maintained (cf. chapters 8 and 10). The interest of organized producers is always to prevent the influx of others who want to share their prosperity or to avoid being driven out from a group by the more efficient producers when demand should decline. By this all strictly economic decisions, that is all new adjustments to unforeseen changes, will be impeded. The viability of a society, however, depends on the smooth and continuous execution of such gradual changes and their not being blocked by obstacles which can only be broken down when sufficient pressure accumulates. All the benefits we receive from the spontaneous order of the market are the results of such changes, and will be maintained only if the changes are allowed to continue. But every change of this kind will hurt some organized interests; and the preservation of the market order will therefore depend on those interests not being allowed to prevent what they dislike. All the time it is thus the interest of most that some be placed under the necessity of doing something they dislike (such as changing their jobs or accepting a lower income), and this general interest will be satisfied only if the principle is recognized that each has to submit to changes when circumstances nobody can control determine that he is the one who is placed under such a necessity. This risk itself is inseparable from the occurrence of unforeseen changes; and the only choice we have is either to allow the effects of such changes to fall, through the impersonal mechanism of the market, on the individuals whom the market will require to make the change or to accept a reduction of income, or to decide, arbitrarily or by a power struggle, who are to be those who must bear the burden which in this case will necessarily be greater than it would have been if we had let the market bring about the necessary change.

The deadlock to which the political determination of prices and wages by organized interests has already led has produced in some countries the demand for an 'incomes policy' which is to substitute an authoritative fixing of the remuneration of the different factors of production for their determination by the market. The demand is based on the recognition that if wages and other incomes are no longer determined by the market but by the political force of the organized groups, some deliberate co-ordination becomes necessary—and particularly that, if such political determination is to be effected with regard to wages, where the political determination had become most conspicuous, this would be possible to achieve only if a similar control was applied to all other incomes also.

The immediate danger which led to the demand for an 'incomes policy' was, however, the process of inflation which the competitive pressure for an increase of all incomes produced. As a means of curbing this upward movement of all money incomes, these 'incomes policies' were bound to fail. And the inflationary policies by which we are at present attempting to overcome those 'rigidities' are no more than palliatives that in the long run will not solve the problem but merely make it worse: because the temporary escape which they provide from the difficulties only allows the rigidities to grow stronger and stronger. No wage and price stop can alter the basic malaise, and every attempt to bring about the necessary alterations in relative prices by authoritative decision must fail, not only because no authority can know which prices are appropriate, but even more because such authority must, in whatever it does, endeavour to appear to be just, though the changes that will be required will have nothing whatever to do with justice. In consequence, all the measures of 'incomes policy' that have been taken have not even come near to solving the really central problem, that of restoring the process by which the relative incomes of the different groups are adjusted to changing conditions; and by treating this as a matter of political decisions they have, if anything, made matters only worse. As we have seen, the only definite content that can be given to the concept of 'social justice' is the preservation of the relative positions of the different groups; but these are what must be altered if adjustment to changed conditions is to be achieved. If change can be brought about only by political decision, the effect can only be, since there exists no basis for real agreement, an increasing rigidity of the whole economic structure.

Since Great Britain was the only big country which, at a time when a thorough readaptation of the deployment of her resources was required, found itself in the grip of extreme rigidity produced by an essentially politically determined wage structure, the resulting difficulties have come to be known as the 'English disease'. But in many other countries, where the situation is not very different, similar methods are now being tried in vain to solve the same kind of difficulties.

What is not yet generally recognized is that the real exploiters in our present society are not egotistic capitalists or entrepreneurs, and in fact not separate individuals, but organizations which derive their power from the moral support of collective action and the feeling of group loyalty. It is the built-in bias of our existing institutions in favour of organized interests which gives these organizations an artificial preponderance over the market forces and which is the main cause of real injustice in our society and of distortion of its economic structure. More real injustice is probably done in the name of group loyalty than from any selfish individual motives. Once we recognize that the degree of organizability of an interest has no relation to its importance from any social point of view, and that interests can be effectively organized only if they are in a position to exercise anti-social powers of coercion, the naive conception that, if the power of organized interests is checked by 'countervailing power',[14] this will produce a viable social order, appears as an absurdity. If by 'regulatory mechanism', of which the chief expounder of these ideas speaks, is meant a mechanism conducive to the establishment of an advantageous or rational order, 'countervailing powers' certainly produces no such mechanism. The whole conception that the power of organized interests can or will be made innocuous by 'countervailing power' constitutes a relapse into the methods of settling conflicts which once prevailed among individuals and from which the development and enforcement of rules of just conduct has gradually freed us. The problem of developing similar rules of just conduct for organized groups is still largely a problem for the future, and the main concern in the efforts to solve it will have to be the protection of the individuals against group pressure.

Organizable and non-organizable interests

During the last half century or so the dominant opinion which has guided policy has been that the growth of organized interests for the purpose of bringing pressure on government is inevitable, and that its obviously harmful effects are due to the fact that only some interests are yet so organized; this defect, it is thought, will disappear as soon as all important interests are equally organized so as to balance each other. Both views are demonstrably false. In the first instance, it is worth bringing pressure on government only if government has the power to benefit particular interests and this power exists only if it has authority to lay down and enforce aimed and discriminatory rules. In the second instance, as has been shown in an important study by M. Olson,[15] except in the case of relatively small groups, the existence of common interests will normally *not* lead to the spontaneous formation of a comprehensive organization of such interests, and has in fact done so only when government either positively assisted the efforts to organize all members of such groups, or has at least tolerated the use of coercion or discrimination to bring about such organization. It can be shown that these methods, however, can never bring about a comprehensive organization of all important interests but will always produce a condition in which the non-organizable interests will be sacrificed to and exploited by the organizable interests.

Olson's demonstration that, *first*, only relatively small groups will in general spontaneously form an organization, *second*, that the organizations of the great economic interests which today dominate government to a large extent have come about only with the help of the power of that government, and, *third*, that it is impossible in principle to organize all interests and that in consequence the organization of certain large groups assisted by government leads to a persistent exploitation of unorganized and unorganizable groups is here of fundamental importance. To the latter seem to belong such important groups as the consumers in general, the taxpayers, the women, the aged, and many others who together constitute a very substantial part of the population. All these groups are bound to suffer from the power of organized group interests.

SIXTEEN

THE MISCARRIAGE OF THE DEMOCRATIC IDEAL: A RECAPITULATION

An nescis, mi fili, quantilla prudentia regitur orbis?

Axel Oxenstjerna (1648)

The miscarriage of the democratic ideal

It is no longer possible to ignore that more and more thoughtful and well-meaning people are slowly losing their faith in what was to them once the inspiring ideal of democracy.

This is happening at the same time as, and in part perhaps in consequence of, a constant extension of the field to which the principle of democracy is being applied. But the growing doubts are clearly not confined to these obvious abuses of a political ideal: they concern its true core. Most of those who are disturbed by their loss of trust in a hope which has long guided them, wisely keep their mouths shut. But my alarm about this state makes me speak out.

It seems to me that the disillusionment which so many experience is not due to a failure of the principle of democracy as such but to our having tried it the wrong way. It is because I am anxious to rescue the true ideal from the miscredit into which it is falling that I am trying to find out the mistake we made and how we can prevent the bad consequences of the democratic procedure we have observed.

To avoid disappointment, of course, any ideal has to be approached in a sober spirit. In the case of democracy in particular we must not forget that the word refers solely to a particular method of government. It meant orginally no more than a certain procedure for arriving at political decisions, and tells us nothing about what the aims of government ought to be. Yet as the only method of peaceful change of government which men have yet discovered it is nevertheless precious and worth fighting for.

98

A 'bargaining' democracy

Yet it is not difficult to see why the outcome of the democratic process in its present form must bitterly disappoint those who believed in the principle that government should be guided by the opinion of the majority. *not actually majority interests*

Though some claim this is now the case, it is too obviously not true to deceive observant persons. Never, indeed, in the whole of history were governments so much under the necessity of satisfying the particular wishes of numerous special interests as is true of government today. Critics of present democracy like to speak of 'mass-democracy'. But if democratic government were really bound to what the masses agree upon there would be little to object to. The cause of complaints is not that the governments serve an agreed opinion of the majority, but that they are bound to serve the several interests of a conglomerate of numerous groups. It is at least conceivable, though unlikely, that an autocratic government will exercise self-restraint; but an omnipotent democratic government simply cannot do so. If its powers are not limited, it simply cannot confine itself to serving the agreed views of the majority of the electorate. It will be forced to bring together and keep together a majority by satisfying the demands of a multitude of special interests, each of which will consent to the special benefits granted to other groups only at the price of their own special interests being equally considered. Such a bargaining democracy has nothing to do with the conceptions used to justify the principle of democracy.

The playball of group interests

No to omnipotent demo

When I speak here of the necessity of democratic government being limited, or more briefly of limited democracy, I do not, of course, mean that the part of government conducted democratically should be limited, but that *all* government, specially if democratic, should be limited. The reason is that democratic government, if nominally omnipotent, becomes as a result of unlimited powers exceedingly weak, the playball of all the separate interests it has to satisfy to secure majority support.

How has the situation come about?

For two centuries, from the end of absolute monarchy to the rise of unlimited democracy the great aim of constitutional government had been to limit all governmental powers. The chief principles

All gvt. should be limited

gradually established to prevent all arbitrary exercise of power were the separation of powers, the rule or sovereignty of law, government under the law, the distinction between private and public law, and the rules of judicial procedure. They all served to define and limit the conditions under which any coercion of individuals was admissible. Coercion was thought to be justified only in the general interest. And only coercion according to uniform rules equally applicable to all was thought to be in the general interest.

All these great liberal principles were given second rank and were half forgotten when it came to be believed that democratic control of government made unnecessary any other safeguards against the arbitrary use of power. The old principles were not so much forgotten as their traditional verbal expression deprived of meaning by a gradual change of the key words used in them. The most important of the crucial terms on which the meaning of the classical formulae of liberal constitution turned was the term 'Law'; and all the old principles lost their significance as the content of this term was changed.

Laws versus directions

To the founders of constitutionalism the term 'Law' had had a very precise narrow meaning. Only from limiting government by law in this sense was the protection of individual liberty expected. The philosophers of law in the nineteenth century finally defined it as rules regulating the conduct of persons towards others, applicable to an unknown number of future instances and containing prohibitions delimiting (but of course not specifying) the boundaries of the protected domain of all persons and organized groups. After long discussions, in which the German jurisprudents in particular had at last elaborated this definition of what they called 'law in the material sense', it was in the end suddenly abandoned for what now must seem an almost comic objection. Under this definition the rules of a constitution would not be law in the material sense.

They are, of course, not rules of conduct but rules for the organization of government, and like all public law are apt to change frequently while private (and criminal) law can last.

Law was meant to prevent unjust conduct. Justice referred to principles equally applicable to all and was contrasted to all specific commands or privileges referring to particular individuals and groups. But who still believes today, as James Madison could two hundred years ago, that the House of Representatives would be unable to make 'law which will not have its full operation on themselves and their friends, as well as the great mass of society'?

What happened with the apparent victory of the democratic ideal was that the power of laying down laws and the governmental power of issuing directions were placed into the hands of the same assemblies. The effect of this was necessarily that the supreme governmental authority became free to give itself currently whatever laws helped it best to achieve the particular purposes of the moment. But it necessarily meant the end of the principle of government *under* the law. While it was reasonable enough to demand that not only legislation proper but also governmental measures should be determined by democratic procedure, placing both powers into the hands of the same assembly (or assemblies) meant in effect return to unlimited government.

It also invalidated the original belief that a democracy, because it had to obey the majority, could only do what was in the general interest. This would have been true of a body which could give only *general* laws or decide on issues of truly *general* interest. But this is not only *not* true but outright *impossible* for a body which has unlimited powers and must use them to buy the votes of particular interests, including those of some small groups or even powerful individuals. Such a body, which does not owe its authority to demonstrating its belief in the justice of its decisions by committing itself to general rules, is constantly under the necessity of rewarding the support by the different groups by conceding special advantages. The 'political necessities' of contemporary democracy are far from all being demanded by the majority!

Laws and arbitrary government

The result of this development was not merely that government was no longer under the law. It also brought it about that the concept of law itself lost its meaning. The so-called legislature was no longer (as John Locke had thought it should be) confined to giving laws in the sense of general rules. *Everything* the 'legislature' resolved came to be called 'law', and it was no longer called legislature because it gave laws, but 'laws' became the name for everything which emanated from the 'legislature'. The hallowed term 'law' thus lost all its old meaning, and it became

101

the name for the commands of what the fathers of constitutionalism would have called arbitrary government. Government became the main business of the 'legislature' and legislation subsidiary to it.

The term 'arbitrary' no less lost its classical meaning. The word had meant 'rule-less' or determined by particular will rather than according to recognized rules. In this true sense even the decision of an autocratic ruler may be lawful, and the decision of a democratic majority entirely arbitrary. Even Rousseau, who is chiefly responsible for bringing into political usage the unfortunate conception of 'will', understood at least occasionally that, to be just, this will must be *general in intent*. But the decision of the majorities in contemporary legislative assemblies need, of course, not have that attribute. Anything goes, so long as it increases the number of votes supporting governmental measures.

An omnipotent sovereign parliament, not confined to laying down general rules, means that we have an arbitrary government. What is worse, a government which cannot, even if it wished, obey any principles, but must maintain itself by handing out special favours to particular groups. It must buy its authority by discrimination. Unfortunately the British Parliament which had been the model for most representative institutions also introduced the idea of the sovereignty (i.e. omnipotence) of Parliament. But the sovereignty of the *law* and the sovereignty of an unlimited *Parliament* are irreconcilable. Yet today, when Mr Enoch Powell claims that 'a Bill of Rights is incompatible with the free constitution of this country', Mr Gallagher hastens to assure him that he understands that and agrees with Mr Powell.[1]

It turns out that the Americans two hundred years ago were right and an almighty Parliament means the death of the freedom of the individual. Apparently a free constitution no longer means the freedom of the individual but a *licence to the majority in Parliament to act as arbitrarily as it pleases*. We can either have a free Parliament or a free people. Personal freedom requires that all authority is restrained by long-run principles which the opinion of the people approves.

From unequal treatment to arbitrariness

It took some time for those consequences of unlimited democracy to show themselves.

For a while the traditions developed during the period in which liberal constitutionalism operated as a restraint on the extent of governmental power. Wherever these forms of democracy were imitated in parts of the world where no such tradition existed, they invariably, of course, soon broke down. But in the countries with longer experience with representative government the traditional barriers to arbitrary use of power were at first penetrated from entirely benevolent motives. Discrimination to assist the least fortunate did not seem to be discrimination. (More recently we even invented the nonsense word 'under-privileged' to conceal this.) But in order to put into a more equal material position people who are inevitably very different in many of the conditions on which their wordly success depends it is necessary to treat them unequally.

Yet to break the principle of *equal treatment under the law* even for charity's sake inevitably opened the floodgates to arbitrariness. To disguise it the pretence of the formula of 'social justice' was resorted to; nobody knows precisely what it means, but for that very reason it served as the magic wand which broke down all barriers to partial measures. Dispensing gratuities at the expense of somebody else *who cannot be readily identified* became the most attractive way of buying majority support. But a parliament or government which becomes a charitable institution thereby becomes exposed to irresistible blackmail. And it soon ceases to be the 'deserts' but becomes exclusively the 'political necessity' which determines which groups are to be favoured at general expense.

This legalized corruption is not the fault of the politicians; they cannot avoid it if they are to gain positions in which they can do any good. It becomes a built-in feature of any system in which majority support authorizes a special measure assuaging particular discontent. Both a legislature confined to laying down general rules and a governmental agency which can use coercion only to enforce general rules which it cannot change can resist such pressure; an omnipotent assembly cannot. Deprived of all power of discretionary coercion, government might, of course, still discriminate in rendering services - but this would be less harmful and could be more easily prevented. But once central government possesses no power of discriminatory coercion, most services could be and probably should be delegated to regional or local corporations competing for inhabitants by providing better services at lower costs.

Separation of powers to prevent unlimited government

It seems clear that a nominally unlimited ('sovereign') representative assembly must be progressively driven into a steady and unlimited extension of the powers of government. It appears equally clear that this can be prevented only by dividing the supreme power between two distinct democratically elected assemblies, i.e. by applying the principle of the separation of powers on the highest level.

Two such distinct assemblies would, of course, have to be differently composed if the *legislative* one is to represent the *opinion* of the people about which sorts of government actions are just and which are not, and the other *governmental* assembly were to be guided by the *will* of the people on the particular measures to be taken within the frame of rules laid down by the first. For this second task - which has been the main occupation of existing parliaments - the practices and organization of parliaments have become well adapted, especially with their organization on party lines which is indeed indispensable for conducting government.

But it was not without reason that the great political thinkers of the eighteenth century were without exception deeply distrustful of party divisions in a true legislature. It can hardly be denied that the existing parliaments are largely unfit for legislation proper. They have neither the time nor the right frame of mind to do it well.

SEVENTEEN

A MODEL CONSTITUTION

In all cases it must be advantageous to know what is the most perfect in the kind, that we may be able to bring any real constitution or form of government as near it as possible, by such gentle alterations and innovations as may not give too great a disturbance to society.

David Hume*

The wrong turn taken by the development of representative institutions

What can we do today, in the light of the experience gained, to accomplish the aims which, nearly two hundred years ago, the fathers of the Constitution of the United States of America for the first time attempted to secure by a deliberate construction? Though our aims may still be the same, there is much that we ought to have learnt from the great experiment and its numerous imitations. We know now why the hope of the authors of those documents, that through them they could effectively limit the powers of government, has been disappointed. They had hoped by a separation of the legislative from executive as well as the judicial powers to subject government and the individuals to rules of just conduct. They could hardly have forseen that, because the legislature was also entrusted with the direction of government, the task of stating rules of just conduct and the task of directing particular activities of government to specific ends would come to be hopelessly confounded, and that law would cease to mean only such universal and uniform rules of just conduct as would limit all arbitrary coercion. In consequence, they never really achieved that separation of powers at which they had aimed. Instead they produced in the USA a system under which, often to the detriment of the efficiency of government, the power of organizing and directing government was divided between

105

the chief executive and a representative assembly elected at different times and on different principles and therefore frequently at loggerheads with each other.

We have already seen that the desire to have the laying down of rules of just conduct as well as the direction of current government in the hands of representative bodies need not mean that both these powers should be entrusted to the same body. The possibility of a different solution of the problem[1] is in fact suggested by an earlier phase of the development of representative institutions. The control of the conduct of government was, at least at first, brought about mainly through the control of revenue. By an evolution which started in Britain as early as the end of the fourteenth century the power of the purse had progressively devolved upon the House of Commons. When at last at the end of the seventeenth century the exclusive right of the Commons over 'money bills' was definitely conceded by the House of Lords, the latter, as the highest court in the country, still retained ultimate control of the development of the rules of common law. What would have been more natural than that, in conceding to the Commons sole control of the current conduct of government, the second chamber should have in return claimed the exclusive right to alter by statute the enforceable rules of just conduct?

Such a development was not really possible so long as the upper house represented a small privileged class. But in principle a division by functions instead of a division according to the different classes represented might have led to a situation in which the Commons would have obtained full power over the apparatus of government and all the material means put at its disposal, but would have been able to employ coercion only within the limits of the rules laid down by the House of Lords. In organizing and directing what was properly the task of government they would have been entirely free. To guide the actions of the officers of government concerning what was the property of the state they could have laid down any rules they agreed upon. But neither they nor their servants could have coerced private citizens except to make them obey the rules recognized or laid down by the Upper House. It would then have been entirely logical if the current affairs of government were conducted by a committee of the Lower House, or rather of its majority. Such a government would then in its powers over citizens have been entirely under a law which it would have had no power to alter in order to make it suit its particular purposes.

106

Such a separation of tasks would have required and gradually produced a sharp distinction between rules of just conduct and instructions to government. It would soon have shown the need for a superior judicial authority, capable of deciding conflicts between the two representative bodies, and by doing so, gradually building up an ever more precise distinction between the two kind of rules; the private (including criminal) and the public law, which are now confused because they are described by the same term, 'law'.

Instead of such a progressive clarification of the fundamental distinction the combination of wholly different tasks in the hands of one and the same body has led to an increasing vagueness of the concept of law. We have seen that the distinction is not an easy one to draw and that the task presents even modern legal thought with some hard problems. But it is not an impossible task. Though a wholly satisfactory solution may require further advance of our understanding. It is through such advance that all law has grown.

The value of a model of an ideal constitution

Assuming that a distinction between the two kinds of rules which we now call laws can be drawn clearly, its significance will be put into sharper focus if we sketch in some detail the sort of constitutional arrangements which would secure a real separation of powers between two distinct representative bodies whereby law-making in the narrow sense as well as government proper would be conducted democratically, but by different and mutually independent agencies. My purpose in presenting such a sketch is not to propose a constitutional scheme for present application. I certainly do not wish to suggest that any country with a firmly established constitutional tradition should replace its constitution by a new one drawn up on the lines suggested. But apart from the fact that the general principles discussed in the preceding pages will obtain more definite shape if I outline here a constitution embodying them, there are two further reasons which appear to make such a sketch worth while.

In the first instance, very few countries in the world are in the fortunate position of possessing a strong constitutional tradition. Indeed, outside the English-speaking world probably only the smaller countries of Northern Europe and Switzerland have such traditions. Most of the other countries have never preserved a constitution long enough to make it become a deeply entrenched

107

tradition; and in many of them there is also lacking the background of traditions and beliefs which in the more fortunate countries have made constitutions work which did not explicitly state all that they presupposed, or which did not even exist in written form. This is even more true of those new countries which, without a tradition even remotely similar to the ideal of the Rule of Law which the nations of Europe have long held, have adopted from the latter the institutions of democracy without the foundations of beliefs and convictions presupposed by those institutions.

If such attempts to transplant democracy are not to fail, much of that background of unwritten traditions and beliefs, which in the successful democracies had for a long time restrained the abuse of the majority power, will have to be spelled out in such instruments of government for the new democracies. That most of such attempts have so far failed does not prove that the basic conceptions of democracy are inapplicable, but only that the particular institutions which for a time worked tolerably well in the West presuppose the tacit acceptance of certain other principles which were in some measure observed there but which, where they are not yet recognized, must be made as much a part of the written constitution as the rest. We have no right to assume that the particular forms of democracy which have worked with us must also work elsewhere. Experience seems to show that they do not. There is, therefore, every reason to ask how those conceptions which our kind of representative institutions tacitly presupposed can be explicitly put into such constitutions.

In the second instance, the principles embodied in the scheme to be outlined may be of relevance in connection with the contemporary endeavours to create new supra-national institutions. There seems to be a growing feeling that we may hope to achieve some sort of international law but that it is doubtful whether we can, or even whether we should, create a supra-national government beyond some pure service agencies. Yet if anything should be clear it is that, if these endeavours are not to fail, or even not to do more harm than good, these new supra-national institutions will for a long time have to be limited to restraining national governments from actions harmful to other countries, but possess no powers to order them to do particular things. Many of the objections which people understandably have to entrusting an international authority with the power of issuing orders to the several national governments might well be met if such a new authority were to be restricted to the establishment of general rules which merely prohibited certain kinds of actions of the member states or their citizens. But to achieve this we have yet to discover how the power of legislation, in the sense in which it was understood by those who believed in the separation of powers, can be effectively separated from the powers of government.

The basic principles

The basic clause of such a constitution would have to state that in normal times, and apart from certain clearly defined emergency situations, men could be restrained from doing what they wished, or coerced to do particular things, only in accordance with the recognized rules of just conduct designed to define and protect the individual domain of each; and that the accepted set of rules of this kind could be deliberately altered only by what we shall call the Legislative Assembly. This in general would have power only in so far as it proved its intention to be just by committing itself to universal rules intended to be applied in an unknown number of future instances and over the application of which to particular cases it had no further power. The basic clause would have to contain a definition of what can be law in this narrow sense of *nomos* which would enable a court to decide whether any particular resolution of the Legislative Assembly possessed the formal properties to make it law in this sense.

We have seen that such a definition could not rely only on purely logical criteria but would have to require that the rules should be intended to apply to an indefinite number of unknown future instances, to serve the formation and preservation of an abstract order whose concrete contents were unforeseeable, but not the achievement of particular concrete purposes, and finally to exclude all provisions intended or known to affect principally particular identifiable individuals or groups. It would also have to recognize that, though alterations of the recognized body of existing rules of just conduct were the exclusive right of the Legislative Assembly, the initial body of such rules would include not only the products of past legislation but also those not yet articulated conceptions implicit in past decisions by which the courts should be bound and which it would be their task to make explicit.

The basic clause would of course not be intended to define the functions of government but merely to define the limits of its

109

coercive powers. Though it would restrict the means that government could employ in rendering services to the citizens, it would place no direct limit on the content of the services government might render. We shall have to return to this matter when we turn to the functions of the second representative body, the Governmental Assembly.

Such a clause would by itself achieve all and more than the traditional Bills of Rights were meant to secure; and it would therefore make any separate enumeration of a list of special protected fundamental rights unnecessary. This will be clear when it is remembered that none of the traditional Rights of Man, such as the freedom of speech, of the press, of religion, of assembly and association, or of the inviolability of the home or of letters, etc., can be, or ever have been, absolute rights that may not be limited by general rules of law. Freedom of speech does of course not mean that we are free to slander, libel, deceive, incite to crime or cause a panic by false alarm, etc., etc. All these rights are either tacitly or explicitly protected against restrictions only 'save in accordance with the law'. But this limitation, as has become only too clear in modern times, is meaningful and does not deprive the protection of those rights of all efficacy against the 'legislature', only if by 'law' is not meant every properly passed resolution of a representative assembly but only such rules as can be described as laws in the narrow sense here defined.

Nor are the fundamental rights, traditionally protected by Bills of Rights, the only ones that must be protected if arbitrary power is to be prevented, nor can all such essential rights which constitute individual liberty ever be exhaustively enumerated. Though, as has been shown before, the efforts to extend the concept to what are now called social and economic rights were misguided (see appendix to chapter 9), there are many unforeseeable exercises of individual freedom which are no less deserving of protection other than those enumerated by various Bills of Rights. Those which are commonly explicitly named are those which at particular times were specially threatened, and particularly those which seemed to need safeguarding if democratic government was to work. But to single them out as being specially protected suggests that in other fields government may use coercion without being bound by general rules of law.

This, indeed, has been the reason why the original framers of the American Constitution did not at first wish to include in it a Bill of

110

Rights, and why, when it was added, the ineffective and all but forgotten Ninth Amendment provided that 'the enumeration in the Constitution, of certain rights, shall not be construed to deny or disparage others retained by the people'. The enumeration of particular rights as being protected against infringements 'save in accordance with the law' indeed might seem to imply that in other respects the legislature is free to restrain or coerce people without committing itself to a general rule. And the extension of the term 'law' to almost any resolution of the legislature has lately made even this protection meaningless. The purpose of a constitution, however, is precisely to prevent even the legislature from all arbitrary restraints and coercion. And, as has been forcefully pointed out by a distinguished Swiss jurist,[2] the new possibilities which technological developments create may in the future make other liberties even more important than those protected by the traditional fundamental rights.

What the fundamental rights are intended to protect is simply individual liberty in the sense of the absence of arbitrary coercion. This requires that coercion be used only to enforce the universal rules of just conduct protecting the individual domains and to raise means to support the services rendered by government; and since what is implied here is that the individual can be restrained only in such conduct as may encroach upon the protected domain of others, he would under such a provision be wholly unrestricted in all actions which affected only his personal domain or that of other consenting responsible persons, and thus be assured all freedom that can be secured by political action. That this freedom may have to be temporarily suspended when those institutions are threatened which are intended to preserve it in the long run, and when it becomes necessary to join in common action for the supreme end of defending them, or to avert some other common danger to the whole society, is another matter which we shall take up later.

The two representative bodies with distinctive functions

The idea of entrusting the task of stating the general rules of just conduct to a representative body distinct from the body which is entrusted with the task of government is not entirely new. Something like this was attempted by the ancient Athenians when they allowed only the *nomothetae*, a distinct body, to change the fundamental *nomos*.[3] As *nomos* is about the only term which has

111

preserved at least approximately the meaning of general rules of just conduct, and as the term *nomothetae* was revived in a somewhat similar context in seventeenth century England[4] and again by J.S. Mill,[5] it will be convenient occasionally to use it as a name for that purely legislative body which the advocates of the separation of powers and the theorists of the Rule of Law had in mind, whenever it is necessary emphatically to distinguish it from the second representative body which we shall call the Governmental Assembly.

Such a distinctive legislative assembly would evidently provide an effective check on the decisions of an equally representative governmental body only if its membership were not composed in the same way; this would in practice appear to require that the two assemblies must not be chosen in the same manner, or for the same period. If the two assemblies were merely charged with different tasks but composed of approximately the same proportions of representatives of the same groups and especially parties, the legislature would probably simply provide those laws which the governmental body wanted for its purposes as much as if they were one body.

The different tasks also require that the different assemblies should represent the views of the electors in different respects. For the purpose of government proper it seems desirable that the concrete wishes of the citizens for particular results should find expression, or, in other words, that their particular interests should be represented; for the conduct of government a majority committed to a programme of action and 'capable of governing' is thus clearly needed. Legislation proper, on the other hand, should not be governed by interests but by opinion, i.e. by views about what *kind* of action is right or wrong – not as an instrument for the achievement of particular ends but as a permanent rule and irrespective of the effect on particular individuals or groups. In choosing somebody most likely to look effectively after their particular interests and in choosing persons whom they can trust to uphold justice impartially the people would probably elect very different persons: effectiveness in the first kind of task demands qualities very different from the probity, wisdom, and judgment which are of prime importance in the second.

The system of periodic election of the whole body of representatives is well designed not only to make them responsive to the fluctuating wishes of the electorate, but also to make them organize into parties and to render them dependent on the agreed aims of parties committed to support particular interests and particular programmes of actions. But it also in effect compels the individual member to submit to party discipline to get the support of the party for re-election.

To expect from an assembly of representatives charged with looking after particular interests the qualities which were expected by the classical theorists of democracy from a representative sample of the people at large is unreasonable. But this does not mean that if the people were asked to elect representatives who had no power to grant them particular favours they could not be induced to respond by designating those whose judgment they have learnt most to respect, especially if they had to choose among persons who already had made their reputation in the ordinary pursuits of life.

What would thus appear to be needed for the purposes of legislation proper is an assembly of men and women elected at a relatively mature age for fairly long periods, such as fifteen years, so that they would not have to be concerned about being re-elected, after which period, to make them wholly independent of party discipline, they should not be re-eligible nor forced to return to earning a living in the market but be assured of continued public employment in such honorific but neutral positions as lay judges, so that during their tenure as legislators they would be neither dependent on party support nor concerned about their personal future. To assure this only people who have already proved themselves in the ordinary business of life should be elected and the same time to prevent the assembly's containing too high a proportion of old persons, it would seem wise to rely on the old experience that a man's contemporaries are his fairest judges and to ask each group of people of the same age once in their lives, say in the calendar year in which they reached the age of 45, to select from their midst representatives to serve for fifteen years.

The result would be a legislative assembly of men and women between their 45th and 60th years, one-fifteenth of whom would be replaced every year. The whole would thus mirror that part of the population which had already gained experience and had had an opportunity to make their reputation, but who would still be in their best years. It should be specially noted that, although the under 45s would not be represented in such an assembly, the average age of the members - 52½ years - would be less than that of most existing representative bodies, even if the strength of the older part were kept constant by replacement of those dropping out through death and disease, which in the normal course of events would seem unnecessary and would only increase the proportion of those with little experience in the business of legislating.

Various additional safeguards might be employed to secure the entire independence of these *nomothetae* from the pressure of particular interests or organized parties. Persons who had already served in the Governmental Assembly or in party organizations might be made ineligible for the Legislative Assembly. And even if many members might have closer attachment to certain parties, there would be little inducement for them to obey instructions of the party leadership or the government in power.

Members would be removable only for gross misconduct or neglect of duty by some group of their present or former peers on the principles which today apply to judges. The assurance after the end of their tenure and up to the age of retirement with a pension (that is for the time from their 60th to their 70th year) of a dignified position such as that of lay members of judicial courts would be an important factor contributing to their independence; indeed, their salary might be fixed by the Constitution at a certain percentage of the average of, say, the twenty most highly paid posts in the gift of government.

It could be expected that such a position would come to be regarded by each age class as a sort of prize to be awarded to the most highly respected of their contemporaries. As the Legislative Assembly should not be very numerous, comparatively few individuals would have to be elected every year. This might well make it advisable to employ an indirect method of election, with regionally appointed delegates electing the representative from their midst. Thus a further inducement would be provided for each district to appoint as delegates persons of such standing as would have the best chance of being chosen in the second poll.

It might at first seem as if such a purely legislative assembly would have very little work to do. If we think exclusively of those tasks which we have so far stressed, namely the revision of the body of private (including commercial and criminal) law, they would indeed appear to require action only at long intervals, and hardly provide adequate continuous occupation for a select group of highly competent persons. Yet this first impression is misleading. Though we have used private and criminal law as our chief illustrations, it must be remembered that all enforceable rules of conduct would have to have the sanction of this assembly. While, within the compass of this book, we have had little opportunity to go into detail on these matters we have repeatedly pointed out that those tasks include not only the principles of taxation but also all those regulations of safety and health, including regulations of production or construction, that have to be enforced in the general interest and should be stated in the form of general rules. These comprise not only what used to be called safety legislation but also all the difficult problems of creating an adequate framework for a functioning competitive market and the law of corporations which we have mentioned in the last chapter.

Such matters have in the past had to be largely delegated by the legislature which had no time for careful consideration of the often highly technical issues involved, and have in consequence been placed in the hands of the bureaucracy or special agencies created for the purpose. Indeed, a 'legislature' chiefly concerned with the pressing matters of current government is bound to find it difficult to give such matters the attention they require. They are nevertheless matters not of administration but of legislation proper, and the danger that the bureaucracy, if the tasks are delegated to it, will assume discretionary and essentially arbitrary powers is considerable. There are no intrinsic reasons why the regulation of these matters should not take the form of general rules (as was still the rule in Britain before 1914), if it were seriously attempted by a legislature, instead of being considered from the point of view of the convenience of administrators ambitious of acquiring power. Probably most of the powers which bureaucracy has acquired, and which are in effect uncontrollable, are the result of delegation by legislatures.

Yet, though I am not really concerned about the members of the legislature lacking adequate occupation, I will add that I should regard it as by no means unfortunate but rather as desirable if a selected group of men and women, who had already made a reputation in the ordinary business of life, were then freed for part of their lives from the necessity or duty of devoting themselves to tasks imposed on them by circumstances so that they would be able to reflect on the principles of government or might take up whatever cause they thought important. A certain sprinkling of people who have leisure is essential if public spirit is to express itself in those voluntary activities where new ideals can manifest themselves. Such was the function of the man of independent means, and though I believe it to be a strong argument for his preservation, there is no

115

reason why people who have acquired property should be the only ones given such an opportunity. If those who have been entrusted by their contemporaries with the highest confidence they can show were to be free to devote a substantial part of their time to tasks of their own choice, they may contribute much to the development of that 'voluntary sector' which is so necessary if government is not to assume overwhelming power. And if the position of a member of the legislature should not prove to be a very onerous one, it ought nevertheless to be made one of great honour and dignity so that in some respects the members of this democratically elected body would be able to play the role of what Max Weber has called the *honoratiores,* independent public figures who, apart from their functions as legislators, and without party ties, could take a leading part in various voluntary efforts.

So far as the chief task of these *nomothetae* is concerned, it may be felt that the main problem would probably not be whether they had enough work to do, but rather whether there would be a sufficient inducement for them to do it. It might be feared that the very degree of independence which they enjoyed might tempt them to become lazy. Though it seems to me not very likely that persons who had earlier made their mark in active life, and whose position would henceforth rest on public reputation should, once they were elected for fifteen years to a position in which they were practically irremovable, in such a manner neglect their duties, yet provisions might be made similar to those applying in the case of judges. Though they must be wholly independent of the governmental organization there might well be some supervision by some senate of former members of the body who in the case of neglect of duties might even be entitled to remove representatives. It would also be such a body which at the end of the tenure of membership of the Legislative Assembly would have to assign positions to each retiring member, ranging from that of a president of the Constitutional Court to that of a lay assessor of some minor judicial body.

The Constitution should, however, also guard against the eventuality of the Legislative Assembly becoming wholly inactive by providing that, while it should have exclusive powers to lay down general rules of just conduct, this power might devolve temporarily to the Governmental Assembly if the former did not respond within a reasonable period to a notice given by government that some rules should be laid down on a particular question. Such a constitutional provision would probably by its mere existence make it unnecessary

116

that it should ever have to be invoked. The jealousy of the Legislative Assembly would probably operate strongly enough to assure that it would within a reasonable time answer any question of rules of just conduct which was raised.

Further observations on representation by age groups

Although only the general principle of the suggested model constitution is relevant to the main theme of this book, the method of representation by generations proposed for the Legislative Assembly offers so many interesting possibilities for the development of democratic institutions that it seems worthwhile to elaborate on it a little further. The fact that the members of each age class would know that some day they would have an important common task to perform might well lead to the early formation of local clubs of contemporaries, and since this would contribute towards the proper education of suitable candidates, such a tendency would seem to deserve public support, at least through the provision of regular meeting places and facilities for contacts between the groups of different localities. The existence in each locality of only one such publically assisted and recognised group for every age class might also help to prevent a splitting of groups on party lines.

Clubs of contemporaries might well be formed either at school-leaving age or at least when each class entered public life, say at the age of 18. They would possibly be more attractive if men of one age group were brought together with women two years or so younger. This might be achieved, without any objectionable legal discrimination, by allowing men and women at the age of eighteen to join either the then newly formed club or one of those formed in one of the preceding two or three years, in which case probably most men would prefer to join their own new club, while women would seem more likely to join one of those started in the preceding years. Such a choice would of course imply that those opting for the higher age class would permanently belong to it and vote for the delegate and be eligible as delegates and representatives earlier than would otherwise be the case.

The clubs would, by bringing together the contemporaries of all social classes, and preserving contacts between those who were together at school (and perhaps national service), but now go entirely different ways, provide a truly democratic link by serving to provide contacts cutting across all other stratifications and providing an education in, and an incentive for, interest in public institutions as well as training in parliamentry procedures. They would also provide a regular channel for the expression of dissent of those not yet represented in a Legislative Assembly. If they should occasionally also become platforms for party debates, their advantage would be that those leaning towards different parties would be induced to discuss the issues together, and would become conscious that they had the common task of representing the outlook of their generation and to qualify for possible later public service.

Though individual membership ought to be primarily in the local group, it should confer on a member the right to take part as visitors in the clubs of one's age class at places other than that of one's permanent residence; and if it were known that in each locality a particular age class met regularly at a particular time and place (as it is the case with Rotarians and similar organizations), this might become an important means of inter-local contacts. In many other respects such clubs would probably introduce an important element of social coherence, especially to the structure of urban society, and do much to reduce the existing occupational and class distinctions.

The rotating chairmanship of these clubs would provide the members with an opportunity to become acquainted with the suitability of potential candidates for election as delegates or representatives; in the case of indirect elections they might therefore be based on personal knowledge even in the second round and the delegates ultimately selected might thereafter act not only as chairmen but also as voluntary but officially recognized spokesmen of their respective age groups, a sort of special honorary 'ombudsmen', who would protect the interests of their age groups against authorities. The advantage of their performing such functions would be that in voting for them the members would be more likely to elect somebody whose integrity they trusted.

Though after the election of the representatives these clubs would have few further formal tasks they would probably continue as means of social contact which might in fact also be called upon in case of need to restore the number of representatives if by some unusual accidents it had been depleted much below normal strength – perhaps not to the full original number but at least so that the numerical strength of their age group was adequately represented.

The governmental assembly

We need say little here about the second or Governmental Assembly because for it the existing parliamentary bodies, which have developed mainly to serve governmental tasks, could serve as model. There is no reason why it should not be formed by periodic re-elections of the whole body on party lines,[6] and why its chief business should not be conducted by an executive committee of the majority. This would constitute the government proper and operate subject to the control and criticism of an organized opposition ready to offer an alternative government. Concerning the various possible arrangements with regard to methods of election, periods for which the representatives are elected, etc., the arguments to be considered would be more or less the same as those currently discussed and need not detain us here. Perhaps the case for securing an effective majority capable of conducting government would under this scheme even more strongly than it does now outweigh the case for an exact mirroring of the proportional distribution of the different interests in the population at large, and the case against proportional representation would therefore, in my opinion, become even stronger.

The one important difference between the position of such a representative Governmental Assembly and the existing parliamentary bodies would of course be that in all that it decided it would be bound by the rules of just conduct laid down by the Legislative Assembly, and that, in particular, it could not issue any orders to private citizens which did not follow directly and necessarily from the rules laid down by the latter. Within the limits of these rules the government would, however, be complete master in organizing the apparatus of government and deciding about the use of material and personal resources entrusted to the government.

A question which should be reconsidered is whether, with regard to the right to elect representatives to this Governmental Assembly, the old argument does not assume new strength that employees of government and all who received pensions or other support from government should have no vote. The argument was clearly not conclusive so long as it concerned the vote for a representative assembly whose primary task was conceived to be the laying down of universal rules of just conduct. Undoubtedly the civil servant or government pensioner is as competent to form an opinion on what is just as anybody else, and it would have appeared as invidious for such persons to be excluded from a right granted to many who are less informed and less educated. But it is an altogether different matter when what is at issue is not an opinion but frankly interest in seeing particular results achieved. Here neither the instruments of policy nor those who, without contributing to the means, merely share in the results, seem to have the same claim as the private citizen. That civil servants, old age pensioners, the unemployed, etc., should have a vote on how they should be paid out of the pocket of the rest, and their vote be solicited by a promise of a rise in their pay, is hardly a reasonable arrangement. Nor would it seem reasonable that, in addition to formulating projects for action, the government employees should also have a say on whether their projects should be adopted or not, or that those who are subject to orders by the Governmental Assembly should have a part in deciding what these orders ought to be.

The task of the governmental machinery, though it would have to operate within the framework of a law it could not alter, would still be very considerable. Though it would be under an obligation not to discriminate in the services it renders, the choice, organization, and aims of these services would still give it great power, limited only so far as coercion or other discriminatory treatment of the citizens was excluded. And though the manner in which it could raise funds would thus be restricted, the amount or the general purposes for which they are spent would not be, except indirectly.

The constitutional court

The whole arrangement rests on the possibility of drawing a sharp distinction between the enforceable rules of just conduct to be developed by the Legislative Assembly and binding the government and citizens alike, and all those rules of the organization and conduct of government proper which, within the limits of the law, it would be the task of the Governmental Assembly to determine. Though we have endeavoured to make the principle of the distinction clear, and the basic clause of the constitution would have to attempt to define what is to be considered law in the relevant sense of rules of just conduct, in practice the application of the distinction would undoubtedly raise many difficult problems, and all its implications could be worked out only through the continuous efforts of a special court. The problems would arise chiefly in the form of a conflict of competence between the two assemblies, generally through the questioning by one of the validity of the resolution passed by the other.

To give the court of last instance in these matters the required authority, and in view of the special qualification needed by its members, it would probably be desirable to establish it as a separate Constitutional Court. It would seem appropriate that in addition to professional judges its membership should include former members of the Legislative and perhaps also of the Governmental Assembly. In the course of gradually building up a body of doctrine it should probably be bound by its own former decisions, while whatever reversal of such decisions might seem necessary had best been left to an amending procedure provided by the constitution.

The only other point about this Constitutional Court that needs to be stressed here is that its decisions often would have to be, not that either of the two Assemblies were competent rather than the other to take certain kinds of action, but that nobody at all was entitled to take certain kinds of coercive measures. This would in particular apply, except in periods of emergency to be considered later, to all coercive measures not provided for by general rules of just conduct which were either traditionally recognized or explicitly laid down by the Legislative Assembly.

The scheme proposed also raises all kinds of problems concerning the organization of the administration of justice in general. To organize the judicial machinery would clearly seem an organizational and therefore governmental task, yet to place it into the hands of government might threaten the complete independence of the courts. So far as the appointment and promotion of judges is concerned, this might well be placed into the hands of that committee of former members of the Legislative Assembly which we suggested should decide about the employment of their fellows as lay judges and the like. And the independence of the individual judge might be secured by his salary being determined in the same manner as that which we have proposed for the determination of the salaries of the members of the Legislative Assembly, namely as a certain percentage of the average salary of a fixed number of the highest positions in the gift of government.

121

Quite a different problem is that of the technical organization of the courts, their non-judicial personnel and their material needs. To organize these might seem more clearly a matter of government proper, yet there are good reasons why in the Anglo-Saxon tradition the conception of a Ministry of Justice responsible for such matters has long been suspect. It might at least be considered whether such a task, which clearly should not be performed by the Legislative Assembly, might not be entrusted to that committee selected from its former members which we have already mentioned, and which thereby would become the permanent organizational body for the third, the judicial power, commanding for its purposes a block grant of financial means assigned to it by government.

All this is closely connected with another important and difficult issue which we have not yet considered and that even here we can barely touch upon. It is the whole question of competence for laying down the law of procedure as against substantive law. In general this, as all rules subsidiary to the enforcement of justice, should be a matter for the Legislative Assembly, though some points of a more organizational character that today are also regulated in the codes of procedure might well seem matters to be decided either by the special body suggested or by the Governmental Assembly. These are, however, technical questions which we cannot further consider here.

The general structure of authority

The function of the Legislative Assembly must not be confused with that of a body set up to enact or amend the Constitution. The functions of these two bodies would indeed be entirely different. Strictly speaking, a Constitution ought to consist wholly of organizational rules, and need touch on substantive law in the sense of universal rules of just conduct only by stating the general attributes such laws must possess in order to entitle government to use coercion for their enforcement.

But though the Constitution must define what can be substantive law in order to allocate and limit powers among the parts of the organization it sets up, it leaves the content of this law to be developed by the legislature and judiciary. It represents a protective superstructure designed to regulate the continuous process of developing an existing body of law and to prevent any confusion of the powers of government in enforcing the rules on which the spontaneous order of society rests, and those of using the material means entrusted to its administration for the rendering of services to the individuals and groups.

There is no need here to enter into a discussion of the appropriate procedure for establishing and amending the Constitution. But perhaps the relation between the body called upon for this task and those established *by* the Constitution can be further elucidated by our saying that the proposed scheme replaces the existing two-tiered arrangement with a three-tiered one: while the Constitution allocates and restricts powers, it should not prescribe positively how these powers are to be used. The substantive law in the sense of rules of just conduct would be developed by the Legislative Assembly which would be limited in its powers only by the provision of the Constitution defining the general attributes which enforceable rules of just conduct must possess. The Governmental Assembly and its government as its executive organ on the other hand would be restricted both by the rules of the Constitution and by the rules of just conduct laid down or recognized by the Legislative Assembly. This is what government under the law means. The government, the executive organ of the Governmental Assembly, would of course also be bound by the decision of that Assembly and might thus be regarded as the fourth tier of the whole structure, with the administrative bureaucratic apparatus as the fifth.

If it be asked where under such an arrangement 'sovereignty' rests, the answer is nowhere – unless it temporally resides in the hands of the constitution-making or constitution-amending body. Since constitutional government is limited government there can be no room in it for a sovereign body if sovereignty is defined as unlimited power. We have seen before that the belief that there must always be an unlimited ultimate power is a superstition deriving from the erroneous belief that all law derives from the deliberate decision of a legislative agency. But government never starts from a lawless state; it rests on and derives its support from the expectation that it will enforce the prevailing opinions concerning what is right.

It might be noticed that the hierarchy of tiers of authority is related to the periods for which the different agencies have to make provision. Ideally the Constitution ought to be intended for all time, though of course, as is true of any product of the human

123

mind, defects will be discovered which will need correction by amendment. Substantive law, though also intended for an indefinite period, will need continual development and revision as new and unforeseen problems arise with which the judiciary cannot deal adequately. The administration of the resources entrusted to government for the purpose of rendering services to the citizens is in its nature concerned with short-term problems and has to provide satisfaction of particular needs as they arise, and commanding as means for this task not the private citizen but only the resources explicity placed under its control.

Emergency powers

The basic principle of a free society, that the coercive powers of government are restricted to the enforcement of universal rules of just conduct, and cannot be used for the achievement of particular purposes, though essential to the normal working of such a society, may yet have to be temporarily suspended when the long-run preservation of that order is itself threatened. Though normally the individuals need be concerned only with their own concrete aims, and in pursuing them will best serve the common welfare, there may temporarily arise circumstances when the preservation of the overall order becomes the overruling common purpose, and when in consequence the spontaneous order, on a local or national scale, must for a time be converted into an organization. When an external enemy threatens, when rebellion or lawless violence has broken out, or a natural catastrophe requires quick action by whatever means can be secured, powers of compulsory organization, which normally nobody possesses, must be granted to somebody. Like an animal in flight from mortal danger society may in such situations have to suspend temporarily even vital functions on which in the long run its existence depends if it is to escape destruction.

The conditions under which such emergency powers may be granted without creating the danger that they will be retained when the absolute necessity has passed are among the most difficult and important points a constitution must decide on. 'Emergencies' have always been the pretext on which the safeguards of individual liberty have been eroded – and once they are suspended it is not difficult for anyone who has assumed such emergency powers to see to it that the emergency will persist. Indeed if all needs felt by important groups that can be satisfied only by the exercise of dictatorial powers constitute an emergency, every situation is an emergency situation. It has been contended with some plausibility that whoever has the power to proclaim an emergency and on this ground to suspend any part of the constitution is the true sovereign.[7] This would seem to be true enough if any person or body were able to arrogate to itself such emergency powers by declaring a state of emergency.

It is by no means necessary, however, that one and the same agency should possess the power to declare an emergency and to assume emergency powers. The best precaution against the abuse of emergency powers would seem to be that the authority that can declare a state of emergency is made thereby to renounce the powers it normally possesses and to retain only the right of revoking at any time the emergency powers it has conferred on another body. In the scheme suggested it would evidently be the Legislative Assembly which would not only have to delegate some of its powers to the government, but also to confer upon this government powers which in normal circumstances nobody possesses. For this purpose an emergency committee of the Legislative Assembly would have to be in permanent existence and quickly accessible at all times. The committee would have to be entitled to grant limited emergency powers until the Assembly as a whole could be convened which itself then would have to determine both the extent and duration of the emergency powers granted to government. So long as it confirmed the existence of an emergency, any measures taken by government within the powers granted to it would have full force, including such specific commands to particular persons as in normal times nobody would have the power to issue. The Legislative Assembly, however, would at all times be free to revoke or restrict the powers granted, and after the end of the emergency to confirm or to revoke any measures proclaimed by the government, and to provide for compensation to those who in the general interest were made to submit to such extraordinary powers.

Another kind of emergency for which every constitution should provide is the possible discovery of a gap in its provisions, such as the appearance of questions of authority to which the constitutional rules do not give an answer. The possibility of a discovery of such lacunae in any scheme, however carefully thought out, can never be excluded: and there may well arise questions which require a prompt authoritative answer if the whole machinery of government is not to be paralysed. Yet though somebody should have the power to provide a temporary answer to such questions by *ad hoc* decisions, these decisions should remain in effect only until the Legislative Assembly, the Constitutional Court, or the normal apparatus for amending the Constitution has filled the gap by an appropriate regulation. Until then a normally purely ceremonial Head of State might well be given power to fill such gaps by provisional decisions.

The division of financial powers

The field in which the constitutional arrangements here sketched would produce the most far-reaching changes would be that of finance. It is also the field in which the nature of these consequences can be best illustrated in such a condensed outline as is attempted here.

The central problem arises from the fact that the levying of contributions is necessarily an act of coercion and must therefore be done in accordance with general rules laid down by the Legislative Assembly, while the determination of both the volume and the direction of expenditure is clearly a governmental matter. Our scheme would therefore require that the uniform rules according to which the total means to be raised are apportioned among the citizens be laid down by the Legislative Assembly, while the total amount of expenditure and its direction would have to be decided by the Governmental Assembly.

Nothing would probably provide a more salutary discipline of expenditure than such a condition in which everybody voting for a particular outlay would know that the costs would have to be borne by him and his constituents in accordance with a predetermined rule which he could not alter. Except in those cases where the beneficiaries of a particular outlay could be clearly identified (although, once the service was provided for all it could not be withheld from those not voluntarily paying for it and the costs would therefore have to be raised by compulsion) as is the case with a motor tax for the provision of roads, or a wireless tax, or the various local and communal taxes for the finance of particular services, all expenditure decided upon would automatically lead to a corresponding increase of the general burden of taxes for all under the general scheme determined by the Legislative Assembly. There could then be no support for any expenditure based on the expectation that the burden could afterwards be shifted on to

126

other shoulders: everyone would know that of all that would be spent he had to bear a fixed share.

Current methods of taxation have been shaped largely by the endeavour to raise funds in such a manner as to cause the least resistance or resentment on the part of the majority who had to approve the expenditure. They certainly were not designed to assure responsible decisions on expenditure, but on the contrary to produce the feeling that somebody else would pay for it. It is regarded as obvious that the methods of taxation should be adjusted to the amount to be raised, since in the past the need for additional revenue regularly led to a search for new sources of taxation. Additional expenditure thus always raised the question of who should pay for it. The theory and practice of public finance has been shaped almost entirely by the endeavour to disguise as far as possible the burden imposed, and to make those who will ultimately have to bear it as little aware of it as possible. It is probable that the whole complexity of the tax structure we have built up is largely the result of the efforts to persuade citizens to give the government more than they would knowingly consent to do.

To distinguish effectively the legislation on the general rules by which the tax burden is to be apportioned among the individuals from the determination of the total sums to be raised, would require such a complete re-thinking of all the principles of public finance that the first reaction of those familiar with the existing institutions will probably be to regard such a scheme as wholly impracticable. Yet nothing short of such a complete reconsideration of the institutional setting of financial legislation can probably stop that trend towards a continuing and progressive rise of that share of the income of society which is controlled by government. This trend, if allowed to continue, would before long swallow up the whole of society in the organization of government.

It is evident that taxation in accordance with a uniform rule can have no place for any overall progression of the total tax burden, although, as I have discussed elsewhere,[8] some progression of the direct taxes may not only be permissible but necessary to offset the tendency of indirect taxes to be regressive. I have in the same place also suggested some general principles by which we might so limit taxation as to prevent the shifting of the burden by a majority to the shoulders of a minority, but at the same time leave open the unobjectionable possibility of a majority conceding to a weak minority certain advantages.

127

EIGHTEEN

THE CONTAINMENT OF POWER AND THE DETHRONEMENT OF POLITICS

We are living at a time when justice has vanished. Our parliaments light-heartedly produce statutes which are contrary to justice. States deal with their subjects arbitrarily without attempting to preserve a sense of justice. Men who fall under the power of another nation find themselves to all intents and purposes outlawed. There is no longer any respect for their natural right to their homeland or their dwelling place or property, their right to earn a living or to sustenance, or to anything whatever. Our trust in justice has been wholly destroyed.

Albert Schweitzer

Limited and unlimited power

The effective limitation of power is the most important problem of social order. Government is indispensable for the formation of such an order only to protect all against coercion and violence from others. But as soon as, to achieve this, government successfully claims the monopoly of coercion and violence, it becomes also the chief threat to individual freedom. To limit this power was the great aim of the founders of constitutional government in the seventeenth and eighteenth centuries. But the endeavour to contain the powers of government was almost inadvertently abandoned when it came to be mistakenly believed that democratic control of the exercise of power provided a sufficient safeguard against its excessive growth.[1]

We have since learnt that the very omnipotence conferred on democratic representative assemblies exposes them to irresistible pressure to use their power for the benefit of special interests, a pressure a majority with unlimited powers cannot resist if it is to remain a majority. This development can be prevented only by depriving the governing majority of the power to grant discriminat-

128

ory benefits to groups or individuals. This has generally been believed to be impossible in a democracy because it appears to require that another will be placed above that of the elected representatives of a majority. In fact democracy needs even more severe restraints on the discretionary powers government can exercise than other forms of government, because it is much more subject to effective pressure from special interests, perhaps of small numbers, on which its majority depends.

The problem seemed insoluble, however, only because an older ideal had been forgotten, namely that the power of all authorities exercising governmental functions ought to be limited by long run rules which nobody has the power to alter or abrogate in the service of particular ends: principles which are the terms of association of the community that recognizes an authority because this authority is committed to such long-term rules. It was the constructivistic-positivist superstition which led to the belief that there must be some single unlimited supreme power from which all other power is derived, while in fact the supreme authority owes its respect to restraint by limiting general rules.

What today we call democratic government serves, as a result of its construction, not the opinion of the majority but the varied interests of a conglomerate of pressure groups whose support the government must buy by the grant of special benefits, simply because it cannot retain its supporters when it refuses to give them something it has the power to give. The resulting progressive increase of discriminating coercion now threatens to strangle the growth of a civilization which rests on individual freedom. An erroneous constructivistic interpretation of the order of society, combined with mistaken understanding of the meaning of justice, has indeed become the chief danger to the future not only of wealth, but of morals and peace. Nobody with open eyes can any longer doubt that the danger to personal freedom comes chiefly from the left, not because of any particular ideals it pursues, but because the various socialist movements are the only large organized bodies which, for aims which appeal to many, want to impose upon society a preconceived design. This must lead to the extinction of all moral responsibility of the individual and has already progressively removed, one after the other, most of those safeguards of individual freedom which had been built up through centuries of the evolution of law.

To regain certain fundamental truths which generations of

129

demagoguery have obliterated, it is necessary to learn again to understand why the basic values of a great or open society must be negative, assuring the individual of the right within a known domain to pursue his own aims on the basis of his own knowledge. Only such negative rules make possible the formation of a self-generating order, utilizing the knowledge, and serving the desires, of the individuals. We shall have to reconcile ourselves to the still strange fact that in a society of free men the highest authority must in normal times have no power of positive commands whatever. Its sole power should be that of prohibition according to rule, so that it would owe its supreme position to its commitment with every act to a general principle.

Peace, freedom and justice: the three great negatives

The fundamental reason why the best that a government can give a great society of free men is negative is the unalterable ignorance of any single mind, or any organization that can direct human action, of the immeasurable multitude of particular facts which must determine the order of its activities. Only fools believe that they know all, but there are many. This ignorance is the cause why government can only assist (or perhaps make possible) the formation of an abstract pattern or structure in which the several expectations of the members approximately match each other, through making these members observe certain negative rules or prohibitions which are independent of particular purposes. It can only assure the abstract character and not the positive content of the order that will arise from the individuals' use of their knowledge for their purpose by delimiting their domains against each other by abstract and negative rules. Yet this very fact that in order to make most effective the use by the individuals of the information they possess for their own purposes, the chief benefit government can offer them must be 'merely' negative, most people find difficult to accept. In consequence all constructivists try to chisel on the original conception of these ideals.

Perhaps the only one of the great ideals with regard to which people are generally prepared to accept its negative character and would at once reject any attempt at chiselling its peace. I hope, at least, that if, say, a Krushchev had used the popular socialist gambit to agree to peace provided it was 'positive peace', everybody would have understood that this simply meant peace only if he could do what he liked. But few seem to recognize that if the intellectual chisellers demand that liberty, or justice, or law be made 'positive', this is a similar attempt to pervert and abuse the basic ideals. As in the case of many other good things, such as quiet, health, leisure, peace of mind, or a good conscience, it is the absence of certain evils rather than the presence of positive goods which is the pre-condition of the success of individual endeavours.

Current usage, which has come to employ 'positive' and 'negative' almost as equivalent to 'good' and 'bad', and makes people feel that a 'negative value' is the opposite of a value, a dis-value or a harm, blinds many people to the crucial character of the greatest benefits our society can offer to us.

The three great negatives of Peace, Freedom and Justice are in fact the sole indispensable foundations of civilization which government must provide. They are necessarily absent in the 'natural' condition of primitive man, and man's innate instincts do not provide them for his fellows. They are, as we shall see in the postscript, the most important yet still only imperfectly assured products of the rules of civilization.

Coercion can assist free men in the pursuit of their ends only by the enforcement of a framework of universal rules which do not direct them to particular ends, but, by enabling them to create for themselves a domain protected against unpredictable disturbance caused by other men – including agents of government – to pursue their own ends. And if the greatest need is security against infringement of such a protected sphere by others, including government, the highest authority needed is one who can merely say 'no' to others but has itself no 'positive' powers.

The conception of a highest authority which cannot issue any commands sounds strange and even contradictory to us because it has come to be believed that a highest authority must be an all-comprehensive, omnipotent authority which comprises all the powers of the subordinate authorities. But there is no justification at all for this 'positivist' belief. Except when as a result of external human or natural forces the self-generating order is disturbed and emergency measures are required to restore the conditions for its operation, there is no need for such 'positive' powers of the supreme authority. Indeed, there is every reason to desire as the highest authority such a one that all its powers rest on its committing itself to the kind of abstract rules which, independently of the particular consequences, require it to prevent interference with the acquired rights of the individuals by government or private agencies. Such an authority which normally is committed to certain recognized principles and then can order enforcement of such general rules, but so long as society is not threatened by outside forces has no other coercive powers whatever, may still be above all governmental powers – even be the only common power over a whole territory, while all the properly governmental powers might be separate for the different regions.

Centralization and decentralization

The amount of centralization which we take for granted and in which the supreme legislature and the supreme governmental power are part of the same unitary organization of what we call a nation or a state (and which is little reduced even in federal states), is essentially the effect of the need of making this organization strong for war. But now, when at least in Western Europe and North America we believe we have excluded the possibility of war between the associated nations and are relying for defence (we hope effectively) on a supranational organization, we ought gradually to discover that we can reduce the centralization and cease to entrust so many tasks to the national government, merely to make that government strong against external enemies.

It was necessary, in the interest of clarity, in the context of this book to discuss the changes in the constitutional structure, required if individual freedom is to be preserved, with reference to the most familiar type of a unitary state. But they are in fact even more suitable for a decentralized hierarchic structure on federal lines. We can here mention only a few major aspects of this.

The bicameral system, usually regarded as essential for a federal constitution, has under the scheme proposed here been preempted for another purpose; but its function in a federation could be achieved by other means, such as a system of double counting of votes, at least in the governmental assembly: once according to heads and once according to the number of states represented in the central assembly. It would probably be desirable to restrict federal arrangements to government proper and to have a single legislative assembly for the whole federation. But it is not really necessary always to have both legislative assemblies and governmental assemblies on the same level of the hierarchy, provided that the governmental power, whether extending to a smaller or a larger territory than the legislative power, is always limited by the latter.

This would seem to make it desirable that the legislative power should extend over a larger territory than the governmental one; but there exist of course several instances (Great Britain with a different system of private law in England and Scotland, the USA with the common law in most states and the Code Napoleon in one) with a central governmental executive ruling over territories with different law, and a few (the British Commonwealth of Nations to some extent and for a period) where the highest power determining the law (the court of last instance) was common to a number of otherwise wholly independent governments.

More important for our purposes are, however, the desirable devolutions which would become possible once the power of a supranational authority to say 'no' to actions harmful to associated states had reduced the necessity of a strong central national government for defence purposes. Most service activities of government might then indeed with advantage be delegated to regional or local authorities, wholly limited in their coercive powers by the rules laid down by a higher legislative authority.

There exists, of course, neither on the national nor on the international level, a moral ground why poorer regions should be entitled to tap for their purposes the wealth of richer regions. Yet centralization advances, not because the majority of the people in the large region are anxious to supply the means for assistance to the poorer regions, but because the majority, to be a majority, needs the additional votes from the regions which benefit from sharing in the wealth of the larger unit. And what is happening in the existing nations is beginning to happen on an international scale, where, by a silly competition with Russia, the capitalist nations, instead of lending capital to enterprise in countries which pursue economic policies which they regard as promising, are actually subsidizing on a large scale the socialist experiments of underdeveloped countries where they know that the funds that they supply will be largely wasted.

The rule of the majority versus *the rule of laws approved by the majority*

Not only peace, justice and liberty, but also democracy is basically a negative value, a procedural rule which serves as protection against despotism and tyranny, and certainly no more but not much less important than the first Three Great Negatives – or, to put it differently, a convention which mainly serves to prevent harm. But,

133

like liberty and justice, it is now being destroyed by endeavours to give it a 'positive' content. I am fairly certain that the days of unlimited democracy are numbered. We will, if we are to preserve the basic values of democracy, have to adopt a different form of it, or sooner or later lose altogether the power of getting rid of an oppressive government.

As we have seen (chapters 12, 13 and 16), under the prevailing system it is not the common opinion of a majority that decides on common issues, but a majority that owes its existence and power to the gratifying of the special interests of numerous small groups, which the representatives cannot refuse to grant if they are to remain a majority. But while agreement of the majority of a great society on general rules is possible, the so-called approval by the majority of a conglomerate of measures serving particular interests is a farce. Buying majority support by deals with special interests, though this is what contemporary democracy has come to mean, has nothing to do with the original ideal of democracy, and is certainly contrary to the more fundamental moral conception that all use of force ought to be guided and limited by the opinion of the majority. The vote-buying process which we have come to accept as a necessary part of the democracy we know, and which indeed is inevitable in a representative assembly which has the power both to pass general laws and to issue commands, is morally indefensible and produces all that which to the outsider appears as contemptible in politics. It is certainly not a necessary consequence of the ideal that the opinion of the majority should rule, but is in conflict with it.

This error is closely connected with the misconception that the majority must be free to do what it likes. A majority of the representatives of the people based on bargaining over group demands can never represent the opinion of the majority of the people. Such 'freedom of Parliament' means the oppression of the people. It is wholly in conflict with the conception of a constitutional limitation of governmental power, and irreconcilable with the ideal of a society of free men. The exercise of the power of a representative democracy beyond the range where voters can comprehend the significance of its decisions can correspond to (or be controlled by) the opinion of the majority of the people only if in all its coercive measures government is confined to rules which apply equally to all members of the community.

So long as the present form of democracy persists, decent government cannot exist, even if the politicians are angels or profoundly convinced of the supreme value of personal freedom. We have no right to blame them for what they do, because it is we who, by maintaining the present institutions, place them in a position in which they can obtain power to do any good only if they commit themselves to secure special benefits for various groups. This has led to the attempt to justify these measures by the construction of a pseudo-ethics, called 'social justice', which fails every test which a system of moral rules must satisfy in order to secure a peace and voluntary co-operation of free men.

It is the crucial contention of this book that what in a society of free men can alone justify coercion is a predominant opinion on the principles which ought to govern and restrain individual conduct. It is obvious that a peaceful and prosperous society can exist only if some such rules are generally obeyed and, when necessary, enforced. This has nothing to do with any 'will' aiming at a particular objective.

What to most people still seems strange and even incomprehensible is that in such a society the supreme power must be a limited power, not all-comprehensive but confined to restraining both organized government and private persons and organizations by the enforcement of general rules of conduct. Yet it can be the condition of submission which creates the state that the only authorization for coercion by the supreme authority refers to the enforcement of general rules of conduct equally applicable to all. Such a supreme power ought to owe the allegiance and respect which it claims to its commitment to the general principles, to secure obedience to which is the sole task for which it may use coercion. It is to make these principles conform to general opinion that the supreme legislature is made representative of the views of the majority of the people.

Moral confusion and the decay of language

Under the influence of socialist agitation in the course of the last hundred years the very sense in which many of the key words describing political ideals are used has so changed meaning that one must today hesitate to use even words like 'liberty', 'justice', 'democracy' or 'law', because they no longer convey the meaning they once did. But, as Confucius is reported to have said, 'when words lose their meaning, people will lose their liberty'. It was, unfortunately, not only ignorant propagandists but often grave social philosophers who contributed to this decay of language by twisting well established words to seduce people to serve what they imagined to be good purposes. When a John Dewey defines liberty as 'the effective power to do specific things'[2] this might seem a devious trick to delude innocents. But if another social philosopher argues in discussing democracy that 'the most promising line of approach is to say that democracy . . . is considered good because on the whole it is the best device for securing certain elements of social justice',[3] it is evidently just incredible naivety.

The younger generation of social philosophers apparently do not even know what the basic concepts once meant. Only thus can it be explained when we find a young scholar seriously asserting that the usage of speaking of a 'just state of affairs . . . must be regarded as the primary one, for when we describe a man as just we mean that he usually attempts to act in such a way that a just state of affairs results'[4] and even adding a few pages later that 'there appears [!] to be a category of "private justice" which concerns the dealing of a man with his fellows where he is not acting as a participant in one of the major social institutions.'[5] This may perhaps be accounted for by the fact that today a young man will first encounter the term 'justice' in some such connection, but it is of course a travesty of the evolution of the concept. As we have seen, a state of affairs which has not been deliberately brought about by men can possess neither intelligence nor virtue, nor justice, nor any other attribute of human values – not even if it is the unpredictable result of a game which people have consented to play by entering in their own interest into exchange relations with others. Justice is, of course, not a question of the aims of an action but of its obedience to rules which it obeys.

These instances, culled almost at random, of the current abuse of political terms in which those who have skill with words, by shifting the meaning of concepts they have perhaps never quite understood, have gradually emptied them of all clear content, could be increased indefinitely. It is difficult to know what to do when the enemies of liberty describe themselves as liberals, as is today common practice in the USA – except calling them persistently, as we ought to do, pseudo-liberals – or when they appeal to democracy when they mean egalitarianism. It is all part of that 'Treason of the Intellectuals' which Julien Benda castigated forty years ago, but which has since succeeded in creating a reign of untruthfulness which has become habitual in discussing issues of 'social' policy, and in the current language of politicians who habitually employ this make-believe without themselves knowing it as such.

But it is not merely the confessed socialists who drive us along that road. Socialist ideas have so deeply penetrated general thought that it is not even only those pseudo-liberals who merely disguise their socialism by the name they have assumed, but also many conservatives who have assumed socialist ideas and language and constantly employ them in the belief that they are an established part of current thought. Nor is it only people who have strong views on, or take an active part in public affairs.[7] Indeed the most active spreading of socialist conceptions still takes place through what David Hume called the fiction of poets,[8] the ignorant literati who are sure that the appealing words they employ have definite meaning. Only because we are so habituated to this can it be explained that, for instance, hundreds of thousands of business men all over the world still allow over their doorsteps journals which in their literary part will resort even to obscene language (such as 'the excremental abundance of capitalist production' in *Time* magazine of 27 June 1977) to ridicule capitalism.[9] Though the principle of freedom requires that we tolerate such scandalous scurrilities, one might have hoped that the good sense of the readers would soon learn what publications they can trust.[10]

Democratic procedure and egalitarian objectives

Perhaps the worst sufferer in this process of the emptying of the meaning of words has in recent times been the word 'democracy' itself. Its chief abuse is to apply it not to a procedure of arriving at agreement on common action, but to give it a substantive content prescribing what the aim of those activities ought to be. However absurd this clearly is, many of the current invocations of democracy amount to telling democratic legislatures what they ought to do. Except so far as organization of government is concerned, the term 'democratic' says nothing about the particular aims people ought to vote for.

The true value of democracy is to serve as a sanitary precaution protecting us against an abuse of power. It enables us to get rid of a government and try to replace it by a better one. Or, to put it differently, it is the only convention we have yet discovered to make peaceful change possible. As such it is a high value well worth

137

fighting for, since any government the people cannot get rid of by such an agreed procedure is bound to fall sooner or later into bad hands. But it is far from being the highest political value, and an unlimited democracy may well be worse than limited governments of a different kind.

In its present unlimited form democracy has today largely lost the capacity of serving as a protection against arbitrary power. It has ceased to be a safeguard of personal liberty, a restraint on the abuse of governmental power which it was hoped it would prove to be when it was naively believed that, when all power was made subject to democratic control, all the other restraints on governmental power could be dispensed with. It has, on the contrary, become the main cause of a progressive and accelerating increase of the power and weight of the administrative machine.

The omnipotent and omnicompetent single democratic assembly, in which a majority capable of governing can maintain itself only by trying to remove all sources of discontent of any supporter of that majority, is thereby driven to take control of all spheres of life. It is forced to develop and impose, in justification of the measures it must take to retain majority support, a non-existing and in the strict sense of the word inconceivable code of distributive justice. In such a society, to have political pull becomes much more rewarding than adding to the means of satisfying the needs of one's fellows. As everything tends to become a political issue for which the inter- ference of the coercive powers of government can be invoked, an ever larger part of human activity is diverted from productive into political efforts – not only of the political machinery itself but, worse, of that rapidly expanding apparatus of para-government designed to bring pressure on government to favour particular interests.

What is still not understood is that the majority of a representa- tive assembly with unlimited powers is neither able, nor constrain- ed, to confine its activities to aims which all the members of the majority desire, or even approve of.[11] If such an assembly has the power to grant special benefits, a majority can regularly be kept together only by paying off each of the special groups by which it is composed. In other words, we have under the false name of demo- cracy created a machinery in which not the majority decides, but each member of the majority has to consent to many bribes to get majority support for his own special demands. However admirable the principle of majority decisions may be with respect to matters which necessarily concern all, so vicious must be the result of an application of this procedure to distributing the booty which can be extracted from a dissident minority.

It seems to be inevitable that if we retain democracy in its present form, the concept itself is bound to become discredited to such an extent that even the legitimate case for majority decisions on questions of principle will go by default. Democracy is in danger because the particular institutions by which we have tried to realize it have produced effects which we mistake for those of the genuine article. As I have myself suggested before, I am even no longer certain that the name democracy can still be freed from the distaste with which increasing numbers of people for good reasons have come to regard it, even though few yet dare publicly to express their disillusionment.[12]

The root of the trouble is, of course, to sum up, that in an unlimited democracy the holders of discretionary powers are forced to use them, whether they wish it or not, to favour particular groups on whose swing-vote their powers depend. This applies as much to government as to such democratically organized institutions as trades unions. Even if, in the case of government, some of these powers may serve to enable it to do much that might be desirable in itself, we must renounce conferring them since such discretionary powers inevitably and necessarily place the authority into a position in which it will be forced to do even more that is harmful.

'State' and 'society'

If democracy is to maintain a society of free men, the majority of a political body must certainly not have the power to 'shape' a society, or make its members serve particular ends – i.e. ends other than the abstract order which it can secure only by enforcing equally abstract rules of conduct. The task of government is to create a framework within which individuals and groups can successfully pursue their respective aims, and sometimes to use its coercive powers of raising revenue to provide services which for one reason or other the market cannot supply. But coercion is justified only in order to provide such a framework within which all can use their abilities and knowledge for their own ends so long as they do not interfere with the equally protected individual domains of others. Except when 'Acts of God or the King's enemies' make it necessary to confer temporary emergency powers on an authority which can at any time be revoked by the agency which has conferred them, nobody need possess power of discriminating coercion. (Where such powers may have to be used to prevent suspected crime, the person to whom it has been erroneously applied ought to be entitled to full compensation for all injury suffered.)

Much confusion of this issue is due to a tendency (particularly strong in the Continental tradition, but with the spreading of socialist ideas growing rapidly also in the Anglo-Saxon world) to identify 'state' and 'society'. The state, the organization of the people of a territory under a single government, although an indispensible condition for the development of an advanced society, is yet very far from being identical with society, or rather with the multiplicity of grown and self-generating structures of men who have any freedom that alone deserves the name of society. In a free society the state is one of many organizations – the one which is required to provide an effective external framework within which self-generating orders can form, but an organization which is confined to the government apparatus and which does not determine the activities of the free individuals. And while this organization of the state will contain many voluntary organizations, it is the spontaneously grown network of relationships between the individuals and the various organizations they create that constitutes societies. Societies form but states are made. This is why so far as they can produce the needed services, or self-generating structures, societies are infinitely preferable, while the organizations based on the power of coercion tend to become a straitjacket that proves to be harmful as soon as it uses its powers beyond the enforcement of the indispensibly abstract rules of conduct.

It is in fact very misleading to single out the inhabitants or citizens of a particular political unit as the prototype of a society. There exists, under modern conditions, no single society to which an individual normally belongs, and it is highly desirable that this should not be so. Each of us is fortunately a member of many different overlapping and interlacing societies to which he may belong more or less strongly or lastingly. Society is a network of voluntary relationships between individuals and organized groups, and strictly speaking there is hardly ever merely one society to which any person exclusively belongs. For practical purposes it may be innocuous to single out, in a particular context, some part of the complex order of often hierarchically related networks as specially relevant for the topic discussed, and to assume that it will be understood to which part of this complex the speaker or writer refers as 'the society'. But it should never be forgotten that today many persons and organizations belong to networks which extend over national boundaries as well as that within any nation any one may be an element in many different structures of this kind.

Indeed, the operation of the spontaneous ordering forces, and of the rules of conduct making possible the formations of such orderly structures which we describe as societies, becomes fully intelligible (and at the same time our inability to comprehend their functioning in detail evident) only if we are aware of the multiplicity of such overlapping structures.

Anyone aware of the complex nature of this net of relationships determining the processes of society should also readily recognize the erroneous anthropomorphism of·conceiving of society as 'acting' or 'willing' anything. Originally it was of course an attempt of socialists to disguise the fact that their proposals amounted to an endeavour to enhance the coercive powers of government when they prefered to speak of 'socialization' rather than 'nationalization' or 'politicalization' of the means of production, etc. But this led them deeper and deeper into the anthropomorphic interpretation of society – that tendency of interpreting the results of spontaneous processes as being directed by some 'will', or being produced or producible by design, which is so deeply engrained in the structure of primitive human thinking.

Not only do most processes of social evolution take place without anybody willing or foreseeing them – it is only because of this that they lead to cultural evolution. Out of a directed process nothing greater can emerge than the directing mind can foresee. He will be the only one who would be allowed to profit from experience. A developing society does not advance by government impressing new ideas on it, but by new ways and methods constantly being tried in a process of trial and error. It is, to repeat once more, the favourable general conditions that will assist unknown persons in unknown circumstances which produce the improvement which no supreme authority could bring about.

A game according to rules can never know justice of treatment

It was in effect the discovery that playing a game according to rules improved the *chances* of all, even at the risk that the outcome for some might be worse than it would be otherwise, which made classical liberalism aim at the complete elimination of power in determining relative incomes earned in the market. Combined with the provision of cushioning the risk by providing *outside* the market a uniform minimum income for all those who for some reason are unable to earn at least that much in the market, it leaves no moral justification for a use of force to determine relative incomes by government or any other organized group. Indeed, it becomes the clear moral duty of government not only itself to refrain from any such interference in the game, but also to prevent the arrogation of such power by any organized group.

In such an order in which the use of force to determine relative or absolute material positions is on principle excluded, it can be as little a matter of justice what at any given moment a person ought to be induced to do in the general interest, as how much he ought to be offered in remuneration. The relative social usefulness of the different activities of any one person, and even of the various activities which different persons may pursue, is unfortunately not a matter of justice but the result of events which cannot be foreseen or controlled. What the public, and, I am afraid, even many reputed economists, fail to understand is that the prices offered for services in this process serve not as remunerations of the different people for what they have done, but as signals telling them what they ought to do, in their own as well as in the general interest.

It is simply silly to represent the different prizes which different persons will draw in the game that we have learnt to play because it secures the fullest utilization of dispersed knowledge and skills, as if the participants were 'treated' differently by society – even if the initial position is determined by the accidental circumstances of previous history, during which the game may not always have been played honestly, if the aim is to provide maximum opportunity to men as they are, without any arbitrary coercion, we can achieve our ends only by treating them according to the same rules irrespective of their factual differences, leaving the outcome to be decided by those constant restructurings of the economic order which are determined by circumstances nobody can foresee.

The basic conception of classical liberalism, which alone can make decent and impartial government possible, is that government must *regard* all people as equal, however unequal they may in fact be, and that in whatever manner the government restrains (or assists) the action of one, so it must, under the same abstract rules, restrain (or assist) the actions of all others. Nobody has special claims on government because he is either rich or poor, beyond the assurance of protection against all violence from anybody and the assurance of a certain flat minimum income if things go wholly wrong. Even to take notice of the factual inequality of individuals, and to make this the excuse of any discriminating coercion, is a breach of the basic terms on which free man submits to government.

This game serves not only the winner, because his gain from having served the others best is always only part of what he has added to the social product; and it is only by playing according to the rules of this game that we can assure that high degree of utilization of resources which no other known method can achieve.

The para-government of organized interests and the hypertrophy of government

Many of the gravest defects of contemporary government, widely recognized and deplored but believed to be inevitable consequences of democracy, are in fact the consequences only of the unlimited character of present democracy. The basic fact is still not clearly seen that under this form of government whatever the government has constitutional power to do it can be forced to do, even against its better judgment, if those benefiting by the measure are 'swing groups' on whose support the majority of the government depends. The consequence is that the apparatus of organized particular interests designed solely to bring pressure on government is becoming the worst incubus forcing government to be harmful.

The pretence can hardly be taken seriously that all these features of incipient corporativism which make up the para-government are necessary to advise government on the probable effects of its decisions. I will not attempt here to estimate how large a proportion of the ablest and best informed members of society are already absorbed into these essentially anti-social activities beyond emphasizing that both sides of what are now euphemistically called 'social partners' (*Sozialpartner*) are frequently forced to divert some of their best people from supplying what the public needs to the task of stultifying each other's efforts. I have little to add to the masterly description of the mechanism of this process of government by coalitions of organized interests which Professor Mancur Olson, Jr, has given in his book on *The Logic of Collective Action*, [13] and will merely recapitulate a few points.

Of course, all pressure on government to make it use its coercive

143

powers to benefit particular groups is harmful to the generality. But it is inexcusable to pretend that in this respect the position is the same on all sides and that in particular the pressure which can be brought by the large firms or corporations is comparable to that of the organization of labour which in most countries have been authorized by law or jurisdiction to use coercion to gain support for their policies. By conferring, for supposedly 'social' reasons, on the trades unions unique privileges, which hardly government itself enjoys, organizations of workers have been enabled to exploit other workers by altogether depriving them of the opportunity of good employment. Though this fact is conventionally still ignored, the chief powers of the trades unions rests today entirely on their being allowed to use power to prevent other workers from doing work they would wish to do.

But quite apart from the fact that by the exercise of this power particular trade unions can achieve only a relative improvement of the wages of their members, at the price of reducing the general productivity of labour and thus the general level of real wages, combined with the necessity in which they can place a government that controls the quantity of money to inflate, this system is rapidly destroying the economic order. Trades unions can now put governments in a position in which the only choice they have is to inflate or to be blamed for the unemployment which is caused by the wage policy of the trades unions (especially their policy of keeping relations between wages of different unions constant). This position must before long destroy the whole market order, probably through the price controls which accelerating inflation will force governments to impose.

As little as the whole role of the growing para-government can I at this stage begin to discuss the threat created by the incessant growth of the government machinery, i.e. the bureaucracy. Democracy, at the same time at which it seems to become all-engulfing, becomes on the governmental level an impossibility. It is an illusion to believe that the people, or their elected representatives, can govern a complex society in detail. Government relying on the general support from a majority will of course still determine the major steps, so far as it is not merely driven to these by the momentum of its previous proceedings. But Government is already becoming so complex that is is inevitable that its members, as heads of the various departments, are increasingly becoming puppets of the bureaucracy, to which they will still give 'general directions', but

144

on the operation of which the execution of all the detail depends. It is not without reason that socialist governments want to politicize this bureaucracy, because it is by it and not in any democratic body that more and more of the crucial decisions are made. No totalitarian power can be achieved without this.

Unlimited democracy and centralization

Nowhere are the effects of unlimited democracy more clearly shown than in the general increase of the power of central government by the assumption of functions formerly performed by regional or local authorities. Probably with the sole exception of Switzerland, central government has almost everywhere not only become *the* government *par excellence,* but it is steadily drawing more and more activities into its exclusive competence. That a nation is governed chiefly from its national capital and that this central power not only gives it a common structure of law (or at least secures that there is a determinable law regulating the relations between all its inhabitants), but that also more and more of the services which government renders to the people are directed from a single centre of command, has come to be regarded as inevitable and natural – even though recently in many parts of the world tendencies to secessionism show an increasingly resentment of this situation.

Recently the growth of the powers of central government has also been much assisted by those central planners who, when their schemes failed on a local or regional level, regularly claimed that in order to be effective they must be applied on a larger scale. The failure to master even the problems of a moderate range was often made the excuse for attempting still more ambitious schemes still less suitable for the central direction or control by authority.

But the decisive ground of the growing preponderance of central government in modern times is that only on that level, at least in unitary states, the legislation possessed the unlimited power which no legislation ought to possess and which enabled it so to fashion its 'laws' as to empower the administration to use the discretionary and discriminatory measures which are necessary to achieve the desired control of the economic process. If the central government can order many things which a local government cannot, it becomes the easiest way to meet group demands to push the decision up to the authority that possesses these powers. To deprive the national (and in federations the state) legislatures of the power to use legislation for conferring discretionary powers on the administration would therefore remove the chief cause of the progressive centralization of all government.

The devolution of internal policy to local government[14]

Without those arbitrary powers inadvertently conferred on 'legislatures', the whole structure of governments would undoubtedly have developed on very different lines. If all administration were under a uniform law it could not alter, and which nobody could change to make it serve specific administrative purposes, the abuse of legislation in the service of special interests would cease. Most service activities now rendered by central government could be devolved to regional or local authorities which would possess the power to raise taxes at a rate they could determine but which they could levy or apportion only according to general rules laid down by a central legislature.

I believe the result would be the transformation of local and even regional governments into quasi-commercial corporations competing for citizens. They would have to offer a combination of advantages and costs which made life within their territory at least as attractive as elsewhere within the reach of its potential citizens. Assuming their powers to be so limited by law as not to restrict free migration, and that they could not discriminate in taxation, their interest would be wholly to attract those who in their particular condition could make the greatest contribution to the common product.

To re-entrust the management of most service activities of government to smaller units would probably lead to the revival of a communal spirit which has been largely suffocated by centralization. The widely felt inhumanity of the modern society is not so much the result of the impersonal character of the economic process, in which modern man of necessity works largely for aims of which he is ignorant, but of the fact that political centralization has largely deprived him of the chance to have a say in shaping the environment which he knows. The Great Society can only be an abstract society – an economic order from which the individual profits by obtaining the means for all his ends, and to which he must make his anonymous contribution. This does not satisfy his emotional, personal needs. To the ordinary individual it is much more

146

important to take part in the direction of his local affairs that are now taken largely out of the hands of men he knows and can learn to trust, and transferred to a remoter bureaucracy which to him is an inhuman machine. And while within the sphere which the individual knows, it can only be beneficial to rouse his interest and induce him to contribute his knowledge and opinion, it can produce only disdain for all politics if he is mostly called upon to express views on matters which do not recognizably concern him.[15]

The abolition of the government monopoly of services

There is of course no need for central government to decide who should be entitled to render the different services, and it is highly undesirable that it should possess mandatory powers to do so. Indeed, though it may in some instances for the time being be true that only governmental agencies with compulsory powers of levying contributions can render certain services, there is no justification for any governmental agency possessing the exclusive right of supplying any particular service. Though it might turn out that the established supplier of some services is in so much better a position to render it than any possible competitor from private enterprise, and thus will achieve a *de facto* monopoly, there is no social interest in giving him a legal monopoly of any kind of activity. This means of course that any governmental agency allowed to use its taxing power to finance such services ought to be required to refund any taxes raised for these purposes to all those who prefer to get the services in some other way. This applies without exception to all those services of which today government possesses or aspires to a legal monopoly, with the only exception of maintaining and enforcing the law and maintaining for this purpose (including defence against external enemies) an armed force, i.e. all those from education to transport and communications, including post, telegraph, telephone and broadcasting services, all the so-called 'public utilities', the various 'social' insurances and, above all, the issue of money. Some of these services may well for the time being most efficiently be performed by a *de facto* monopoly; but we can neither insure improvement nor protect ourselves against extortion unless the possibility exists of somebody else offering better services of any of these kinds.

As with most of the topics touched upon in this final chapter, I cannot enter here into any more detailed discussion of the service activities which are today rendered by government; but in some of these cases the question whether the government ought to possess an exclusive right to them is of decisive importance, not merely a question of efficiency but of crucial significance of the preservation of a free society. In these cases the objection against any monopoly powers of government must preponderate, even if such a monopoly should promise services of higher quality. We may still discover for example, that a government broadcasting monopoly may prove as great a threat to political freedom as an abolition of the freedom of the press would be. The postal system is another instance where the prevailing government monopoly is the result solely of the striving of government for control over private activity and has in most parts of the world produced a steadily deteriorating service.

Above all, however, I am bound to stress that in the course of the work on this book I have been, by the confluence of political and economic considerations, led to the firm conviction that a free economic system will never again work satisfactorily and we shall never remove its most serious defects or stop the steady growth of government, unless the monopoly of the issue of money is taken from government. I have found it necessary to develop this argument in a separate book,[16] indeed I fear now that all the safeguards against oppression and other abuses of governmental power which the restructuring of government on the lines suggested in this volume are intended to achieve, would be of little help unless at the same time the control of government over the supply of money is removed. Since I am convinced that there are now no longer any rigid rules possible which would secure a supply of money by government by which at the same time the legitimate demands for money are satisfied and the value of that money kept stable, there appears to me to exist no other way of achieving this than to replace the present national moneys by competing different moneys offered by private enterprise, from which the public would be free to choose that which serves best for their transactions.

This seems to me so important that it would be essential for the constitution of a free people to entrench this principle by some special clause such as: 'Parliament shall make no law abridging the right of anybody to hold, buy, sell or lend, make and enforce contracts, calculate and keep their accounts in any kind of money they choose.' Although this is in fact implied in the basic principle that government can enforce or prohibit kinds of action only by general abstract rules, applying equally to everyone, including

148

government itself, this particular application of the principle is still too unfamiliar to expect courts to comprehend that the age-old prerogative of government is no longer to be recognized, unless this is explicitly spelled out in the constitution.

The dethronement of politics

Though I had wished at the end of this work to give some indication of the implications of the principles developed for international affairs, I find it impossible to do so without letting the exposition grow to undue length. It would also require further investigations which I am loath to undertake at this stage. I believe the reader will have no difficulty in seeing in what manner the dismantling of the monolithic state, and the principle that all supreme power must be confined to essentially negative tasks – powers to say no – and that all positive powers must be confined to agencies which have to operate under rules they cannot alter, must have far-reaching applications to international organization. As I have suggested earlier,[17] it seems to me that in this century our attempts to create an international government capable of assuring peace have generally approached the task from the wrong end: creating large numbers of specialized authorities aiming at particular regulations rather than aiming at a true international law which would limit the powers of national governments to harm each other. If the highest common values are negative, not only the highest common rules but also the highest authority should essentially be limited to prohibitions.

It can scarcely be doubted that quite generally politics has become much too important, much too costly and harmful, absorbing much too much mental energy and material resources, and that at the same time it is losing more and more the respect and sympathetic support of the public at large who have come to regard it increasingly as a necessary but incurable evil that must be borne. Yet the present magnitude and remoteness and still all-pervasiveness of the whole apparatus of politics is not something men have chosen, but the outcome of a self-willed mechanism they have set up without foreseeing its effects. Government is now of course not a human being one can trust, as the inherited ideal of the good ruler still suggests to the naive mind. Nor is it the result of the joint wisdom of trusted representatives the majority of whom can agree on what is best. It is a machinery directed by 'political necessities' which are only remotely affected by the opinions of the majority.

149

While legislation proper is a matter of long-run principles and not particular interests, all particular measures which government may take must become issues of day-to-day politics. It is an illusion to believe that such specific measures are normally determined by objective necessities on which all reasonable people ought to be able to agree. There are always costs to be balanced against the objectives aimed at, and there is no objective tests of the relative importance of what may be achieved and what will have to be sacrificed. It is the great difference between general laws which aim at improving the chances of all by securing an order in which there are good prospects of finding a partner for a transaction favourable to both sides, and coercive measures aiming at benefiting particular people or groups. So long as it is legitimate for government to use force to effect a redistribution of material benefits – and this is the heart of socialism – there can be no curb on the rapacious instincts of all groups who want more for themselves. Once politics becomes a tug-of-war for shares in the income pie, decent government is impossible. This requires that all use of coercion to assure a certain income to particular groups (beyond a flat minimum for all who cannot earn more in the market) be outlawed as immoral and strictly anti-social.

Today the only holders of power unbridled by any law which binds them and who are driven by the political necessities of a self-willed machine are the so-called legislators. But this prevailing form of democracy is ultimately self-destructive, because it imposes upon governments tasks on which an agreed opinion of the majority does not and cannot exist. It is therefore necessary to restrain these powers in order to protect democracy against itself.

A constitution like the one here proposed would of course make all socialist measures for redistribution impossible. This is no less justified than any other constitutional limitations of power intended to make impossible the destruction of democracy and the rise of totalitarian powers. At least at the time, which I believe is not far off, when the traditional beliefs of socialism will be recognized as an illusion, it will be necessary to make provision against the ever-recurring infection with such illusions that is bound again and again to cause an inadvertent slide into socialism.

For this it will not be sufficient to stop those who desire to destroy democracy in order to achieve socialism, or even only those wholly committed to a socialist programme. The strongest support of the trend towards socialism comes today from those who claim that they want neither capitalism nor socialism but a 'middle way', or a 'third world'. To follow them is a certain path to socialism, because once we give licence to the politicians to interfere in the spontaneous order of the market for the benefit of particular groups, they cannot deny such concessions to any group on which their support depends. They thus initiate that cumulative process which by inner necessity leads, if not to what the socialists imagine, then to an ever-growing domination over the economic process by politics.

There exists no third principle for the organization of the economics process which can be rationally chosen to achieve any desirable ends, in addition to either a functioning market in which nobody can conclusively determine how well-off particular groups or individuals will be, or a central direction where a group organized for power determines it. The two principles are irreconcilable, since any combination prevents the achievement of the aims of either. And while we can never reach what the socialists imagine, the general licence to politicians to grant special benefits to those whose support they need still must destroy that self-forming order of the market which serves the general good, and replace it by a forcibly imposed order determined by some arbitrary human wills. We face an inescapable choice between two irreconcilable principles, and however far we may always remain from fully realizing either, there can be no stable compromise. Whichever principle we make the foundation of our proceedings, it will drive us on, no doubt always to something imperfect, but more and more closely resembling one of the two extremes.

Once it is clearly recognized that socialism as much as fascism or communism inevitably leads into the totalitarian state and the destruction of the democratic order, it is clearly legitimate to provide against our inadvertently sliding into a socialist system by constitutional provisions which deprive government of the discriminating powers of coercion even for what at the moment may generally be regarded as good purposes.

However little it may often appear to be true, the social world is governed in the long run by certain moral principles on which the people at large believe. The only moral principle which has ever made the growth of an advanced civilization possible was the principle of individual freedom, which means that the individual is guided in his decisions by rules of just conduct and not by specific commands. No principles of collective conduct which bind the individual can exist in a society of free men. What we have achieved we owe to securing to the individuals the chance of creating for themselves a protected domain (their 'property') within which they can use their abilities for their own purposes. Socialism lacks any principles of individual conduct yet dreams of a state of affairs which no moral action of free individuals can bring about.

The last battle against arbitrary power is still ahead of us – the fight against socialism and for the abolition of all coercive power to direct individual efforts and deliberately to distribute its results. I am looking forward to a time when this totalitarian and essentially arbitrary character of all socialism will be as generally understood as that of communism and of fascism and therefore constitutional barriers against any attempt to acquire such totalitarian powers on any pretext will be generally approved.

What I have been trying to sketch in these volumes (and the separate study of the role of money in a free society) has been a guide out of the process of degeneration of the existing form of government, and to construct an intellectual emergency equipment which will be available when we have no choice but to replace the tottering structure by some better edifice rather than resort in despair to some sort of dictatorial regime. Government is of necessity the product of intellectual design. If we can give it a shape in which it provides a beneficial framework for the free growth of society, without giving to any one power to control this growth in the particular, we may well hope to see the growth of civilization continue.

We ought to have learnt enough to avoid destroying our civilization by smothering the spontaneous process of the interaction of the individuals by placing its direction in the hands of any authority. But to avoid this we must shed the illusion that we can deliberately 'create the future of mankind', as the characteristic hubris of a socialist sociologist has recently expressed it.[18] This is the final conclusion of the forty years which I have now devoted to the study of these problems since I became aware of the process of the Abuse and Decline of Reason which has continued throughout that period.[19]

THE THREE SOURCES OF
HUMAN VALUES

Prophete rechts, Prophete links,
Das Weltkind in der Mitten

J. W. Goethe**

The errors of sociobiology

The challenge which made me re-order my thoughts on the present subject was an unusually explicit statement of what I now recognize as a widespread error implicit in much current discussion. I met it in an interesting new work of what is regarded as the new American science of sociobiology, Dr G. E. Pugh's *The Biological Origin of Human Values*,[1] a book which has received great praise from the recognized head of this school, Professor Edward O. Wilson of Harvard University.[2] The startling point about it is that its whole argument is based on the express assumption that there are only two kinds of human values which Dr Pugh designates as 'primary' and 'secondary', meaning by the first term those which are genetically determined and therefore innate, while he defines the secondary ones as 'products of rational thought'.[3]

Social biology is, of course, the outcome of what is now already a fairly long development. Older members of the London School of Economics will remember that more than forty years ago a chair of social biology was established there. We have since had the great development of the fascinating study of ethology, founded by Sir Julian Huxley,[4] Konrad Lorenz,[5] and Niko Tinbergen,[6] now rapidly developed by their many gifted followers,[7] as well as a large number of American students. I must admit that even in the work of my Viennese friend Lorenz, which I have been following closely for fifty years, I have occasionally felt uneasy about an all-too-rapid application of conclusions drawn from the observation of animals to the explanation of human conduct. But none of these has done me the favour to state as a basic assumption and to proceed consistently on what with the others seemed occasional careless formulations, namely that those two kinds of values are the only kinds of human values.

What is so surprising about this view occurring so frequently among biologists,[8] is that one might rather have expected that they would be sympathetic to that analogous yet in important respects different process of selective evolution to which is due the formation of complex cultural structures. Indeed, the idea of cultural evolution is undoubtedly older than the biological concept of evolution. It is even probable that its application by Charles Darwin to biology was, through his grandfather Erasmus, derived from the cultural evolution concept of Bernard Mandeville and David Hume, if not more directly from the contemporary historical schools of law and language.[9] It is true that, after Darwin, those 'social Darwinists' who had needed Darwin to learn what was an older tradition in their own subjects, had somewhat spoiled the case by concentrating on the selection of congenitally more fit individuals, the slowness of which makes it comparatively unimportant for cultural evolution, and at the same time neglecting the decisively important selective evolution of rules and practices. But there was certainly no justification for some biologists treating evolution as solely a genetic process,[10] and completely forgetting about the similar but much faster process of cultural evolution that now dominates the human scene and presents to our intelligence problems it has not yet learnt to master.

What I had not foreseen, however, was that a close examination of this mistake, common among some specialists, would lead right to the heart of some of the most burning moral and political issues of our time. What at first may seem a question of concern only to specialists, turns out to be a paradigm of some of the gravest ruling misconceptions. Though I rather hope that most of what I shall have to say is somewhat familiar to cultural anthropologists – and the concept of cultural evolution has of course been stressed not only by L. T. Hobhouse and his followers[11] and more recently particularly by Sir Julian Huxley,[12] Sir Alexander Carr-Saunders[13] and C. H. Waddington[14] in Britain and even more by G. G. Simpson, Theodosius Dobzhansky[15] and Donald T. Campbell[16] in the USA, it seems to me that the attention of moral philosophers, political scientists and economists still needs to be emphatically drawn to its importance. What has yet to be more widely recognized is that the present order of society has largely arisen, not by design, but by the prevailing of the more effective institutions in a process of competition.

Culture is neither natural nor artificial, neither genetically transmitted nor rationally designed. It is a tradition of learnt rules of conduct which have never been 'invented' and whose functions the acting individuals usually do not understand. There is surely as much justification to speak of the wisdom of culture as of the wisdom of nature – except, perhaps, that, because of the powers of government, errors of the former are less easily corrected.

It is here that the constructivistic Cartesian approach[17] has made thinkers accept as 'good' for a long time only what were either innate or deliberately chosen rules, and to regard all merely grown formations as mere products of accident or caprice. Indeed, 'merely cultural' has now to many the connotation of changeable at will, arbitrary, superficial, or dispensable. Actually, however, civilization has largely been made possible by subjugating the innate animal instincts to the non-rational customs which made possible the formation of larger orderly groups of gradually increasing size.

The process of cultural evolution

That cultural evolution is not the result of human reason consciously building institutions, but of a process in which culture and reason developed concurrently is, perhaps, beginning to be more widely understood. *It is probably no more justified to claim that thinking man has created his culture than that culture created his reason*[18] As I have repeatedly had occasion to point out, the mistaken view has become deeply embedded in our thinking through the false dichotomy between what is 'natural' and what is 'artificial' which we have inherited from the ancient Greeks.[19] The structures formed by traditional human practices are neither natural in the sense of being genetically determined, nor artificial in the sense of being the product of intelligent design, but the result of a process of winnowing or sifting,[20] directed by the differential advantages gained by groups from practices adopted for some unknown and perhaps purely accidental reasons. We know now that not only among animals such as birds and particularly apes, learnt habits are transmitted by imitation, and even that different 'cultures' may develop among different groups of them,[21] but also that such acquired cultural traits may affect physiological evolution – as is obvious in the case of language: its rudimentary appearance undoubtedly made the physical capacity of clear articulation a great advantage, favouring genetic selection of a suitable speech apparatus.[22]

Nearly all writings on this topic stress that what we call cultural evolution took place during the last 1 per cent of the time during which *Homo sapiens* existed. With respect to what we mean by cultural evolution in a narrower sense, that is, the fast and accelerating development of civilization, this is true enough. Since it differs from genetic evolution by relying on the transmission of acquired properties, it is very fast, and once it dominates, it swamps genetic evolution. But this does not justify the misconception that it was the developed mind which in turn directed cultural evolution. This took place not merely after the appearance of *Homo sapiens*, but also during the much longer earlier existence of the genus *Homo* and its hominid ancestors. To repeat: *mind and culture developed concurrently and not successively*. Once we recognize this, we find that we know so little about precisely how this development took place, of which we have so few recognizable fossils, that we are reduced to reconstruct it as a sort of conjectural history in the sense of the Scottish moral philosophers of the eighteenth century. The facts about which we know almost nothing are the evolution of those rules of conduct which governed the structure and functioning of the various small groups of men in which the race developed. On this the study of still surviving primitive people can tell us little. Though the conception of conjectural history is somewhat suspect today, when we cannot say precisely how things did happen, to understand how they could have come about may be an important insight. The evolution of society and of language and the evolution of mind raise in this respect the same difficulty: the most important part of cultural evolution, the taming of the savage, was completed long before recorded history begins. It is this cultural evolution which man alone has undergone that now distinguishes him from the other animals. As Sir Ernest Gombrich put it somewhere: 'The history of civilization and of culture was the history of man's rise from a near animal state to polite society, the cultivation of arts, the adoption of civilized values and the free exercise of reason.[23]

To understand this development we must completely discard the conception that man was able to develop culture because he was endowed with reason. What apparently distinguished him was the capacity to imitate and to pass on what he had learned. Man probably began with a superior capacity to learn what to do – or even more, what not to do – in different circumstances. And much if not most of what he learnt about what to do he probably learnt by learning the meaning of words.[24] Rules for his conduct which made him adapt what he did to his environment were certainly more important to him than 'knowledge' about how other things behaved. In other words: man has certainly more often learnt to do the right thing without comprehending why it was the right thing, and he still is often served better by custom than by understanding. Other objects were primarily defined for him by the appropriate way of conduct towards them. It was a repertoire of learnt rules which told him what was the right and what was the wrong way of acting in different circumstances that gave him his increasing capacity to adapt to changing conditions – and particularly to co-operate with the other members of his group. Thus a tradition of rules of conduct, existing apart from any one individual who had learnt them, began to govern human life.[25] It was when these learnt rules, involving classifications of different kinds of objects, began to include a sort of model of the environment that enabled man to predict and anticipate in action external events, that what we call reason appeared.[26] There *was then probably much more 'intelligence' incorporated in the system of rules of conduct than in man's thoughts about his surroundings.*

It is therefore misleading to represent the individual brain or mind as the capping stone of the hierarchy of complex structures produced by evolution, which then designed what we call culture. The mind is embedded in a traditional impersonal structure of learnt rules, and its capacity to order experience is an acquired replica of cultural patterns which every individual mind finds given. *The brain is an organ enabling us to absorb, but not to design culture.* This 'world 3', as Sir Karl Popper has called it,[27] though at all times kept in existence by millions of separate brains participating in it, is the outcome of a process of evolution distinct from the biological evolution of the brain, the elaborate structure of which became useful when there was a cultural tradition to absorb. Or, to put it differently, mind can exist only as part of another independently existing distinct structure or order, though that order persists and can develop only because millions of minds constantly absorb and modify parts of it. If we are to understand it, we must direct our attention to that process of sifting of practices which sociobiology

157

systematically neglects. This is the third and most important source of what in the title of this lecture I have called human values and about which we necessarily know little, but to which I still want to devote most of what I have to say. Before I turn, however, to the specific questions of how such social structures evolved, it may be helpful if I briefly consider some of the methodological issues which arise in all attempts to analyse such grown complex structures.

The evolution of self-maintaining complex structures

We understand now that *all* enduring structures above the level of the simplest atoms, and up to the brain and society, are the results of, and can be explained only in terms of, processes of selective evolution,[28] and that the more complex ones maintain themselves by constant adaptation of their internal states to changes in the environment. 'Wherever we look, we discover evolutionary processes leading to diversification and increasing complexity' (Nicolis and Prigogine; see n. 33). These changes in structure are brought about by their elements possessing such regularities of conduct, or such capacities to follow rules, that the result of their individual actions will be to restore the order of the whole if it is disturbed by external influences. Hence what on an earlier occasion I have called the twin concepts of evolution and spontaneous order[29] enables us to account for the persistence of these complex structures, not by a simple conception of one-directional laws of cause and effect, but by a complex interaction of patterns which Professor Donald Campbell described as 'downward causation'.[30]

This insight has greatly altered our approach to the explanation of, and our views about the achievable scope of our endeavours to explain, such complex phenomena. There is now, in particular, no justification for believing that the search for quantitative relationships, which proved so effective for accounting for the interdependence of two or three different variables, can be of much help in the explanation of the self-maintaining structures that exist only because of their self-maintaining attributes.[31] One of the most important of these self-generating orders is the wide-ranging division of labour which implies the mutual adjustment of activities of people who do not know each other. This foundation of modern civilization was first understood by Adam Smith in terms of the operation of feedback mechanism by which he anticipated what we now know as cybernetics.[32] The once popular organismic interpretations of social phenomena, that tried to account for one unexplained order by the analogy with another equally unexplained, has now been replaced by system theory, originally developed by yet another Viennese friend, Ludwig von Bertalanffy, and his numerous followers.[33] This has brought out the common features of those diverse complex orders which are also discussed by information and communication theory and semiotics.[34]

In particular, in order to explain the economic aspects of large social systems, we have to account for the course of a flowing stream, constantly adapting itself as a whole to changes in circumstances of which each participant can know only a small fraction, and not for a hypothetical state of equilibrium determined by a set of ascertainable data. And the numerical measurements with which the majority of economists are still occupied today may be of interest as historical facts; but for the theoretical explanation of those patterns which restore themselves, the quantitative data are about as significant as it would be for human biology if it concentrated on explaining the different sizes and shapes of such human organs as stomachs and livers of different individuals which happen to appear in the dissecting room very different from, and to resemble only rarely, the standard size or shapes in the textbooks.[35] With the functions of the system these magnitudes have evidently very little to do.

The stratification of rules of conduct[36]

But, to return to my central theme: the differences between the rules which have developed by each of the three distinct processes has led to a *super-imposition of not merely three layers of rules, but of many more,* according as traditions have been preserved from the successive stages through which cultural evolution has passed. The consequence is that modern man is torn by conflicts which torment him and force him into ever-accelerating further changes. There is, of course, in the first instance, the solid, i.e. little changing foundation of genetically inherited, 'instinctive' drives which are determined by his physiological structure. There are then all the remains of the traditions acquired in the successive types of social structures through which he has passed – rules which he did not deliberately choose but which have spread because some practices enhanced the prosperity of certain groups and led to their expansion, perhaps less by more rapid procreation than by the attraction of outsiders. And there is, third, on top of all this, the thin layer of rules, deliberately adopted or modified to serve known purposes.

The transition from the small band to the settled community and finally to the open society and with it to civilization was due to men learning to obey the same abstract rules instead of being guided by innate instincts to pursue common perceived goals. The innate natural longings were appropriate to the condition of life of the small band during which man had developed the neural structure which is still characteristic of *Homo sapiens*. These innate structures built into man's organization in the course of perhaps 50,000 generations were adapted to a wholly different life from that which he has made for himself during the last 500, or for most of us only 100, generations or so. It would probably be more correct to equate these 'natural' instincts with 'animal' rather than with characteristically human or good instincts. Indeed, the general use of 'natural' as a term of praise is becoming very misleading, because one of the main functions of the rules learned later was to restrain the innate or natural instincts in the manner that was required to make the Great Society possible. We are still inclined to assume that what is natural must be good; but it may be very far from good in the Great Society. What has made men good is neither nature nor reason but tradition. There is not much common humanity in the biological endowment of the species. But most groups had to acquire certain similar traits to form into larger societies; or, more probably, those who did not were exterminated by those who did. And though we still share most of the emotional traits of primitive man, he does not share all ours, or the restraints which made civilization possible. Instead of the direct pursuit of felt needs or perceived objects, the obedience to learnt rules has become necessary to restrain those natural instincts which do not fit into the order of the open society. It is this 'discipline' (one of the lexical meanings of this word is 'systems of rules of conduct') against which man still revolts.

The morals which maintain the open society do not serve to gratify human emotions – which never was an aim of evolution – but they served only as the signals that told the individual what he ought to do in the kind of society in which he had lived in the dim past. What is still only imperfectly appreciated is that the cultural selection of new learnt rules became necessary chiefly in order to repress some of the innate rules which were adapted to the hunting and gathering life of the small bands of fifteen to forty persons, led by a headman and defending a territory against all outsiders. From that stage practically all advance had to be achieved by infringing or repressing some of the innate rules and replacing them by new ones which made the co-ordination of activities of larger groups possible. Most of these steps in the evolution of culture were made possible by some individuals breaking some traditional rules and practising new forms of conduct – not because they understood them to be better, but because the groups which acted on them prospered more than others and grew.[37] We must not be surprised that these rules often took the form of magic or ritual. The conditions of admission to the group was to accept all its rules, though few understood what depended on the observance of any particular one. There was just in each group only one acceptable way of doing things, with little attempt to distinguish between effectiveness and moral desirability.

Customary rules and economic order

It would be interesting, but I cannot attempt here, to account for the succession of the different economic orders through which civilization has passed in terms of changes in the rules of conduct. They made that evolution possible mostly by relaxations of prohibitions: an evolution of individual freedom and a development of rules which protected the individual rather than commanded it to do particular things. There can be little doubt that from the toleration of bartering with the outsider, the recognition of delimited private property, especially in land, the enforcement of contractural obligations, the competition with fellow craftsmen in the same trade, the variability of initially customary prices, the lending of money, particularly at interest, were all initially infringements of customary rules – so many falls from grace. And the law-breakers, who were to be path-breakers, certainly did not introduce the new rules because they recognized that they were beneficial to the community, but they simply started some practices advantageous to them which then did prove beneficial to the group in which they prevailed. There can, for instance, be little doubt that Dr Pugh is right when he observes,

> within primitive human society 'sharing' is a way of life. . . .
> The sharing is not limited to food, but extends to all kinds of
> resources. The practical result is that scarce resources are
> shared within the society approximately in proportion to

need. This behaviour may reflect some innate and uniquely human values that evolved during the transition to a hunting economy.[38]

That was probably true enough in that stage of development. But these habits had to be shed again to make the transition to the market economy and the open society possible. The steps of this transition were all breaches of that 'solidarity' which governed the small group and which are still resented. Yet they were the steps towards almost all that we now call civilization. The greatest change which man has still only partially digested came with the transition from the face-to-face society[39] to what Sir Karl Popper has appropriately called the abstract society:[40] a society in which no longer the known needs of known people but only abstract rules and impersonal signals guide action towards strangers. This made a specialization possible far beyond the range any one man can survey.

Even today the overwhelming majority of people, including, I am afraid, a good many supposed economists, do not yet understand that this extensive social division of labour, based on widely dispersed information, has been made possible entirely by the use of those impersonal signals which emerge from the market process and tell people what to do in order to adapt their activities to events of which they have no direct knowledge. That in an economic order involving a far-ranging division of labour it can no longer be the pursuit of perceived common ends but only abstract rules of conduct – and the whole relationship between such rules of individual conduct and the formation of an order which I have tried to make clear in earlier volumes of this work – is an insight which most people still refuse to accept. That neither what is instinctively recognized as right, nor what is rationally recognized as serving specific purposes, but inherited traditional rules, or that what is neither instinct nor reason but tradition should often be most beneficial to the functioning of society, is a truth which the dominant constructivistic outlook of our times refuses to accept. If modern man finds that his inborn instincts do not always lead him in the right direction, he at least flatters himself that it was his reason which made him recognize that a different kind of conduct will serve his innate values better. The conception that man has, in the service of his innate desires, consciously constructed an order of society is, however, erroneous, because without the cultural evolution which lies between instinct and the capacity of rational design he would not have possessed the reason which now makes him try to do so.

162

Man did not adopt new rules of conduct because he was intelligent. He became intelligent by submitting to new rules of conduct. The most important insight which so many rationalists still resist and are even inclined to brand as a superstition, namely that man has not only never invented his most beneficial institutions, from language to morals and law, and even today does not yet understand why he should preserve them when they satisfy neither his instincts nor his reason, still needs to be emphasized. The basic tools of civilization – language, morals, law and money – are all the result of spontaneous growth and not of design, and of the last two organized power has got hold and thoroughly corrupted them.

Although the Left is still inclined to brand all such efforts as apologetics, it may still be one of the most important tasks of our intelligence to discover the significance of rules we never deliberately made, and the obedience to which builds more complex orders than we can understand. I have already pointed out that the pleasure which man is led to strive for is of course not the end which evolution serves but merely the signal that in primitive conditions made the individual do what was usually required for the preservation of the group, but which under present conditions may no longer do so. The constructivistic theories of utilitarianism that derive the now valid rules from their serving individual pleasure are therefore completely mistaken. The rules which contemporary man has learnt to obey have indeed made possible an immense proliferation of the human race. I am not so certain that this has also increased the pleasure of the several individuals.

The discipline of freedom

Man has not developed in freedom. The member of the little band to which he had had to stick in order to survive was anything but free. *Freedom is an artefact of civilization* that released man from the trammels of the small group, the momentary moods of which even the leader had to obey. Freedom was made possible by the gradual evolution of *the discipline of civilization which is at the same time the discipline of freedom.* It protects him by impersonal abstract rules against arbitrary violence of others and enables each individual to try to build for himself a protected domain with which nobody else is allowed to interfere and within which he can use his own knowledge for his own purposes. We owe our freedom to restraints of freedom. 'For', Locke wrote, 'who could be free when every other man's humour might domineer over him?' (2nd Treatise, sect. 57.)

The great change which produced an order of society which became increasingly incomprehensible to man, and for the preservation of which he had to submit to learnt rules which were often contrary to his innate instincts, was the transition from the face-to-face society, or at least of groups consisting of known and recognizable members, to the open abstract society that was no longer held together by common concrete ends but only by the obedience to the same abstract rules.[41] What man probably found most difficult to comprehend was that the only common values of an open and free society were not concrete objects to be achieved, but only those common abstract rules of conduct that secured the constant maintenance of an equally abstract order which merely assured to the individual better prospects of achieving his individual ends but gave him no claims to particular things.[42]

The conduct required for the preservation of a small band of hunters and gatherers, and that presupposed by an open society based on exchange, are very different. But while mankind had hundreds of thousands of years to acquire and genetically to embody the responses needed for the former, it was necessary for the rise of the latter that he not only learned to acquire new rules, but that some of the new rules served precisely to repress the instinctive reactions no longer appropriate to the Great Society. These new rules were not supported by the awareness that they were more effective. *We have never designed our economic system. We were not intelligent enought for that.* We have stumbled into it and it has carried us to unforeseen heights and given rise to ambitions which may yet lead us to destroy it.

This development must be wholly unintelligible to all those who recognize only innate drives on the one hand and deliberately designed systems of rules on the other. But if anything is certain it is that no person who was not already familiar with the market could have designed the economic order which is capable of maintaining the present numbers of mankind.

This exchange society and the guidance of the co-ordination of a far-ranging division of labour by variable market prices was made possible by the spreading of certain gradually evolved moral beliefs which, after they had spread, most men in the Western world learned to accept. These rules were inevitably learned by all the members of a population consisting chiefly of independent farmers, artisans and merchants and their servants and apprentices who shared the daily experiences of their masters. They held an ethos that esteemed the prudent man, the good husbandman and provider who looked after the future of his family and his business by building up capital, guided less by the desire to be able to consume much than by the wish to be regarded as successful by his fellows who pursued similar aims.[43] It was the thousands of individuals who practised the new routine more than the occasional successful innovators whom they would imitate that maintained the market order. Its mores involved withholding from the known needy neighbours what they might require in order to serve the unknown needs of thousands of unknown others. Financial gain rather than the pursuit of a known common good became not only the basis of approval but also the cause of the increase of general wealth.

The re-emergence of suppressed primordial instincts

At present, however, an ever increasing part of the population of the Western World grow up as members of large organizations and thus as strangers to those rules of the market which have made the great open society possible. To them the market economy is largely incomprehensible; they have never practised the rules on which it rests, and its results seem to them irrational and immoral. They often see in it merely an arbitrary structure maintained by some sinister power. In consequence, the long-submerged innate instincts have again surged to the top. Their demand for a just distribution in which organized power is to be used to allocate to each what he deserves, is thus strictly an *atavism*, based on primordial emotions. And it is these widely prevalent feelings to which prophets, moral philosophers and constructivists appeal by their plan for the deliberate creation of a new type society.[44]

But, though they all appeal to the same emotions, their arguments take very different and in some respects almost contradictory forms. A first group proposes a return to the older rules of conduct which have prevailed in the distant past and are still dear to men's sentiments. A second wants to construct new rules which will better serve the innate desires of the individuals. Religious prophets and ethical philosophers have of course at all times been mostly reactionaries, defending the old against the new principles. Indeed, in most parts of the world the development of an open market economy has long been prevented by those very morals preached by prophets and philosophers, even before governmental measures did the same. *We must admit that modern civilization has become largely possible by the disregard of the injunctions of those indignant moralists.* As has been well said by the French historian Jean Baechler, *'the expansion of capitalism owes its origins and raison d'être to political anarchy'.*[45] That is true enough of the Middle Ages, which, however, could draw on the teaching of the ancient Greeks who – in some measure also as a result of political anarchy – had not only discovered individual liberty and private property,[46] but also the inseparability of the two,[47] and thereby created the first civilization of free men.

When the prophets and philosophers, from Moses to Plato and St Augustine, from Rousseau to Marx and Freud, protested against the prevailing morals, clearly none of them had any grasp of the extent to which the practices which they condemned had made possible the civilization of which they were part. They had no conception that the system of competitive prices and remunerations signalling to the individual what to do, had made possible that extensive specialization by informing the individuals how best to serve others of whose existence they might not know – and to use in this opportunities of the availability of which they also had no direct knowledge. Nor did they understand that those condemned moral beliefs were less the effect than the cause of the evolution of the market economy.

But the gravest deficiency of the older prophets was their belief that the intuitively perceived ethical values, divined out of the depth of man's breast, were immutable and eternal. This prevented them from recognizing that all rules of conduct served a particular kind of order to society, and that, though such a society will find it necessary to enforce its rules of conduct in order to protect itself against disruption, it is not society with a given structure that creates the rules appropriate to it, but the rules which have been practised by a few and then imitated by many which created a social order of a particular kind. Tradition is not something constant but the product of a process of selection guided not by reason but by success. It changes but can rarely be deliberately changed. Cultural selection is not a rational process; it is not guided by but it creates reason.

The belief in the immutability and permanence of our moral rules receives of course some support from the recognition that as little as we have designed our whole moral system, is it in our power to change it as a whole.[48] We do not really understand how it maintains the order of actions on which the co-ordination of the activities of many millions depends.[49] And since we owe the order of our society to a tradition of rules which we only imperfectly understand, *all progress must be based on tradition.* We must build on tradition and can only tinker with its products.[50] It is only by recognizing the conflict between a given rule and the rest of our moral beliefs that we can justify our rejection of an established rule. Even the success of an innovation by a rule-breaker, and the trust of those who follow him, has to be bought by the esteem he has earned by the scrupulous observation of most of the existing rules. To become legitimized, the new rules have to obtain the approval of society at large – not by a formal vote, but by gradually spreading acceptance. And though we must constantly re-examine our rules and be prepared to question every single one of them, we can always do so only in terms of their consistency or compatibility with the rest of the system from the angle of their effectiveness in contributing to the formation of the same kind of overall order of actions which all the other rules serve.[51] There is thus certainly room for improvement, but we cannot redesign but only further evolve what we do not fully comprehend.

The successive changes in morals were therefore not a moral decline, even though they often offended inherited sentiments, but a necessary condition to the rise of the open society of free men. The confusion prevailing in this respect is most clearly shown by the common identification of the terms 'altruistic' and 'moral',[52] and the constant abuse of the former, especially by the sociobiologists,[53] to describe any action which is unpleasant or harmful to the doer but beneficial to society. Ethics is not a matter of choice. We have not designed it and cannot design it. And perhaps all that is innate is the fear of the frown and other signs of disapproval of our fellows. The rules which we learn to observe are the result of cultural evolution. We can endeavour to improve the system of rules by seeking to reconcile its internal conflicts or its conflicts with our emotions. But instinct or intuition do not entitle us to reject a particular demand of the prevailing moral code, and only a responsible effort to judge it as part of the system of other requirements may make it morally legitimate to infringe a particular rule.

There is, however, so far as present society is concerned, no 'natural goodness', because with his innate instincts man could never have built the civilization on which the numbers of present mankind depend for their lives. To be able to do so, he had to

167

shed many sentiments that were good for the small band, and to submit to the sacrifices which the discipline of freedom demands but which he hates. The abstract society rests on learnt rules and not on pursuing perceived desirable common objects: and wanting to do good to known people will not achieve the most for the community, but only the observation of its abstract and seemingly purposeless rules. Yet this little satisfies our deeply engrained feelings, or only so long as it brings us the esteem of our fellows.[54]

Evolution, tradition and progress

I have so far carefully avoided saying that evolution is identical with progress, but when it becomes clear that it was the evolution of a tradition which made civilization possible, we may at least say that spontaneous evolution is a necessary if not a sufficient condition of progress. And though it clearly produces also much that we did not foresee and do not like when we see it, it does bring to ever-increasing numbers what they have been mainly striving for. We often do not like it because the new possibilities always also bring a new discipline. *Man has been civilized very much against his wishes.* It was the price he had to pay for being able to raise a larger number of children. We especially dislike the economic disciplines and economists are often accused of over-rating the importance of the economic aspects of the process. The indispensable rules of the free society require from us much that is unpleasant, such as suffering competition from others, seeing others being richer than ourselves, etc., etc. But it is a misunderstanding when it is suggested that the economists want everything to serve economic goals. Strictly speaking, no final ends are economic, and the so-called economic goals which we pursue are at most inter-mediate goals which tell us how to serve others for ends which are ultimately non-economic.[55] And it is the discipline of the market which forces us to calculate, that is, to be responsible for the means we use up in the pursuit of our ends.

Unfortunately social usefulness is not distributed according to any principles of justice – and could be so distributed only by some authority assigning specific tasks to particular individuals, and rewarding them for how industriously and faithfully they have carried out orders, but depriving them at the same time of the use of their own knowledge for their own values. Any attempt to make the remuneration of the different services correspond to our atavistic conception of distributive justice must destroy the effective utilization of the dispersed individual knowledge, and what we know as a pluralistic society.

That progress may be faster than we like, and that we might be better able to digest it if it were slower, I will not deny. But, unfortunately, *progress cannot be dosed*, (nor, for that matter, economic growth!) All we can do is to create conditions favourable to it and then hope for the best.[56] It may be stimulated or damped by policy, but nobody can predict the precise effects of such measures; to pretend to know the desirable direction of progress seems to me to be the extreme of hubris. Guided progress would not be progress. But civilization has fortunately outstripped the possibility of collective control, otherwise we would probably smother it.

I can already hear our modern intellectuals hurling against such an emphasis on tradition their deadly thunderbolt of 'conservative thinking'. But to me there can be no doubt that it were favourable moral traditions which made particular groups strong rather than intellectual design that made the progress of the past possible and will do so also in the future. To confine evolution to what we can foresee would be to stop progress; and it is due to the favourable framework which is provided by a free market but which I cannot further describe here that the new which is better has a chance to emerge.

The construction of new morals to serve old instincts: Marx

The real leaders among the reactionary social philosophers are of course all the socialists. Indeed the whole of socialism is a result of that revival of primordial instincts, though most of its theorists are too sophisticated to deceive themselves that in the great society those old instincts could be satisfied by re-instating the rules of conduct that governed primitive man. So these recidivists join the opposite wing and endeavour to construe new morals serving the instinctive yearnings.

The extent to which particularly Karl Marx was completely unaware of the manner in which appropriate rules of individual conduct induce the formation of an order in the Great Society is best seen when we inquire what made him speak of the 'chaos' of capitalist production. What prevented him from appreciating the signal-function of prices through which people are informed what they ought to do was, of course, his labour theory of value. His vain search for a physical cause of value made him regard prices as determined by labour costs, that is, by what people had done in the past rather than as the signal telling them what they must do in order to be able to sell their products. In consequence, any Marxist is to the present day wholly incapable of understanding that self-generating order, or to see how a selective evolution that knows no laws that determine its direction can produce a self-directing order. Apart from the impossibility of bringing about by central direction an efficient social division of labour by inducing the constant adaptation to the ever-changing awareness of events possessed by millions of people, his whole scheme suffers from the illusion that in a society of free individuals in which the remuneration offered tells the people what to do, the products could be distributed by some principles of justice.

But if the illusion of social justice must be sooner or later disappointed,[57] the most destructive of the constructivistic morals is egalitarianism – for which Karl Marx can certainly *not* be blamed. It is wholly destructive because it not only deprives the individuals of the signals which alone can offer to them the opportunity of a choice of the direction of their efforts, but even more through eliminating the one inducement by which free men can be made to observe any moral rules: the differentiating esteem by their fellows. I have no time to analyse here the dreadful confusion which leads from the fundamental presupposition of a free society, that all must be judged and treated by others according to the same rules (the equality before the law), to the demand that government should treat different people differently in order to place them in the same material position. This might indeed be the only 'just' rule for any socialist system in which the power of coercion must be used to determine both the assignment to kinds of work and the distribution of incomes. An egalitarian distribution would necessarily remove all basis for the individual's decision how they are to fit themselves into the pattern of general activities and leave only outright command as the foundation of all order.

But as moral views create institutions, so institutions create moral views; and under the prevailing form of unlimited democracy in which the power to do so creates the necessity of benefiting particular groups, government is led to concede claims the satisfaction of which destroys all morals. While the realization of socialism would make the scope of private moral conduct dwindle, the political necessity of gratifying all demands of large groups must lead to the degeneration and destruction of all morals.

All morals rest on the different esteem in which different persons are held by their fellows according to their conforming to accepted moral standards. It is this which makes moral conduct a social value. Like all rules of conduct prevailing in a society, and the observance of which makes an individual a member of the society, their acceptance demands equal application to all. This involves that morals are preserved by discriminating between people who observe them and those who do not, irrespective of why particular people may infringe them. *Morals presuppose a striving for excellence and the recognition that in this some succeed better than others*, without inquiring for the reasons which we can never know. Those who observe the rules are regarded as better in the sense of being of superior value compared with those who do not, and whom in consequence the others may not be willing to admit into their company. Without this morals would not persist.

I doubt whether any moral rule could be preserved without the exclusion of those who regularly infringe it from decent company – or even without people not allowing their children to mix with those who have bad manners. It is by the separation of groups and their distinctive principles of admission to them that sanctions of moral behaviour operate. Democratic morals may demand a presumption that a person will conduct himself honestly and decently until he proves the contrary – but they cannot require us to suspend that essential discipline without destroying moral beliefs.

The conscientious and courageous may on rare occasions decide to brave general opinion and to disregard a particular rule which he regards as wrong, if he proves his general respect for the prevailing moral rules by carefully observing the others. But there can be no excuse or pardon for a systematic disregard of accepted moral rules because they have no understood justification. The only base for judging particular rules is their reconcilability or conflict with the majority of other rules which are generally accepted.

It is certainly sad that men can be made bad by their environment, but this does not alter the fact that they are bad and must be treated as such. The repentant sinner may earn absolution, but so long as he continues breaking the rules of morals he must

171

remain a less valued member of society. Crime is not necessarily the result of poverty and not excused by environment. There are many poor people much more honest than many rich, and middle-class morals are probably in general better than those of the rich. But morally a person breaking the rules must be counted bad even if he knows no better. And that often people will have much to learn in order to be accepted by another group is much to the good. Even moral praise is not based on intention but on performance and must be so.

In a culture formed by group selection, the imposition of egalitarianism must stop further evolution. Egalitarianism is of course not a majority view but a product of the necessity under unlimited democracy to solicit the support even of the worst. And while it is one of the indispensable principles of a free society that we value people differently according to the morality of their manifest conduct, irrespective of the, never fully known, reasons of their failures, egalitarianism preaches that nobody is better than anybody else. The argument is that it is nobody's fault that he is as he is, but that all is the responsibility of 'society'. It is by the slogan that 'it is not your fault' that the demagoguery of unlimited democracy, assisted by a scientistic psychology, has come to the support of those who claim a share in the wealth of our society without submitting to the discipline to which it is due. It is not by conceding 'a right to equal concern and respect'[58] to those who break the code that civilization is maintained. Nor can we, for the purpose of maintaining our society, accept all moral beliefs which are held with equal conviction as equally legitimate, and recognize a right to blood feud or infanticide or even theft, or any other moral beliefs contrary to those on which the working of our society rests. What makes an individual a member of society and gives him claims is that he obeys its rules. Wholly contradictory views may give him rights in other societies but not in ours. For the science of anthropology all cultures or morals may be equally good, but we maintain our society by treating others as less so.

Our civilization advances by making the fullest use of the infinite variety of the individuals of the human species, apparently greater than that of any wild animal species,[59] which had generally to adapt to one particular ecological niche. Culture has provided a great variety of cultural niches in which that great diversity of men's innate or acquired gifts can be used. And if we are to make use of the distinct factual knowledge of the individuals inhabiting different locations on this world, we must allow them to be told by the impersonal signals of the market how they had best use them in their own as well as in the general interest.

It would indeed be a tragic joke of history if man, who owes his rapid advance to nothing so much as to the exceptional variety of individual gifts, were to terminate his evolution by imposing a compulsory egalitarian scheme on all.

The destruction of indispensable values by scientific error: Freud

I come finally to what for many years has increasingly become one of my main concerns and causes of apprehension: the progressive destruction of irreplaceable values by scientific error.[60] The attacks do not all come from socialism, although the errors I shall have to consider mostly lead to socialism. It finds support from purely intellectual errors in the associated fields of philosophy, sociology, law and psychology. In the first three fields these errors derive mostly from the Cartesian scientism and constructivism as developed by Auguste Comte.[61] Logical positivism has been trying to show that all moral values are 'devoid of meaning', purely 'emotive'; it is wholly contemptuous of the conception that even emotional responses selected by biological *or* cultural evolution may be of the greatest importance for the coherence of an advanced society. The sociology of knowledge, deriving from the same source, similarly attempts to discredit all moral views by the alleged interested motifs of their defenders.

I must confess here that, however grateful we all must be for some of the descriptive work of the sociologists, for which, however, perhaps anthropologists and historians would have been equally qualified, there seems to me still to exist no more justification for a theoretical discipline of sociology than there would be for a theoretical discipline of naturology apart from the theoretical disciplines dealing with particular classes of natural or social phenomena. I am quite certain, however, that the sociology of knowledge with its desire that mankind should pull itself up by its own bootstraps (a belief characteristically re-asserted now in these very words by the behaviourist B. F. Skinner) has wholly misconceived the process of the growth of knowledge. I have earlier in this work attempted to show why legal positivism, with its belief that every legal rule must be derivable from a conscious act of legislation, and that all conceptions of justice are

173

the product of particular interests, is conceptually as much mistaken as historically.[62]

But the culturally most devastating effects have come from the endeavour of psychiatrists to cure people by releasing their innate instincts. After having lauded earlier my Viennese friends Popper, Lorenz, Gombrich and Bertalanffy, I am afraid I must now concede that the logical positivism of Carnap and the legal positivism of Kelsen are far from the worst things that have come out of Vienna. Through his profound effects on education, Sigmund Freud has probably become the greatest destroyer of culture. Although in his old age, in his *Civilisation and its Discontents*,[63] he seems himself to have become not a little disturbed by some of the effects of his teaching, his basic aim of undoing the culturally acquired repressions and freeing the natural drives, has opened the most fatal attack on the basis of all civilization. The movement culminated about thirty years ago and the generation grown up since has been largely brought up on its theories. I will give you from that date only one particular crass expression of the fundamental ideas by an influential Canadian psychiatrist who later became the first Secretary General of the World Health Organization. In 1946 the late Dr G. B. Chisholm in a work praised by high American legal authority, advocated

> the eradication of the concept of right and wrong which has
> been the basis of child training, the substitution of intelligent
> and rational thinking for the faith in the certainties of old
> people [. . . since] most psychiatrists and psychologists and
> many other respectable people have escaped from these moral
> chains and are able to observe and think freely.

In his opinion it was the task of the psychiatrists to free the human race from 'the crippling burden of good and evil' and the 'perverse concepts of right and wrong' and thereby to decide its immediate future.[64]

It is the harvest of these seeds which we are now gathering. Those non-domesticated savages who represent themselves as alienated from something they have never learnt, and even undertake to construct a 'counter-culture', are the necessary product of the permissive education which fails to pass on the burden of culture, and trusts to the *natural instincts which are the instincts of the savage*. It did not surprise me in the least when, according to a report in *The Times*, a recent international conference of senior police officers and other experts acknowledged that a noticeable proportion of today's terrorists have studied sociology or political and educational sciences.[65] What can we expect from a generation who grew up during the fifty years during which the English intellectual scene was dominated by a figure who had publicly pronounced that he always had been and would remain an immoralist?

We must be grateful that before this flood has finally destroyed civilization, a revulsion is taking place even within the field in which it originated. Three years ago Professor Donald Campbell of Northwestern University, in his presidential address to the American Psychological Association on 'The Conflicts between Biological and Social Evolution', said that

> if, as I assert, there is in psychology today a general background assumption that the human impulses provided by biological evolution are right and optimal, both individually and socially, and that repressive or inhibitory moral traditions are wrong, then in my judgment this assumption may now be regarded as scientifically wrong from the enlarged scientific perspective that comes from the joint consideration of population genetics and social system evolution. . . . Psychology may be contributing to the undermining of the retention of what may be extremely valuable, social-evolutionary inhibitory systems which we do not yet fully understand.[66]

And he added a little later: 'the recruitment of scholars into psychology and psychiatry may be such as to select persons unusually eager to challenge the cultural orthodoxy'.[67] From the furore this lecture caused[68] we can judge how deeply embedded these ideas still are in contemporary psychological theory. There are similar salutary efforts by Professor Thomas Szasz of Syracuse University[69] and by Professor H. J. Eysenck in this country.[70] So all hope is not yet lost.

The tables turned

If our civilization survives, which it will do only if it renounces those errors, I believe men will look back on our age as an age of superstition, chiefly connected with the names of Karl Marx and Sigmund

175

Freud. I believe people will discover that the most widely held ideas which dominated the twentieth century, those of a planned economy with a just distribution, a freeing ourselves from repressions and conventional morals, of permissive education as a way to freedom, and the replacement of the market by a rational arrangement of a body with coercive powers, were all based on superstitions in the strict sense of the word. An age of superstitions is a time when people imagine that they know more than they do. In this sense the twentieth century was certainly an outstanding age of superstition, and the cause of this is an overestimation of what science has achieved – not in the field of the comparatively simple phenomena, where it has of course been extraordinarily successful, but in the field of complex phenomena, where the application of the techniques which proved so helpful with essentially simple phenomena has proved to be very misleading.

Ironically, these superstitions are largely an effect of our inheritance from the Age of Reason, that great enemy of all that *it* regarded as superstitions. If the Enlightenment has discovered that the role assigned to human reason in intelligent construction had been too small in the past, we are discovering that the task which our age is assigning to the rational construction of new institutions is far too big. What the age of rationalism – and modern positivism – has taught us to regard as senseless and meaningless formations due to accident or human caprice, turn out in many instances to be the foundations on which our capacity for rational thought rests. *Man is not and never will be the master of his fate: his very reason always progresses by leading him into the unknown and unforeseen where he learns new things.*

In concluding this epilogue I am becoming increasingly aware that it ought not to be that but rather a new beginning. But I hardly dare hope that for me it can be so.

NOTES

CHAPTER TWELVE MAJORITY OPINION AND
CONTEMPORARY DEMOCRACY

* Xenophon, *Helenica,* I, vii, 12–16. A German translation of an earlier version of what have now become chapters 12 and 13 has appeared under the title 'Anschauungen der Mehrheit und zeitgenössische Demokratie' as long ago as 1965 in *Ordo* XV/ XVI (Düsseldorf and Munich, 1965) and was reprinted in my *Freiburger Studien* (Tübingen, 1969).

1 A significant symptom was an article by Cecil King in *The Times* (London) of 16 September 1968, entitled 'The Declining Reputation of Parliamentary Democracy' in which he argued:

> What is to my mind most disturbing is the world-wide decline in authority and in respect for democratic institutions. A century ago it was generally agreed in the advanced countries of the world that parliamentary government was the best form of government. But today dissatisfaction with parliamentary government is widespread. Nobody can seriously argue that in Europe or America parliaments are adding to their prestige. . . . So low has the reputation of parliamentary government sunk that it is now defended on the grounds that bad as it is, other forms of government are worse.

Of the ever-increasing literature on this topic, some of the more recent books are: Robert Moss, *The Collapse of Democracy* (London, 1975); K. Sontheimer, G. A. Ritter *et al., Der Über-druss an der Demokratie* (Cologne, 1970); C. Julien, *La Suicide de la democratie* (Paris, 1972); and Lord Hailsham, *The Dilemma of Democracy* (London, 1978).

2 Harold D. Lasswell, *Politics–Who get What, When, How* (New York, 1936).

3 J. A. Schumpeter, *Capitalism, Socialism and Democracy* (New York, 1942; 3rd edn., 1950).

4 Demosthenes, *Against Leptines*, 92, Loeb Classical Library edn., trs. J. H. Vince. pp. 552-3. Cf. also on the episode to which the passage from Xenophon at the head of this chapter refers, Lord Acton, *History of Freedom* (London, 1907), p. 12:

> On a memorable occasion the assembled Athenians declared it monstrous that they should be prevented from doing whatever they chose; no force that existed could restrain them; they resolved that no duty should restrain them, and that they would be bound by no laws that were not of their own making. In this way the emancipated people of Athens became a tyrant.

5 Aristotle, *Politics*, IV, iv, 7, Loeb Classical Library edn., trs. H. Rackham (Cambridge, Mass. and London, 1932), pp. 304-5.

6 Giovanni Sartori, *Democratic Theory* (New York), 1965), p. 312. The whole section 7 of chapter 13, pp. 306-14, of this book is highly relevant to the present theme.

7 Richard Wollheim, 'A Paradox in the Theory of Democracy', in Peter Laslett and W. G. Runciman (eds), *Philosophy, Politics and Society*, 2nd series (Oxford, 1962), p. 72.

8 George Burdeau as quoted before in vol. 1, p. 1, note 4.

9 It would seem, and is confirmed by M. J. C. Vile, *Constitutionalism and the Separation of Powers* (Oxford, 1967), p. 217, that James Mill was in this respect the main culprit, though it is difficult to find in his *Essay on Government* a precise statement to that effect. But we can trace his influence clearly in his son when, for instance, J. S. Mill argues in *On Liberty* that 'the nation did not need to be protected against its own will' (Everyman edn., p. 67).

10 The Americans at the time of the revolution fully understood this defect of the British Constitution and one of their most acute thinkers on constitutional questions, James Wilson (as M. J. C. Vile, *op. cit.,* p. 158 reports)

> rejected Blackstone's doctrine of parliamentary sovereignty as outmoded. The British do not understand the idea of a constitution [he argued] which limits and superintends the

operations of legislature. This was an improvement in the science of government reserved to the Americans.

Cf. also the article 'An Enviable Freedom' in *The Economist*, 2 April 1977, p. 38:

> The American system may thus represent what might have developed if Britain had not turned to the doctrine of absolute parliamentary sovereignty – with its corollary, now largely mythical, that the abused citizen can look to parliament for vindication of his rights.

But I doubt whether they succeeded in solving the problem more successfully. Closely examined in fact both the two paradigms of democratic government, Britain and the USA, are really two monstrosities and caricatures of the ideal of the separation of powers, since in the first the governing body incidentally also legislates as it suits its momentary aims but regards as its chief task the supervision of the current conduct of government, while in the second the administration is not responsible to, and the President as the chief executive for the whole of his tenure of office may lack the support of, the majority of the representative assembly largely concerned with governmental problems. For a long time these defects could be overlooked on the ground that the systems 'worked', but they hardly do so any longer.

The power of the British Parliament may be illustrated by the fact that so far as I know Parliament could, if it regarded me as important enough, for the statement in the text order me for contempt of Parliament to be confined in the Tower!

11 Cf. J. L. Talmon, *The Origins of Totalitarian Democracy* (London, 1952) and R. R. Palmer, *The Age of Democratic Revolution* (Princeton, 1959).

12 E. Heimann, 'Rationalism, Christianity and Democracy', *Festgabe für Alfred Weber* (Heidelberg, 1949), p. 175.

13 Cf. Wilhelm Hennis, *Demokratisierung: Zur Problematik eines Begriffs* (Cologne, 1970); also J. A. Schumpeter, *op. cit.,* p. 242.

14 Cf. Ludwig von Mises, *Human Action* (Yale University Press, 1949; 3rd rev. edn., Chicago, 1966), p. 150: Democracy 'provides a method for the peaceful adjustment of government to the will of the majority'; also K. R. Popper, *The Open Society and its Enemies* (London, 1945; 4th edn., Princeton, 1963), vol. 1, p. 124: 'I suggest the term "democracy" as a short handy label for

... governments of which we can get rid without bloodshed – for example, by way of general elections; that is to say, the social institutions provide the means by which the rulers may be dismissed by the ruled'; also J. A. Schumpeter, *op. cit., passim*; also the references in my *The Constitution of Liberty* (London and Chicago, 1960), p. 444, note 9. I rather regret that in that book (p. 108), carried away by de Tocqueville, I described the third of the three arguments in support of democracy which I mentioned, namely that it is the only effective method of educating the majority in political matters, as the 'most powerful' argument. It is very important but of course less important than what I had then mentioned as the first: its function as an instrument of peaceful change.

15 These dangers of democratic government were remarkably well understood by the Old Whigs. See, for instance, the discussion in the very important *Cato's Letters* by John Trenchard and Thomas Gordon which appeared in the London press between 1720 and 1722 and then were reprinted many times as a collection (now most conveniently available in the volume *The English Libertarian Heritage,* ed. David L. Jacobson, Indianapolis, 1965), where the letter of 13 January 1721 (p. 124 of edition quoted) argues that 'when the weight of infamy is divided among many, no one sinks under his own burthen'. It is also true that, while a task which is regarded as a distinction is commonly also felt to impose an obligation, one which is everybody's right is easily regarded as legitimately governed by one's personal caprice.

16 Cf. J. A. Schumpeter, *op. cit.,* p. 258: about

> the little field which the individual citizen's mind can
> encompass with a full sense of its reality. Roughly, it consists
> of the things that directly concern himself, his family, his
> business dealings, his hobbies, his friends and enemies, his
> township or ward, his class, church, trade union or any other
> social group of which he is an active member – the things
> under his personal observation, the things which are familiar
> to him independently of what his newspapers tell him, which
> he can directly influence or manage, and for which he
> develops the kind of responsibility that is induced by a direct
> relation to the favourable or unfavourable effects of a course
> of action.

17 Cf. *Cato's Letters*, letter no. 60 of 6 January 1721, *op. cit.*, p. 121.
Cf. the quotation from William Paley on p. 21 above. On the
influence of *Cato's Letters* on the development of American
political ideals Clinton Rossiter writes in *Seedtime of the
Republic* (New York, 1953) p. 141:

> No one can spend any time in the newspapers, library
> inventories, and pamphlets of colonial America without
> realising that *Cato's Letters* rather than Locke's *Civil
> Government* was the most popular, quotable, esteemed
> source of political ideas in the colonial period.

18 See *Cato's Letters*, letter no. 62 of 20 January 1721, p. 128:

> It is a mistaken notion in government, that the interest of the
> majority is only to be consulted, since in society every man
> has a right to every man's assistance in the enjoyment and
> defence of his private property; otherwise the greater
> number may sell the lesser, and divide their estates among
> themselves; and so, instead of a society where all peaceable
> men are protected, become a conspiracy of the many against
> the majority. With as much equity may one man wantonly
> dispose of all, and violence may be sanctified by mere power.

19 On these matters see particuarly R. A. Dahl, *A Preface to
Democratic Theory* (Chicago, 1950) and R. A. Dahl and C. E.
Lindblom, *Politics, Economics, and Welfare* (New York, 1953).

20 For the full text and reference of this quotation from Immanuel
Kant see the quotation at the head of chapter 9 of volume 2 and
note.

21 Or in Austria, where the head of the association of trade unions
is the undisputed most powerful man in the country and only his
general good sense makes, for the time being, the position
tolerable.

22 C. A. R. Crossland, *The Future of Socialism* (London, 1956),
p. 205.

23 See E. E. Schattschneider, *Politics, Pressure, and the Tariff* (New
York, 1935) and *The Semi-Sovereign People* (New York, 1960).

24 Cf. Mancur Olson Jr, *The Logic of Collective Action* (Harvard,
1965).

25 The most consistent expounder of this view is Lady Wootton
(Mrs Barbara Wootton). See her latest book on the subject,
Incomes Policy (London, 1974).

26 There is in English an appropriate word lacking for describing those growths which can at least approximately be referred to by the German term *Bildungen*, i.e. structures which have emerged from a process of spontaneous evolution. 'Institutions', which one is often tempted to use instead, is misleading because it suggests that these structures have been 'instituted' or deliberately established.

27 See the passage by C. R. A. Crossland quoted at note 22 above.

28 See in this connection the very relevant discussion of the abstract character of society in K. R. Popper, *op. cit.*, p. 175.

CHAPTER THIRTEEN THE DIVISION OF DEMOCRATIC POWERS

* W. H. Hutt, *Politically Impossible . . .?* (London, 1971), p. 43; cf. also H. Schoeck, *Was heisst politisch unmöglich?* (Zürich, 1959), and R. A. Dahl and C. E. Lindblom, *Politics, Economics and Welfare* (New York, 1953), p. 325: 'perhaps the most fateful limit of American capacity for rational action in economic affairs is the enormous extent to which bargaining shapes all our governmental decisions.'

1 M. J. C. Vile, *Constitutionalism and the Separation of Powers* (Oxford, 1967), p. 43. See also the important conclusion, *op. cit.*, p. 347: 'It is the concern with social justice which above all else has disrupted the earlier triad of government functions and agencies, and has added a new dimension to modern government.'

2 *Ibid.*, p. 63.

3 John Trenchard and Thomas Gordon, *Cato's Letters* (1720–2), reprinted in D. L. Jacobsen (ed.), *The English Libertarian Heritage* (Indianapolis, 1965), p. 121.

4 William Paley, *The Principles of Moral and Political Philosophy* (1785: London edn., 1824), pp. 348 ff. Cf. also Thomas Day, 'Speech at the general meeting of the freeholders of the county of Cambridge' 20 March 1782 (quoted Diana Spearman, *Democracy in England*, London 1957, p. 12): 'With us no discriminatory power which can affect the life, the property or the liberty of an individual, is permitted to the sovereign itself.'

5 M. J. C. Vile, *op. cit.*, p. 158. Cf. also the interesting arguments by James Iredell in an article of 1786 quoted in Gerald Stourzh, *Vom Widerstandsrecht zur Verfassungsgerichtsbarkeit: Zum*

Problem der Verfassungswidrigkeit im 18. Jahrhundert (Graz, 1974), p. 31. In the article of 1786, reprinted in Griffith J. McRee, *Life and Correspondence of James Iredell*, vol. II (New York, 1857; reprinted New York, 1949), of which Professor Stourzh has kindly supplied me with a copy, Iredell pleads (pp. 145–8) for the 'subordination of the Legislature to the authority of the Constitution'. He protests against all 'abuse of unlimited power, which was not to be trusted' and particularly against 'the omnipotent power of the British Parliament . . . the theory *of the necessity of the legislature being absolute in all cases*, because it was the great ground of the British pretensions'. He speaks later of 'the principle of *unbounded legislative power* . . . that our Constitution reprobates. In England they are in this condition. In England, therefore, they are less free than we are.' And he concludes: 'It will not be denied, I suppose, that the constitution is a *law of the state*, as well as an *act of Assembly*, with this difference only, that it is *the fundamental law*, and unalterable by the legislature, which derives all its power from it.'

These ideas survived very long among American radicals and were finally used by them as arguments against the restrictions of democracy. Indeed, the manner in which the American Constitution was designed was still correctly, though with a half-critical intention, expounded in the posthumous *Growth and Decadence of Constitutional Government* (New York, 1931; re-edited Seattle, 1972) by Professor J. Allen Smith. In his Introduction to that book Vernon Louis Parrington refers to the earlier work of J. A. Smith on *The Spirit of American Government* (New York, 1907) of which 'to the liberalism of 1907, the most suggestive contribution was the demonstration from the speeches and writings of the time [when the Constitution was written] that the system was devised deliberately for undemocratic ends.' It is not surprising that the concluding chapter of the later book in which the danger to individual liberty of the removal of these barriers to democratic omnipotence are clearly pointed out was much less popular with the American pseudo-liberals. Smith's exposition of how 'The effectiveness of our constitutional guaranties of individual liberty was greatly impaired when the government, and especially the branch of it which was furthest removed from popular influence, the Supreme Court, acquired the recognized right to interpret them' (p. 279), and how 'individual liberty is not necessarily secure where the majority are in control' (p. 282), and his description how 'individual liberty in the United States to-day not only lacks the support of an active, intelligent public opinion, but often encounters a degree of public hostility which renders constitutional guarantees wholly ineffective' (p. 284) reads much like a criticism of the effects of the ideas he once advocated and is still well worth reading.

6 On the recognition of this fact by some earlier German authors such as the philosopher G. W. F. Hegel and the historian of political institutions W. Hasbach see vol. 1, p. 176, notes 17 and 18.

7 On the systematic support of this development by legal positivism see vol. 3, chapter 8.

8 Cf. G. Sartori, *Democratic Theory* (New York, 1965), p. 312:

> Whereas law, as it was formerly understood, effectively served as a solid dam against arbitrary power, legislation, as it is now understood, may be, or may become, no guarantee at all. . . . When the rule of law resolves itself into the rule of the legislators, the way is open, at least in principle, to an oppression 'in the name of law' that has no precedent in the history of mankind.

9 Edmund Burke could still describe a party as a principled union of men 'united for promoting by their joint endeavours the national interest upon some principle in which they are all agreed' (*Thoughts on the Causes of the Present Discontents* (London, 1779)).

10 See above, vol. 2, p. 126.

11 Courtenay Ilbert, *Legislative Methods and Forms* (Oxford, 1901), p. 210.

12 In *Cato's Letters*, 9 February 1722, in the edition of D. L. Jacobson quoted in note 3 above, p. 256.

13 See Gerald Abrahams, *Trade Unions and the Law* (London, 1968).

14 Robert Moss, *The Collapse of Democracy* (London, 1975), p. 102: 'So the Liberals who blithely passed a bill drawn up by the first generation of Labour MPs in keeping of an electoral promise quite literally had no idea what they were doing.'

15 Cf. the quotation from P. Vinogradoff above, vol. 1, p. 179, note 7, and the passage from A. V. Dicey, Lord McDermot and J. A.

Schumpeter quoted in my *The Constitution of Liberty* (London and Chicago, 1960), p. 506, note 3.

16 Cf. the last section of chapter 1 in volume 1 and chapter 8 in volume 2 of the present work as well as K. R. Popper, *The Open Society and its Enemies* (London, 1945; sixth edn., 1966), vol. 1, p. 121.

17 Quoted by C. H. McIlwain, *The High Court of Parliament* (Yale University Press, 1910).

18 See on this Wilhelm Hennis, *Demokratisierung: Zur Problematik eines Begriffs* (Cologne, 1970).

19 Since I first suggested the term 'demarchy' (in a pamphlet on *The Confusion of Language in Political Thought,* Occasional Paper 20 of the Institute of Economic Affairs (London, 1968)) I have noted that the terminological problem has been examined in some detail in the German literature. See particularly the studies by Christian Meier: 'Drei Bemerkungen zur Vor- und Frühgeschichte des Begriffes Demokratie' in *Discordia Concors, Festschrift für Edgar Bonjour* (Basel, 1968); *Die Entstehung des Begriffes 'Demokratie'* (Frankfurt a.M., 1970); and his contribution to the article *'Demokratie'* in O. Brunner, W. Conze and R. Kosselek (eds), *Geschichtliche Grundbegriffe, Historisches Lexikon zur politisch-sozialen Sprache in Deutschland* (Stuttgart, vol. I, 1972), in each of which further references to the discussion will be found.

CHAPTER FOURTEEN THE PUBLIC SECTOR AND THE PRIVATE SECTOR

* The quotation at the head of the chapter is taken from a speech of William Pitt to the House of Commons on 14 January 1766, *Parliamentary History of England* (London, 1813), vol. 16. It deserves notice that to Pitt at that time it appears to have been only measures of taxation which among the subjects coming before Parliament involved coercion of private persons, since the rest of the obligatory rules of just conduct consisted mainly of common and not statute law and therefore appeared to be outside the normal concern of a body occupied chiefly with government rather than with the making of law.

1 Mancur Olson Jr, *The Logic of Collective Action* (Harvard University Press, 1965).

2 On the important recent discussion of the 'minimal state' in

Robert Nozik, *Anarchy, State, and Utopia* (New York, 1974) see the Preface to the present volume.

3 See Mancur Olson Jr, *op. cit.*, and the various important studies by R. H. Coase on this subject.

4 Milton Friedman, *Capitalism and Freedom* (Chicago, 1962).

5 *Ibid.*

6 In Japan, however, museums and the like are to a remarkable extent provided by private enterprise.

7 Cf. Martin Anderson, *The Federal Bulldozer* (Cambridge, Mass., 1964); Jane Jacobs, *The Economy of Cities* (New York, 1969); and Edward C. Banfield, *The Unheavenly City* (Boston, 1970) and *Unheavenly City Revisited* (Boston, 1974).

8 Richard C. Cornuelle, *Reclaiming the American Dream* (New York, 1965). Cornuelle concludes (p. 40):

> If fully mobilized the independent sector could, I believe:
> (1) Put to work everyone who is willing and able to work.
> (2) Wipe out poverty. (3) Find and solve the farm problem.
> (4) Give everyone good medical care. (5) Stop juvenile crime. (6) Renew our towns and cities, and turn anonymous slums into human communities. (7) Pay reasonable retirement benefits to all. (8) Replace hundreds of governmental regulations with more effective codes of conduct, vigorously enforced by each profession and an alert press. (9) Handle the nation's total research effort.
> (10) Turn our foreign policy into a world crusade for human welfare and personal dignity. (11) Lever a wider distribution of stock ownership. (12) Stop air and water pollution. (13) Give every person the education he needs, wants, and can profit by. (14) Provide cultural and educational outlets for everyone who wants them. (15) Wipe out racial segregation. The independent sector has power to do these formidable things. But, curiously, as its strength has increased we have given it less and less to do, and assigned more and more common tasks to government.

I reproduce this remarkable claim to tempt as many readers as possible to consult this unduly neglected book.

9 J. K. Galbraith, *The Affluent Society* (Boston, 1969).

10 Adolf Wagner, *Finanzwissenschaft* (1873; 3rd edn. Leipzig, 1883), Part I, p. 67, and cf. H. Timm, 'Das Gesetz der wachsenden Staatsaufgaben', *Finanzarchiv*, N.F. 21, 1961, as well as H.

Timm and R. Haller (eds), *Beiträge zur Theorie der öffentlichen Ausgaben. Schriften des Vereins für Sozialpolitik*, N. F. 47, 1967. While so far as the coercive activities of government are concerned it has been justly said that we ought to be grateful that we do not get as much government as we pay for, with regard to the services which it renders the opposite is probably true. The size of government expenditure is, of course, no measure whatever of the value of the services actually provided by government. The technical necessity of valuing in all national income statistics government services at costs probably gives a wholly misleading picture of the actual size of the contribution it makes to the stream of services provided for the people.

11 J. K. Galbraith, *op. cit.*, and cf. also Anthony Downs, 'Why Government Budget is too Small in a Democracy', *World Politics*, vol. 12, 1966.

12 See Arthur Seldon, *Taxation and Welfare*, I.E.A. Research Monograph No. 14 (London, 1967), especially the table on p. 18.

13 About the fact that in all advanced European states even at the height of the so-called *laissez faire* period there existed provisions for the maintenance of the poor cf. above, vol. 2, p. 190, note 8.

14 See my *The Constitution of Liberty* (London and Chicago, 1960), chapter 19.

15 Cf. R. H. Coase, 'The British Post Office and the Messenger Companies', *Journal of Law and Economics*, vol. IV, 1961, and the statement of the General Secretary of the British Union of Post Office Workers made at Bournemouth, on 24 May 1976 and reported on the next day in *The Times*, London, that 'Government of both political complexions had reduced a once great public service to the level of a music hall joke'.

16 See my *Denationalization of Money* (Institute of Economic Affairs, 2nd edn., London, 1978).

17 See *The Constitution of Liberty* (London, 1960), chapter 24.

18 See note 4 above.

19 See the book by R. C. Cornuelle quote in note 8 above.

20 Cf. F. A. Mann, 'Outlines of a History of Expropriation', *Law Quarterly Review*, 75, 1958.

21 Cf. Alan F. Westin, *Privacy and Freedom* (New York, 1968). How well founded were the apprehensions which I expressed in *The Constitution of Liberty* (p. 300) concerning the effect of a

universal national health service on the liberty of the private individual has been depressingly confirmed by an article by D. Gould, 'To Hell with Medical Secrecy' in the *New Statesman* of 3 March 1967 in which it is argued that

> ideally, our medical cards ought to be sent to the Ministry of Health, say once a year, and all the information on them should be fed into a computer. Moreover, these cards . . . should list our jobs, past and present, our travels, our relatives, whether and what we smoke and drink, what we eat and do not eat, how much we earn, what sort of exercise we take, how much we weigh, how tall we are, even perhaps the results of regular psychological tests, and a lot of other intimate details. . . .
>
> Proper records, analysed by computer . . . could even reveal the people who ought not to be allowed to drive a motor car, or have a seat in the Cabinet! Ah! What about the sacred freedom of the individual? Freedom, my foot. We survive as a community or not at all, and doctors today are as much servants of the state as their patients. Away with the humbug, and let us admit that all secrets are bad secrets.

CHAPTER FIFTEEN GOVERNMENT POLICY AND THE MARKET

* Ludwig von Mises, *Human Action: A Treatise on Economics* (Yale University Press, 1949), p.239.

1 This chapter, written in more or less the present form about ten years ago and partly published, after having been used for public lectures at Chicago and Kiel, as 'Der Wettbewerb als Entdeckungsverfahren' in *'Kieler Vorträge'*, No. 56 (Kiel, 1969) and in English more recently in my *New Studies in Philosophy, Politics, Economics and the History of Ideas* (London and Chicago, 1977), I have let stand largely unchanged since it already occupies an undue amount of space in the present context and any attempt to deal with more recent developments would in this place have been inappropriate. I should, however, refer here at least to some of the works which have substantially developed the conceptions here sketched, such as Murray Rothbart, *Power and Market* (Menlo Park, 1970), John S. MacGee, *In Defence of Industrial Concentration* (New York, 1971), D. T. Armentano,

The Myth of Antitrust (New Rochelle, N.Y., 1972), and particularly Israel Kirzner, *Competition and Entrepreneurship* (Chicago, 1973) and a number of German essays by Erich Hoppmann, especially 'Missbrauch der Missbrauchaufsicht', *Mitteilungen der List Gesellschaft*, May 1976, and 'Preisunelastizität der Nachfrage als Quelle von Marktbeherrschung', in H. Gutzler and J. H. Kaiser (eds), *Wettbewerb im Wandel* (Baden-Baden, 1976).

2 Among the few who have seen this is the sociologist Leopold von Wiese. See his lecture on 'Die Konkurrenz, vorwiegend in soziologisch-systematischer Betrachtung', *Verhandlungen des 6. Deutschen Soziologentages*, 1929.

3 This seems to have been confused by J. A. Schumpeter, *Capitalism, Socialism, and Democracy* (New York, 1942), p. 101 where he contends that:

> there are superior methods available to the monopolist which either are not available to a crowd of competitors or are not available to them so readily: for their advantages which, though not strictly available on the competitive level of enterprise, are as a matter of fact secured only on the monopoly level, for instance, because monopolization may increase the share of influence of the better, and decrease the share of influence of the inferior brains.

Such a situation may indeed lead to monopoly, but it would not be monopoly but perhaps size which would give the better brains greater influence.

4 Where in both cases we must count as part of these costs of production the alternative products which the particular person or firm could produce instead. It would therefore be compatible with these conditions that somebody who could produce some commodity more cheaply than anybody else will in fact not do so and produce something else instead with respect to which his comparative advantage over other producers is even greater.

5 It may be instructive if I illustrate the kind of obstacles into which one who believes he has discovered a possibility of improving upon existing routines is likely to encounter in modern conditions. The instance of such a frustration which many years I had the opportunity to watch in detail was the case of an American building contractor who, after looking at the prices and rents of houses, the wages and the prices of building materials in a

European city, felt convinced that he could provide better houses at a considerably lower price and still make a substantial profit. What made him in the end give up his plan was that building regulations, trade union rules, cartellized prices of special building equipment and the cost of the bureaucratic procedure of obtaining all the required permissions and approvals precluded the economies in production on which he had based his calculations. I cannot say now whether the obstacles raised directly by government or those due to its toleration of restrictive practices or producers and trade unions were more decisive. What was obvious was that the reason why well-tried possibilities of reducing the costs of houses could not be applied were that those who knew how to use them were not allowed to do so.

6 It deserves observation that an economy in which it is easy to make large profits rapidly, although it is one in which there exist possibilities of rapid growth because there is much that can be quickly remedied, is one which almost certainly has been in a very unsatisfactory state and where the aim of exploiting the obvious opportunities will soon be achieved. This shows, incidentally, how absurd it is to judge relative performance by rate of growth, which is as often as not evidence of past neglect rather than of present achievement. In many respects it is easier and not more difficult for an undeveloped country to grow rapidly once an appropriate framework has been secured.

7 Even the statement of the problem as one of utilizing knowledge dispersed among hundreds of thousands of individuals still over-simplifies its character. It is not merely a task of utilizing information about particular concrete facts which the individuals already possess, but one of using their abilities of discovering such facts as will be relevant to their purposes in the particular situation. This is the reason why all the information accessible to (rather than already possessed by) the individuals can never be put at the disposal of some other agency but can be used only if those who know where the relevant information is to be found are called upon to make the decisions. Every person will discover what he knows or can find out only when faced with a problem where this will help, but can never pass on all the knowledge he commands and still less all the knowledge he knows how to acquire if needed by somebody else.

8 Cf. W. Mieth, 'Unsicherheitsbereiche beim wirtschafts-

politischen Sachurteil als Quelle volkswirtschaftlicher Vorurteile' in W. Strzelewicz (ed.), *Das Vorurteil als Bildungsbarriere* (Göttingen, 1965), p. 192.

9 This has been repeatedly emphasized by Milton Friedman, see, for example, his *Capitalism and Freedom* (Chicago, 1962).

10 W. L. Letwin, *Law and Economic Policy in America* (New York, 1965), p. 281.

11 The *Gesetz gegen Wettbewerbsbeschränkungen* of 27 July 1957.

12 On all this and the issues discussed in the following paragraphs see Mancur Olson Jr, *The Logic of Collective Action* (Harvard University Press, 1933).

13 Gunnar Myrdal, *An International Economy* (New York, 1956), and J. K. Galbraith, *The Affluent Society* (Boston, 1969).

14 J. K. Galbraith, *op. cit.*

15 Mancur Olson Jr, *op. cit.*

CHAPTER SIXTEEN THE MISCARRIAGE OF THE
DEMOCRATIC IDEAL: A RECAPITULATION

* Count Axel Oxenstjerna (1583–1654) in a letter to his son, 1648: 'Dost thou not know, my son, with how little wisdom the world is governed?' Since much of the argument leading to the proposal offered in the next chapter was written, and in part also published, and therefore seen by many readers, a long time ago, I insert here a brief summary in which I believe I have succeeded quite recently in restating the chief points more succinctly. It is an only slightly revised version of an outline published in *Encounter* for March 1978.

1 House of Commons, 17 May 1977. There would in fact be no need for a catalogue of protected rights but merely of a single restriction of all governmental powers that no coercion was permissible except to enforce obedience to laws as defined before. That would include all the recognized fundamental rights and more.

CHAPTER SEVENTEEN A MODEL CONSTITUTION

* David Hume, *Essays*, Part II, Essay XVI, 'The Idea of a Perfect Commonwealth'.

1 The suggestion for the reconstruction of the representative

assemblies has by now occupied me over a long period and I have sketched it in writing on numerous earlier occasions. The first, I believe, was a talk on 'New Nations and the Problem of Power' in the *Listener*, no. 64, London, 10 November 1960. See also 'Libertad bayo la Ley' in *Orientacion Economica*, Caracas, April 1962; 'Recht, Gesetz und Wirtschaftsfreiheit', *Hundert Jahre Industrie – und Handelskammer zu Dortmund 1863–1963* (Dortmund, 1963; reprinted in the *Frankfurter Allgemeine Zeitung* 1/2 May 1963, and in my *Freiburger Studien* (Tübingen, 1969)); 'The Principles of a Liberal Social Order', *Il Politico*, December 1966, and reprinted in *Studies in Philosophy, Politics and Economics* (London and Chicago, 1967); 'Die Anschauungen der Mehrheit und die zeitgenössische Demokratie', *Ordo* 15/16 (Düsseldorf, 1963); 'The Constitution of a Liberal State', *Il Politico* 31, 1967; *The Confusion of Language in Political Thought* (Institute of Economic Affairs, London, 1968); and *Economic Freedom and Representative Government* (Institute of Economic Affairs, London, 1973). Most of the later ones are reprinted in my *New Studies in Philosophy, Politics, Economics and the History of Ideas* (London and Chicago, 1977). The latest statement is in *Three Lectures on Democracy, Justice and Socialism* (Sydney, 1977), also available in German, Spanish and Portuguese translations.

2 Z. Giacommetti, *Der Freiheitskatalog als Kodifikation der Freiheit* (Zürich, 1955).

3 Cf. A. R. W. Harris, 'Law Making at Athens at the End of the Fifth Century B.C.', *Journal of Hellenic Studies*, 1955, and further references given there.

4 E. G. Philip Hunton, *A Treatise on Monarchy* (London, 1643), p. 5.

5 J. S. Mill, *Considerations on Representative Government* (London, 1861), ch. 5.

6 While for the purposes of legislation a division of the assembly on party lines is altogether undesirable, for the purpose of government a two-party system is obviously desirable. There is, therefore, in neither instance a case for proportional representation, the general arguments against which have been powerfully marshalled in a work which, because of the date of its publication, has not received the attention it deserves: F. A. Hermens, *Democracy or Anarchy* (Notre Dame, Ind., 1941).

7 Carl Schmitt, 'Soziologie des Souverainitätsbegriffes und

192

politische Theologie' in M Palyi (ed.), *Hauptprobleme der Soziologie, Erinnerungsgabe für Max Weber*, (Munich, 1923), II, p. 5.

8 See my *The Constitution of Liberty* (London and Chicago, 1960), chapter 20.

CHAPTER EIGHTEEN THE CONTAINMENT OF POWER AND THE DETHRONMENT OF POLITICS

* The quotation at the head of the chapter is translated from the original German version of Albert Schweitzer, *Kultur und Ethik, Kulturphilosophie*, vol. 2 (Bern, 1923), p. xix. In the English translation, published under the title *Civilization and Ethics* (London, 1923), the corresponding passage will be found on p. xviii.

1 Cf. K. R. Popper, *The Open Society and its Enemies* (5th edn., London, 1974), vol. I, p. 124:

For we may distinguish two main types of government. The first type consists of governments of which we can get rid without bloodshed – for example, by way of general elections; that is to say, the social institutions provide means by which the rulers may be dismissed by the ruled, and the social traditions ensure that these institutions will not easily be destroyed by those who are in power. The second type consists of governments which the ruled cannot get rid of except by way of a successful revolution – that is to say, in most cases not at all. I suggest the term 'democracy' as a short-hand label for a government of the first type, and the term 'tyranny' or 'dictatorship' for the second. This, I believe, corresponds to traditional usage.

In connection with what follows concerning the negative character of the highest political values compare also K. R. Popper's *Conjectures and Refutations* (2nd edn., London, 1965), p. 230.

2 John Dewey, 'Liberty and social control', *Social Frontier*, November 1935, and cf. the fuller comments in my *The Constitution of Liberty*, note 21 to chapter 1.

3 Morris Ginsberg in W. Ebenstein (ed.), *Modern Political Thought: The Great Issues* (New York, 1960).

4 David Miller, *Social Justice* (Oxford, 1976), p. 17. Cf. also M. Duverger, *The Idea of Politics* (Indianapolis, 1966), p 171: 'The definition of justice . . . nearly always centers on the dis-

tribution of wealth and social advantages.' One begins to wonder whether these writers have ever heard of John Locke or David Hume or even of Aristotle. See, e.g., John Locke, *Essays Concerning Human Understanding*, IV, iii, 18:

> Where there is no property there is no injustice, is a proposition as certain as any demonstration in Euclid: for the idea of property being a right to anything, and the idea to which the name of 'injustice' is given being the invasion or violation of that right, it is evident that these ideas, being thus established, and these names annexed to them, I can as certainly know the proposition to be true, as that a triangle has three angles equal to two right ones.

5 D. Miller, *op. cit.*, p. 23.

6 J. A. Schumpeter, *History of Economic Analysis* (New York, 1954), p. 394: 'As a supreme, if unintended compliment, the enemies of the system of private enterprise have thought it wise to appropriate its label.'

7 As a friend recently observed to me, if we count all persons who believe in what they call 'social justice' socialists, as we ought, because what they mean by it could be achieved only by the use of governmental power, we must admit that probably something like 90 per cent of the population of the Western democracies are today socialists.

8 David Hume, *A Treatise of Human Nature*, book III, section 2, ed. L. A. Selby-Bigge (Oxford, 1958), p. 495.

9 The literary part of that magazine is full of constant erroneous references to the supposed injustice of our economic order. What, for instance, is supposed to be the causal connection when a little earlier (16 May 1977) a television reviewer speaks about 'how much misery it cost to maintain those ducal shrubs in such well shaved elegance'.

10 In connection with the preceding section see generally my brochure on *The Confusion of Language in Political Thought* (Occasional Paper 20 of the Institute of Economic Affairs, London, 1968).

11 This weakness of the government of an omnipotent democracy was very clearly seen by the extraordinary German student of politics, Carl Schmitt, who in the 1920s probably understood the character of the developing form of government better than most people and then regularly came down on what to me

appears both morally and intellectually the wrong side. Cf. e.g., in his essay on 'Legalität und Legitimität' of 1932 (reprinted in his *Verfassungsrechtliche Aufsätze*, Berlin, 1958, p. 342):

> Ein pluralistischer Parteienstaat wird nicht aus Stärke und Kraft, sondern aus Schwäche 'total'; er interveniert in alle Lebensgebiete, weil er die Ansprüche aller Interessenten erfüllen muss. Insbesondere muss er sich in das Gebiet der bisher staatsfreien Wirtschaft begeben, auch wenn er dort auf jede Leitung und politischen Einfluss verzichtet.

Many of these important conclusions were already stated in 1926 in his *Die geistesgeschichtliche Lage des Parlamentarismus*.

12 See above, p. 38.

13 Harvard University Press, 1965. Cf. also my introduction to the German translation of this book produced by the members of my Freiburg seminar and published as *Die Logik des kollektiven Handelns* (Tübingen, 1968).

14 There are of course many problems arising out of such situations which were intensively discussed by nineteenth-century English liberals in connection with their struggle against the laws of settlement. Much wisdom on these matters will still be found in Edwin Cannan, *The History of Local Rates in England* (2nd edn, London, 1912).

One of the most difficult problems here is perhaps how the desire to attract or retain residents should and can be combined with a freedom of choice whom to accept and whom to reject as a member of a particular community. Freedom of migration is one of the widely accepted and wholly admirable principles of liberalism. But should this generally give the stranger a right to settle down in a community in which he is not welcome? Has he a claim to be given a job or be sold a house if no resident is willing to do so? He clearly should be entitled to accept a job or buy a house if offered to him. But have the individual inhabitants a duty to offer either to him? Or ought it to be an offence if they voluntarily agree not to do so? Swiss and Tyrolese villages have a way of keeping out strangers which neither infringe nor rely on any law. Is this anti-liberal or morally justified? For established old communities I have no certain answers to these questions. But future developments, as I have suggested in *The Constitution of Liberty*, pp. 349–53, seem to me possible on the lines of estate developments with a division of property rights between a freehold ownership of the estate by a corporation and very long leases of the plot owners assuring them of a certain protection against undesirable developments of the neighbourhood. Such a corporation should of course be free to decide to whom it is willing to lease plots.

15 Cf. the passage from J. A. Schumpeter quoted above, chapter 12, note 16.

16 *Denationalization of Money – The Argument Refined* (2nd extended edn, Institute of Economic Affairs, London, 1978).

17 See above pp. 133 ff.

18 Torgny F. Segerstedt, 'Wandel der Gesellschaft', *Bild der Wissenschaft*, VI/5, May 1969.

19 This was the title I had intended to give to a work I had planned in 1939, in which a part on the 'Hubris of Reason' was to be followed by one on 'The Nemesis of the Planned Society'. Only a fragment of this plan was ever carried out and the parts written published first in *Economica* 1941–5 and then reprinted in a volume entitled *The Counter-Revolution of Science* (Chicago, 1952), to the German translation of which I later gave the title *Missbrauch und Verfall der Vernunft* (Frankfurt, 1959) when it became clear that I would never complete it according to the original plan. *The Road to Serfdom* (London and Chicago, 1944) was an advance sketch of what I had intended to make the second part. But it has taken me forty years to think through the original idea.

EPILOGUE: THE THREE SOURCES OF HUMAN VALUES

* Although originally conceived as a Postscript to this volume, I found it easier to write the following pages out as a lecture that was delivered as the Hobhouse Lecture at the London School of Economics on 17 May 1978. In order not further to delay publication of the last volume of this work, I then decided to include it here in the form it was given as a lecture. The lecture has also been published separately by the London School of Economics in 1978.

** J. W. Goethe, *Dichtung und Wahrheit*, book XIV. The date of this passage is 1774.

1 New York, 1977 and London, 1978.

2 See his monumental *Sociobiology, A New Synthesis* (Cambridge, Mass., 1975 and London, 1976) and for a more popular

exposition David P. Barash, *Sociobiology and Behavior* (New York etc., 1977).

3 G. E. Pugh, *op. cit.*, pp. 33 and 341; cf. also on the former page the statement: 'primary values determine what types of secondary criteria the individual will be motivated to adopt.'

4 Huxley's path-breaking work on *The Courtship of the Great Crested Grebe* of 1914 was reprinted (London, 1968) with a foreword by Desmond Morris.

5 Best known of K. Z. Lorenz's works is *King Solomon's Ring* (London, 1952).

6 N. Tinbergen *The Study of Instinct* (Oxford, 1951).

7 See especially I. Eibl-Eibesfeld, *Ethology* (2nd edn, New York, 1975) and particularly Wolfgang Wickler, and Uta Seibt, *Das Prinzip Eigennutz* (Hamburg, 1977), not yet known to me when the text of this book was completed. The original and not sufficiently appreciated works of Robert Ardrey, especially the more recent ones, *The Territorial Imperative*, (London and New York, 1966), and *The Social Contract* (London and New York, 1970) should also be mentioned.

8 See, e.g., also Desmond Morris, *The Naked Ape* (London, 1967), Introduction: '[Man's] old impulses have been with him for millions of years, his new ones only a few thousand at the most.' The transmission of learnt rules probably goes back some hundred thousand years!

9 See my essay 'Dr Bernard Mandeville', *Proceedings of the British Academy*, LII, 1967 and reprinted in *New Studies in Philosophy, Politics, Economics and the History of Ideas* (London and Chicago, 1978).

10 As I had occasion to point out with reference to C. D. Darlington, *The Evolution of Man and Society* (London, 1969), in *Encounter*, February 1971, reprinted in *New Studies*, etc. as note 9 above.

11 L. T. Hobhouse, *Morals in Evolution* (London, 1906) and M. Ginsberg, *On the Diversity of Morals* (London, 1956).

12 J. S. Huxley, *Evolutionary Ethics* (London, 1943).

13 A. M. Carr Saunders, *The Population Problem, A Study in Human Evolution* (Oxford, 1922).

14 C. H. Waddington, *The Ethical Animal* (London, 1960).

15 G. G. Simpson, *The Meaning of Evolution* (Yale University Press, 1949) and T. H. Dobzhansky, *Mankind Evolving: The Evolution of the Human Species* (Yale University Press, 1962)

and 'Ethics and values in biological and cultural evolution', *Zygon*, 8, 1973. See also Stephen C. Pepper, *The Sources of Value* (University of California Press, 1953), pp. 640–56.

16 D. T. Campbell, 'Variation and selective retention in sociocultural evolution' in H. R. Barringer, G. I. Blankstein and R. W. Mack (eds), *Social Change in Developing Areas: A reinterpretation of Evolutionary Theory* (Cambridge, Mass., 1965); 'Social attitudes and other acquired behavior dispositions' in S. Koch (ed.), *Psychology: A Study of a Science*, vol. 6, *Investigations of Man as Socius* (New York, 1963).

17 My long-growing conviction that it was Cartesian influence which has been the chief obstacle to a better understanding of the self-ordering processes of enduring complex structures has been unexpectedly confirmed by the report of a French biologist that it was Cartesian rationalism which produced a 'persistent opposition' to Darwinian evolution in France. See Ernest Boesiger, 'Evolutionary theory after Lamarck', in F. J. Ayala and T. Dobzhansky (eds), *Studies in the Philosophy of Biology* (London, 1974), p. 21.

18 The thesis that culture created man has been first stated by L. A. White in his *The Science of Culture* (New York, 1949) and *The Evolution of Culture* (New York, 1959), but spoilt by his belief in 'laws of evolution'. A belief in selective evolution has, however, nothing to do with a belief in laws of evolution. It postulates merely the operation of a mechanism the results of which depend wholly on the unknown marginal conditions in which it operates. I do not believe there are any laws of evolution. Laws make prediction possible, but the effect of the process of selection depends always on unforeseeable circumstances.

19 See my lecture on 'Dr Bernard Mandeville' quoted in note 9 above, p. 253–4 of the reprint, and *Law, Legislation and Liberty*, vol. 1, p. 20.

20 Cf. Richard Thurnwald (a well known anthropologist and a former student of the economist Carl Menger), 'Zur Kritik der Gesellschaftsbiologie', *Archiv für Sozialwissenschaften*, 52, 1924, and 'Die Gesaltung der Wirtschaftsentwicklung aus ihren Anfängen heraus' in *Die Hauptprobleme der Soziologie, Erinnerungsgabe für Max Weber* (Tübingen, 1923), who speaks of *Siebung*, in contrast to biological selection, though he applies it only to the selection of individuals, not of institutions.

21 See the reference given in *Law, Legislation and Liberty*, vol. 1, p. 163, note 7.

22 I find it difficult to believe, as is usually said, that Sir Alister Hardy in his illuminating book *The Living Stream* (London, 1966) was the first to point out this reverse effect of cultural on biological evolution. But if this should be correct, it would represent a major breakthrough of decisive importance.

23 E. H. Gombrich, *In Search of Cultural History* (Oxford, 1969), p. 4, and cf. Clifford Geertz, *The Interpretation of Cultures* (New York, 1973), p. 44: 'Man is precisely the animal most desperately dependent on much extra-genetic, outside-the-skin control mechanisms, such cultural programs, for organizing behavior'; and *ibid.*, p. 49: 'there is no such thing as a human nature independent of culture. . . . our central nervous system . . . grew up in great part in interaction with culture. . . . We are, in sum, incomplete or unfinished animal who complete or finish ourselves through culture.'

24 See B. J. Whorf, *Language, Truth, and Reality, Selected Writings*, ed. J. B. Carroll (Cambridge, Mass., 1956), and E. Sapir, *Language: an Introduction to the Study of Speech* (New York, 1921); and *Selected writings in Language, Culture and Personality*, ed. D. Mandelbaum (Berkeley and Los Angeles, 1949); as well as F. B. Lenneberg, *Biological Foundations of Language* (New York, 1967).

25 The genetic primacy of rules of conduct of course does not mean, as behaviourists seem to believe, that *we* can still reduce the pattern of the world which now guide our behaviour to rules of conduct. If the guides to conduct are hierarchies of classification of complexes of stimuli which affect our ongoing mental processes so as to put a particular behaviour pattern into effect, we would still have to explain most of what we call mental processes before we could predict behavioural reactions.

26 My colleagues in the social sciences generally find my study on *The Sensory Order. An inquiry into the Foundations of Theoretical Psychology* (London and Chicago, 1952) uninteresting or indigestible. But the work on it has helped me greatly to clear my mind on much that is very relevant to social theory. My conception of evolution, of a spontaneous order and of the methods and limits of our endeavours to explain complex phenomena have been formed largely in the course of the work on that book. As I was using the work I had done in my student days on

theoretical psychology in forming my views on the methodology of the social science, so the working out of my earlier ideas on psychology with the help of what I had learnt in the social science helped me greatly in all my later scientific development. It involved the sort of radical departure from received thinking of which one is more capable at the age of 21 than later, but which, even, though years later, when I published them they received a respectful but not very comprehending welcome by the psychologists. Another 25 years later psychologists seem to discover the book (see W. B. Weimer and D. S. Palermo (eds), *Cognition and Symbolic Processes*, vol. II (New York, 1978)), but I certainly least expected to be discovered by the behaviourists. But see now Rosemary Agonito, 'Hayek revisited: Mind as a process of classification' in *Behaviorism. A Forum for Critical Discussion*, III/2 (University of Nevada, 1975).

27 See most recently Karl R. Popper and John C. Eccles, *The Self and Its Brain. An Argument for Interactionism* (Berlin, New York and London, 1977).

28 Cf. particularly Carsten Bresch, *Zwischenstufe Leben. Evolution ohne Ziel?* (Munich, 1977) and M. Eigen and R. Winkler, *Das Spiel, Naturgesetze steuern den Zufall*, (Munich, 1975).

29 See my lecture on 'Dr Bernard Mandeville' quoted in note 9 above, p. 250 of the reprint.

30 Donald T. Campbell, 'Downward Causation in Hierarchically Organised Biological Systems' in F. J. Ayala and T. Dobzhansky as quoted in note 17 above. See also Karl Popper and John C. Eccles as quoted in note 27 above.

31 On the limited applicability of the concept of law in the explanation of complex self-maintaining structures see the postscript to my article on 'The Theory of Complex Phenomena' in my *Studies in Philosophy, Politics and Economics* (London and Chicago, 1967), pp. 40 ff.

32 *Cf.* Garret Hardin, 'The cybernetics of competition', in P. Shepard and D. McKinley, *The Subversive Science: Essays towards an Ecology of Man* (Boston, 1969).

33 Ludwig von Bertalanffy, *General System Theory: Foundations, Development, Applications* (New York, 1969) and cf. H. von Foerster, and G. W. Zopf Jr (eds), *Principles of Self-Organization* (New York, 1962); G. J. Klir (ed.), *Trends in General System Theory* (New York, 1972); and G. Nicolis and I. Prigogine, *Self-organization in Nonequilibrium Systems* (New York, 1977).

34 See Colin Cherry, *On Human Communication* (New York, 1961), and Noam Chomsky, *Syntactic Structures* (The Hague, 1957).

35 Roger Williams, *You are Extraordinary* (New York, 1967), pp. 26 and 37. People who study statistics, even such very important statistical subjects as demography, do not study society. Society is a structure, not a mass phenomenon, and all its characteristic attributes are those of a constantly changing order or system, and of these orders or system we do not have a sufficient number of specimens to treat the behaviour of the wholes statistically. The belief that within these structures constant quantitative relationships can be discovered by observing the behaviour of particular aggregates or averages is today the worst obstacle to a real understanding of those complex phenomena of which we can study only a few instances. The problems with which the explanation of these structures have to deal have nothing to do with the law of large numbers.

Real masters of the subject have often seen this. See, e.g., G. Udney Yule, *British Journal of Psychology*, XII, 1921/2, p. 107: 'Failing the possibility of measuring that which you desire, the lust for measurement may, for instance, merely result in your measuring something else – and perhaps forgetting the difference – or in ignoring some things merely because they cannot be measured.'

Unfortunately, techniques of research can be readily learnt, and the facility with them lead to teaching positions, by men who understand little of the subject investigated, and their work is then often mistaken for science. But without a clear conception of the problems the state of theory raises, empirical work is usually a waste of time and resources.

The childish attempts to provide a basis for 'just' action by measuring the relative utilities or satisfactions of different persons simply cannot be taken seriously. To show that these efforts are just so much nonsense would require entering into somewhat abstruse argument for which this is not the place. But most economists seem to begin to see that the whole of the so-called 'welfare economics', which pretends to base its arguments on inter-personal comparisons of ascertainable utilities, lacks all scientific foundation. The fact that most of us believe that they can judge which of the several needs of two or more known persons are more important, does not prove either that there is any objective basis for this, nor that we can form such a conceptions about people whom we do not know individually. The idea of basing coercive actions by government on such fantasies is clearly an absurdity.

36 D. S. Shwayder, *The Stratification of Behaviour* (London, 1965) ought to contain much helpful information on this subject of which I have not yet been able to make use.

37 Although the conception of group selection may now not appear as important as it had been thought after its introduction by Sewall Wright in 'Tempo and Mode in Evolution: A Critical Review', *Ecology*, 26, 1945, and V. C. Wynne-Edwards, *Animal Dispersion in Relation to Social Behaviour* (Edinburgh, 1966) – cf. E. O. Wilson, *op. cit.* pp. 106–12, 309–16, and George C. Williams, *Adaptation and Natural Selection, A Critique of Some Current Evolutionary Thought* (Princeton, 1966) and, edited by the same, *Group Selection* (Chicago/New York, 1976), – there can be no doubt that it is of the greatest importance for cultural evolution.

38 G. E. Pugh, *op. cit.*, p. 267, and see now Glynn Isaac, 'The Food-sharing Behaviour of Protohuman Hominids', *Scientific American*, April 1978.

39 This was, of course, not always a peaceful process. It is very likely that in the course of this development a wealthier urban and commercial population often imposed upon larger rural populations a law which was still contrary to the mores of the latter, just as after the conquest by a military band a military land-owning aristocracy imposed in feudal ages upon the urban population a law which had survived from a more primitive stage of economic evolution. This is also one form of the process by which the more powerfully structured society, which can attract individuals by the lures it has to offer in the form of spoils, may displace a more highly civilized one.

40 K. R. Popper, *The Open Society and its Enemies* (5th edn, London, 1966), vol. I, pp. 174–6.

41 The nostalgic character of these longings has been particularly well described by Bertrand de Jouvenel in the passage quoted from his *Sovereignty* (Chicago, 1957, p. 136) in *Law, Legislation and Liberty*, vol. 2, p. 182.

42 In view of the latest trick of the Left to turn the old liberal tradition of human rights in the sense of limits to the powers both of government and of other persons over the individual into

positive claims for particular benefits (like the 'freedom from want' invented by the greatest of modern demagogues) it should be stressed here that in a society of free men the goals of collective action can always only aim to provide opportunities for unknown people, means of which anyone can avail himself for his purposes, but no concrete national goals which anyone is obliged to serve. The aim of policy should be to give all a better chance to find a position which in turn gives each a good chance of achieving his ends than they would otherwise have.

43 *Cf.* David Hume, *A Treatise of Human Nature*, III, ii, ed. L. A. Selby-Bigge, p. 501: 'There is nothing which touches us more nearly than our reputation, and nothing on which our reputation more depends than our conduct with relation to the property of others.' This is perhaps as good a place as any other to point out that our present understanding of the evolutionary determination of the economic order is in a great measure due to a seminal study of Armen Alchian, 'Uncertainty, Evolution and Economics Theory', *Journal of Political Economy*, 58, 1950 and since reprinted in an improved form in the author's *Economic Forces at Work* (Indianapolis, 1977). The conception has now widely spread beyond the circle in which it was initiated and a good survey of the further discussion of these problems and a very full bibliography will be found in the important and scholarly work by Jochem Roepke, *Die Strategie der Innovation* (Tübingen, 1977), which I have not yet been able fully to digest.

44 Long before Calvin the Italian and Dutch commercial towns had practised and later the Spanish schoolmen codified the rules which made the modern market economy possible. See in this connection particularly H. M. Robertson, *Aspects of the Rise of Economic Individualism* (Cambridge, 1933), a book which, if it had not appeared at a time when it practically remained unknown in Germany, should have disposed once and for all of the Weberian myth of the Protestant source of capitalist ethics. He shows that if any religious influences were at work, it was much more the Jesuits than the Calvinists who assisted the rise of the 'capitalist spirit'.

45 Jean Baechler, *The Origin of Capitalism*, trans. Barry Cooper (Oxford, 1975), p. 77 (italics in original).

46 Cf. M. I. Finley, *The Ancient Economy* (London, 1975), pp. 28–9, and 'Between Slavery and Freedom', *Comparative Studies in Society and History*, 6, 1964.

47 See the provision of the ancient Cretan constitution quoted as a motto at the head of chapter 5 of vol. 1 of *Law, Legislation and Liberty*.

48 If rules are adopted, not because their specific effects are understood, but because those groups who practice them are successful, it is not surprising that in primitive society magic and ritual dominate. The condition of admission to the group was to accept all its rules, though few understood what depended on the observation of any particular one. There was merely one accepted way of doing things with little effort to distinguish between effectiveness and moral desirability. If there is anything in which history has almost wholly failed it is in explaining the changes of causes of morals, among which preaching was probably the least important, and which may have been one of the most important factors determining the course of human evolution. Though present morals evolved by selection, this evolution was not made possible by a licence to experiment but on the contrary by strict restraints which made changes of the whole system impossible and granted tolerance to the breaker of accepted rules, who may have turned out a pioneer, only when he did so at his own risk and had earned such licence by his strict observation of most rules which alone could gain him the esteem which legitimized experimentation in a particular direction. The supreme superstition that the social order is created by government is of course just a flagrant manifestation of the constructivistic error.

49 See my lecture on 'Rechtsordnung und Handelnsordnung' in *Zur Einheit der Rechts- und Staatswissenschaften*, ed. E. Streissler, (Karlsruhe, 1967) and reprinted in my *Freiburger Studien* (Tübingen, 1969).

50 The idea is of course the same as what Karl Popper calls 'piecemeal social engineering' (*The Open Society*, etc., as quoted in note 40 above, vol. 2, p. 222), on which I wholly agree, though I still dislike the particular expression.

51 Cf. Ludwig von Mises, *Theory and History* (Yale University Press, 1957) p. 54:

> The ultimate yardstick of justice is conduciveness to the preservation of social co-operation. Conduct suited to preserve social co-operation is just, conduct detrimental to the preservation of society is unjust. There cannot be any

question of organizing society according to the postulate of
an arbitrary preconceived idea of justice. The problem is to
organize society for the best possible realization of those
ends which men want to attain by social co-operation. Social
utility is the only standard of justice. It is the sole guide of
legislation.

Though this is more rationalistically formulated than I would
care to do, it clearly expresses an essential idea. But Mises was of
course a rationalist utilitarian in which direction, for reasons
given, I cannot follow him.

52 This confusion stems in modern times at least from Emile Durk-
heim, whose celebrated work *The Division of Labour in Society*
(trans. George Simpson, London, 1933, see especially p. 228)
shows no comprehension of the manner in which rules of conduct bring about a division of labour and who tends, like the
sociobiologist, to call all action 'altruistic' which benefits others,
whether the acting person intends or even knows this. But compare the sensible position in the textbook *Evolution* by T. Dobzhansky, F. J. Ayala, G. L. Stebbins and J. W. Valentine (San
Francisco, 1977), pp. 456 ff.:

> Certain kinds of behavior found in animals would be ethical
> or altruistic, and others unethical and egotistic, *if these
> behaviors were exhibited by men.* . . . unlike any other
> species, every human generation inherits and also transmits a
> body of knowledge, customs, and beliefs that are not coded
> in the genes. . . . the mode of transmission is quite unlike that
> of biological heredity. . . . For perhaps as long as two million
> years cultural changes were increasingly preponderant over
> genetic ones;

also the passage quoted by them in this context from G. G.
Simpson, *This View of Life* (New York, 1964):

> It is nonsensical to speak of ethics in connection with any
> animal other than man. . . . There is really no point in
> discussing ethics, indeed one might say that the concept of
> ethics is meaningless, unless the following conditions exist:
> (a) There are alternative modes of action; (b) man is capable
> of judging the alternatives in ethical terms; and (c) he is free
> to choose what he judges to be ethically good. Beyond that, it
> bears repeating that the evolutionary functioning of ethics

depends on man's capacity, unique at least in degree, of predicting the results of his actions.

53 See E. O. Wilson, *op. cit.*, p. 117:

> When a person (or animal) increases the fitness of another of the species at the expense of his own fitness, he can be said to have performed an act of *altruism*. Self-sacrifice for the benefit of offspring is altruism in the conventional but not in the strict genetic sense, because individual fitness is measured by the number of surviving offspring. But self-sacrifice on behalf of second cousins is true altruism on both levels, and when directed at total strangers such abnegating behaviour is so surprising (that is, 'noble') as to demand some kind of theoretical explanation.

Cf. also D. P. Barash, *op. cit.*, who discovers even 'altruistic viruses' (p. 77) and R. Trivers, 'The evolution of reciprocal altruism', *Q. Rev. Biol*, 46, 1971.

54 If today the preservation of the present order of the market economy depends, as Daniel Bell and Irving Kristol (eds), *Capitalism Today* (New York, 1970) in effect argue, that the people rationally understand that certain rules are indispensible to preserve the social division of labour, it may well be doomed. It will always be only a small part of the population who will take the trouble to do so, and the only persons who could teach the people, the intellectuals who write and teach for the general public, certainly rarely make an attempt to do so.

55 See Lionel C. Robbins, *An Essay on the Nature and Significance of Economic Science* (London, 1932).

56 It is perhaps sad that culture is inseparable from progress, but the same forces which maintain culture also drive us into progress. What is true of economics is also true of culture generally: it cannot remain stationary and when it stagnates it soon declines.

57 See particularly H. B. Acton, *The Morals of the Market* (London, 1971).

58 Ronald Dworkin, *Taking Rights Seriously* (London, 1977), p. 180

59 See Roger J. Williams, *Free and Unequal: The Biological Basis of Individual Liberty* (University of Texas Press, 1953), pp. 23 and 70; also J. B. S. Haldane, *The Inequality of Men* (London, 1932), P. B. Medawar, *The Uniqueness of the Individual* (Lon-

don, 1957), and H. J. Eysenck, *The Inequality of Man* (London, 1973).

60 The problem had certainly occupied me for some time before I first used the phrase in print in the lecture on 'The Moral Element in Free Enterprise' (1961), reprinted in my *Studies in Philosophy, etc.* (London and Chicago, 1967), p. 232.

61 On the nineteenth-century history of scientism and the associated views which I now prefer to call constructivism see my *The Counter-Revolution of Science. Studies in the Abuse of Reason* (Chicago, 1952).

62 See vol. 2, chapter 8, of *Law, Legislation and Liberty*. The contrast between legal positivism and its opposite, 'the classical theories of Natural law' which, in the definition of H. L. A. Hart (*The Concept of Law*, Oxford University Press, 1961, p. 182), hold 'that there are certain principles of human conduct, *awaiting discovery by human reason,* with which man-made law must conform to be valid' (italics added), is indeed one of the clearest instances of the false dichotomy between 'natural' and 'artificial'. Law is, of course, neither an unalterable fact of nature, nor a product of intellectual design, but the result of a process of evolution in which a system of rules developed in constant interaction with a changing order of human actions which is distinct from it.

63 Sigmund Freud, *Civilisation and its Discontents* (London, 1957), and *cf.* Richard La Pierre, *The Freudian Ethic* (New York, 1959). If for a life-long student of the theory of money who had fought his intellectual struggles with Marxism and Freudianism in the Vienna of the 1920s and had later dabbled in psychology, any evidence had still been necessary that eminent psychologists, including Sigmund Freud, could talk utter nonsense on social phenomena, it has been provided for me by the selection of some of their essays, edited by Ernest Borneman, under the title *The Psychoanalysis of Money* (New York, 1976, a translation of *Die Psychoanalyse des Geldes*, Frankfurt, 1973), which also in a great measure accounts for the close association of psychoanalysis with socialism and especially Marxism.

64 G. B. Chisholm, 'The re-establishment of a peace-time society', *Psychiatry*, vol. 6, 1946. Characteristic for the literary views of that time is also a title like Herbert Read, *To Hell with Culture. Democratic Values are New Values* (London, 1941).

65 *The Times*, 13 April 1978.

66 Donald T. Campbell, 'On the conflicts between biological and social evolution', *American Psychologist*, 30 December 1975, p. 1120.

67 *Ibid.*, p. 1121.

68 The *American Psychologist* of May 1975 carried forty pages of mostly critical reactions to Professor Campbell's lecture.

69 Apart from Thomas Szasz, *The Myth of Mental Illness* (New York, 1961), see particularly his *Law, Liberty and Psychiatry*, (New York, 1971).

70 H. J. Eysenck, *Uses and Abuses of Psychology* (London, 1953).

INDEX OF AUTHORS CITED
IN VOLUMES 1-3

Note: In this index the roman numerals indicate the volume number; the arabic number refers to the pages in the volume.

209

214

Subject Index to Volumes 1–3

Prepared by Vernelia A. Crawford

Note: This index includes the titles of chapters and sections, each listed under the appropriate subject classification. The Roman numeral indicates the volume number; the Arabic number refers to the pages in the volume.

217

Market economy—*contd.*
social justice in, II: 67–70
strangers of, III: 165–8
supply and demand, I: 63; II:
116–17, 120–2; III: 80–5,
91–3
term of, I: 62
threat to, III: 89–93
values in, II: 123–5; *see also*
Valuation (Value judgment)
voluntarism in, III: 50–1
Marxism, II: 103; III: 168–73, 207
n.63
Mathematics, I: 148 n.14; II:
118–19, 130; III: 188 n.21,
201 n.35
Means and ends
abstract rules and, II: 142–4
action, II: 39–42
adaptation of, I: 149 n.15
administration and, III: 22–5,139
choice-making by, II: 9–11
economic, II: 113, 186–7 n.13
Great Society, II: 109–14
individual, II: 8–9, 15–17
law and, I: 158 n.16
market order and, II: 70–3, 94,
107–13
outcome of, I: 10, 147 n.4
particular, II: 14–17, 109–11,
114–15
utility and, II: 18–23
values of, II: 15–17
Measurement, I: 148 n.14; III:
188 n.21, 201 n.35
Merit
earned, II: 62–5, 176(5)
market economy and, II: 70–3,
94
reward for, II: 69–73, 179 n.21
spontaneous order and, II:
151–2
uncertainty of, II: 62, 175*
Middle Ages, law of, I: 83–4, 52,
157 n.13
Migrations, III: 56, 195 n.14
Mind and society, I: 17–19
Minorities, III: 11, 52; *see also*
Majority

Monarchy, I: 84, 166 n.25
Money theory, III: 56–8, 207 n.63
Monopoly
abolition of, III: 147–8
attitude toward, III: 83–5, 88
communication and, III: 147–8
discrimination by, III: 81–5
legislation and, II: 14, 154 n.10,
175*; III: 85–8
power of, III: 77–80
prices, III: 83
protectionism and, III: 79–80,
85–6
services, III: 56–60
source of, III: 72–4, 189 n.3
survival of, III: 189 n.3
Morality (Morals)
attitude toward, I: 25–6; II:
26–7, 88–91
behaviour and, I: 75, 164 n.8
belief in, III: 165–8
conflicts in, II: 97–100; III:
135–7
conscience and, I: 18, 149 n.15
consequences of, II: 135–6
defense of, II: 24–7
destruction of, II: 99, 183 n.43
duty of, II: 32
evolution of, III: 204 n.48
Great Society, II: 144–7
instincts and, III: 168–73
law and, II: 36, 56–9, 162–4 n.9
open and closed society, II:
144–7
philosophy of, II: 43, 166 n.24
preservation of, III: 170–1
principles of, II: 14, 154 n.10,
175*
rewards of, II: 74
rules and, II: 18–24, 58, 83–4,
148
social justice and, II: 62–7
theory of, II: 43, 166–7 n.24
traditional, II: 110–11
tribal, II: 145, 147–9
values in, II: 66–7
virtue and, I: 21, 15 n.25; II: 22, 36,
157 n.23, 162–4 n.9, 175*
see also Justice/Injustice